GENEALOGY FOR BEGINNERS

GENEALOGY FOR BEGINNERS

Katherine Pennavaria

ROWMAN & LITTLEFIELD
Lanham • Boulder • New York • London

Published by Rowman & Littlefield
An imprint of The Rowman & Littlefield Publishing Group, Inc.
4501 Forbes Boulevard, Suite 200, Lanham, Maryland 20706
www.rowman.com

6 Tinworth Street, London SE11 5AL

British Library Cataloguing in Publication Information Available

Library of Congress Cataloging-in-Publication Data

Name: Pennavaria, Katherine, 1959–, author.
Title: Genealogy for Beginners / Katherine Pennavaria.
Description: Lanham : Rowman & Littlefield, [2020] | Includes bibliographical references and index. | Summary: "This book covers everything you need to get started researching your family history or continue a project you've already started. It offers practical suggestions from an experienced genealogist and detailed, step-by-step instructions for carrying out a quality family history research"—Provided by publisher.
Identifiers: LCCN 2019043515 (print) | LCCN 2019043516 (ebook) | ISBN 9781538125489 (cloth) | ISBN 9781538125496 (epub)
Subjects: LCSH: Genealogy.
Classification: LCC CS16 .P443 2020 (print) | LCC CS16 (ebook) | DDC 929.1—dc23
LC record available at https://lccn.loc.gov/2019043515
LC ebook record available at https://lccn.loc.gov/2019043516

To Rosemary Long Meszaros, my good friend and WKU colleague. Couldn't have done it without you, comrade. *Laissez les bon temps rouler!*

CONTENTS

LIST OF FIGURES

ACKNOWLEDGMENTS

I owe the following my sincerest thanks:

- My colleagues in the library at Western Kentucky University, especially Michael Franklin and Morgan Moran at the Visual and Performing Arts Library, for listening and for multiple assists while I worked on this book; Rosemary Meszaros, to whom this book is dedicated, for comradely collaborating over many years, for legal citation and government records expertise, and for reading my drafts; and Brian Coutts, former WKU Libraries department head, for always encouraging me to think big.
- The genealogists I've spoken with at conferences and presentations, for their never-ending enthusiasm about the process.
- The staff at the Bowling Green Kentucky Family History Center, for the microfilms and other research help, especially Carol Ann Stott (deceased), Gail Jackson Miller, Frances Naegel, Loretta Hook, Dorothy Campbell, Linda MacDonald, Bill Copas, Jim Steen, Leland Stott, and John Cullen (deceased).
- The volunteers all over the world whose hours of dedicated effort over many years has turned difficult-to-access genealogical records into online gold.
- Robin Rae Harris, editor of *Kentucky Libraries*, and the rest of the editorial staff, for steady support and for liking my genealogy column idea.

- M. Sandra Wood, former series editor for Rowman & Littlefield, for patient encouragement and sharp editing during our initial collaborations on this subject.
- Elizabeth Shown Mills, professional genealogist and author of *Evidence Explained*, for corrections and suggestions on an earlier version of this book.
- Linda Ehrsam Voigts, former University of Missouri–Kansas City graduate advisor, for showing me how to be a researcher.
- Cynthia Cornell, former DePauw University undergraduate advisor, for inspiring me all those years ago.
- My entire family, especially my dad, Russell James Pennavaria, and my son, Adam Russell Pennavaria. I know it's TMI sometimes, guys.
- And finally, Donna McKay Kasznel, my partner, for being wonderful and for always believing in me.

INTRODUCTION

Every day in America, someone makes the big decision to start researching his or her family history. Perhaps it's long been on the "to do" list, or maybe watching *Who Do You Think You Are?* got the project going. Are you one of those people? If so, welcome to the fascinating world of family history research!

Commercials for Ancestry.com indicate that the process of genealogy is fairly simple; you just "plug in" what you know, and the database does the rest. Well, those ads might sell subscriptions, but they are rather misleading. Getting beyond the low-hanging fruit is not easy; collecting original records, analyzing them, and reaching accurate conclusions requires time, organization, and informed research.

Fortunately, help exists. With dedication and a modest outlay of time, money, and effort, you can succeed in building something beyond what you already know. The history you piece together will form part of the legacy you leave to your immediate and extended family.

Not all beginning genealogists have the same goals. Perhaps you want to track your direct ancestry going back several generations, or maybe you want to focus on capturing the lives and stories of people currently living and the preceding generation. Some people are determined to track down every person connected to their family, no matter how remote. Whatever your goals (and they will change), think beyond merely compiling a "tree"; the real goal is to conduct historical research according to the best genealogy research standards. As you look for and collect records, try to think like a historian rather than a hobbyist; aim

for creating an evidence-based history of the various families you research. And don't give up when the going gets tough. The work you do
now will someday be found and appreciated by family members you
most likely have never met or will never meet.

Tracing a family's history is not easy for Americans. We inhabit a
"melting pot" culture where movement and self-reinvention have long
been part of the national ethos. Except for those individuals descended
entirely from native peoples of North and South America, U.S. citizens
have immigrants in their ancestry who came to this land within the past
five hundred years, whether those people traveled by choice or were
forced to make the trip.

Every genealogy project is built on *records*. Records come in all
shapes and sizes, but most of the ones you'll need were originally on
paper, most likely created by a government entity. Finding these
records is part of the initial challenge, as they are not all online and
some can be difficult to get to. Once you have the records, you'll need
to analyze and interpret them.

Conducting good genealogy research has a great deal to do with
decisions you make early on; this book concentrates on those early days,
especially what you need to succeed and how to make things easier for
yourself. But while it is aimed at beginners, this book also contains
plenty of advice for advanced family historians about resources and the
research process.

It begins with an overview of genealogy as a hobby and passionate
interest for millions of Americans. You'll learn how the Internet, that
magical genie in our computers that has so changed our daily lives, can
be credited with sparking the genealogy boom. But credit also goes in
large part to the Church of Jesus Christ of Latter-day Saints, and its
contribution is duly noted. Chapter 1 finally lets you into the secret of
family secrets and family names and describes what arrival in America
was like for millions of European immigrants.

In chapter 2, things get practical. You can follow step-by-step advice
for getting your genealogy project successfully launched. The best way
to start, as the old writing tip goes, is to write what you know. From
there, you'll get more ideas on interviewing family members, finding
old family pictures and papers, and conducting research both on- and
offline. This last bit covers the best research practices recommended by
professional genealogists today. You don't have to be a professional to

practice good research methods; this chapter tells you how to do so at a beginner's level.

Chapter 3 takes practicality a step further as it outlines how to tackle the mounds of pictures and paper records you'll encounter, both how to preserve them and how to store them. You'll also learn about scanning and audiovisual conversion projects as well as dealing with the subsequent digital files, from labeling to editing and storing. Tips on keeping research organized, especially labeling files effectively and keeping track of your sources, finish off the chapter.

In chapter 4, we take a step back from practicality and look at the many types of genealogy records (federal, county, military, religious, court, etc.) you'll work with. You'll examine serious problems with record creation, indexing, and handling that might prevent you from finding records unless you do some careful searching.

Chapter 5 introduces the fascinating, complex world of online searching for genealogy records. Learn the difference between public and private records (it's not as obvious as you'd think) and explore online sites grouped by whether they are *essential*, *useful*, or *worth exploring*. Finish up the chapter with some search tips guaranteed to get results.

In chapter 6, things get a little more advanced. Find out about getting access to unpublished material, using special maps and researching property records, and finding and working with non-U.S. records. Chapter 7 takes you into specific resources for ethnic and cultural heritage research and walks you through the rapidly evolving world of DNA testing for genealogy results. Closing out the book, chapter 8 offers up-to-date information on how to keep abreast of changes in the genealogy world through blogs, podcasts, and online forums. You'll also find ideas for educating yourself on the subject and sharing the results of your hard work.

Let the journey begin!

I

GENEALOGY—AN OVERVIEW

This chapter addresses:

- The Internet revolution and genealogy
- The role of the Church of Jesus Christ of Latter-day Saints
- Family secrets and family names
- The immigrant experience

A revolution has taken place in America, again. The first one resulted in a brand-new country; this latest one takes us into an undiscovered country: the past.

The arrival of the Internet in the 1990s brought many changes to our global society, and one of those changes was a massive increase in the number of people researching their family histories. Before the availability of online indexes and records, genealogists had to work the old-fashioned way: spending many hours at archives and libraries, combing through printed indexes, and sending inquiry letters to far-off repositories. They operated, in short, the same way all researchers did pre-Internet, which makes sense because genealogy has always been, essentially, historical research based on the scientific model—that is, the researcher gathers data, analyzes it, draws conclusions, and shares results.

The difficulties in researching genealogy pre-Internet did not dissuade people from doing it, but the number of practitioners was always small, and the work seemed slightly eccentric—appropriate for people attempting to gain entry into the Daughters of the American Revolution or the Mayflower Society, perhaps, but not really important for everyone else.

The Internet changed everything about family history research because it opened the door to novices. People could now successfully pursue family history research without any expertise and without labor-intensive effort. But a revolution cannot occur in a vacuum. For the Internet revolution to change the way genealogy was done, some entity first had to create searchable data for researchers to find, and that entity is a quintessentially American one.

GENEALOGY AND THE LDS CHURCH

The Church of Jesus Christ of Latter-day Saints (LDS) can rightly claim a major role in establishing the way genealogy is done today in North America.[1] Its primary motivation for establishing genealogy as a priority for church members comes from the church's doctrine that "family relationships are intended to continue beyond this life."[2] LDS members, like most Americans, can trace their family lines back to a generation who came, or were brought, to the United States. Trying to find out more about that immigrant generation presented members with a challenge, however, because the records were in other countries. So the church decided to implement a massive project to photograph and digitize local church and civil records all over the world and in the United States—a project that continues to this day.

For many decades, LDS members have visited cities and towns throughout the world as part of their required two-year missionary service. While there, many of these missionary teams double as documenting agents, spending countless hours laying out and photographing old record books with the assistance of local record keepers. Their focus has primarily been on records that reveal kinship, especially those known as "vital" records (births, marriages, deaths), plus some census, court, and property records.

After completing photography on a record set, the field workers send the film or digital images to Salt Lake City for processing. In the past, the photographic film was turned into microfilm; today they go straight to digital images. Volunteers spend many hours name-indexing the records and making them available in the searchable database called

FamilySearch, which is part of the Family History Library in Salt Lake City. In all, the LDS church controls about *three billion* pages of family history records.[3]

The LDS church started committing vital records to microfilm in 1938, when that technology was brand-new. But the church has been involved in genealogy in a highly organized way since 1894, when the Genealogical Society of Utah was founded to assist LDS members in compiling their lineage. Church leaders decided at that time to build a library in Salt Lake City to house the gathered records and provide a place for research to be carried out. Today, the Family History Library is the largest of its kind in the world and is open to the public free of charge. It sees roughly 1,500 visitors a day and has many professional staff members dedicated to answering phone, chat, and e-mail inquiries. The Family History Library in Salt Lake is every genealogist's mecca—the place where it all started and the place to do research using the stored microfilms and a print collection not available online.

The Genealogical Society of Utah evolved into FamilySearch International, the entity that today manages the Family History Library and its storage facility, the Granite Mountain vault; FamilySearch International continues to provide *free access* to the billions of records that it holds. The microfilms created by the LDS church are now almost completely digitized and online—full digitization of the records is expected by the end of 2020.

The premier subscription site Ancestry was founded in 1983 as a print publisher. In 1997, it was purchased by InfoBases, a company that had been selling packages of records on floppy disk and grew into a giant. Today, Ancestry offers its subscribers about five billion digitized records, the majority from the United States; the most comprehensive nationally significant record sets available are the passenger lists for immigrants coming into the United States from many different ports, the completely digitized U.S. federal census (1790–1940), draft registration cards, and city directories (all discussed in chapter 4).

Photographing and preserving records all over the world is only a part of what the LDS church has done to promote genealogy. When the Internet age arrived, the LDS church began making its indexes available online at no charge. With the arrival of online searching, information that had once been difficult to access was now available on screens across America. Suddenly, records that most genealogists in the United

States thought they would never see were yielding data: names and dates for marriages, births, and deaths of people who lived generations ago, even ancestors who never saw the shores of America. For Americans descended from people whose records had been photographed by the diligent LDS members, this newly available information changed everything about who did genealogy and why. No longer was genealogy the province of potential Daughters of the American Revolution members; now anyone could potentially trace their family history back many generations.

In short, all genealogists today owe a debt of gratitude to the LDS church, whether they know it or not. Credit for the genealogy boom also goes to the National Genealogical Society (created in 1903), for its journal and book publications and its decades of educational programs. Also significant is the New England Historic Genealogy Society, founded in 1845. Their journal and book publications, along with their active members, played a monumental role in the development of genealogical scholarship.

FAMILY SECRETS

You probably heard lots of family stories while you were growing up and might be thinking that your genealogy research can help you confirm those stories, or at least provide more details.[4] Just remember that every family also has stories that were suppressed or hidden by those involved. As Steve Luxenberg says in the beginning of *Annie's Ghosts* (2009), his moving story about uncovering his mother's "hidden" sister, "Secrets . . . have a way of working themselves free of their keepers." As you do family history research, you won't know exactly what you'll find, but one thing is certain: you will uncover things kept hidden by previous generations. If you are just getting started, you might want to prepare yourself for this eventuality. All experienced genealogists have had a few *Wow!* moments during the process. Such revelations can be painful.

All families have secrets. As you go along, you might find evidence of such things as premarital births, divorces, suicides, abandoned children, and misattributed paternity. You will certainly uncover information that does not match everything you were told about your family's past. And sometimes you'll find clear signs that information has been deliberately kept secret for years. Perhaps these secrets should stay buried, perhaps not. The point is that often you uncover them inadvertently, not suspecting they are there. Then you face a choice about whether to share that information.

THE IMMIGRANT EXPERIENCE

Most Americans today are descended from European or African forebears who arrived on the shores of North America after an ocean voyage across either the Atlantic or Pacific; many others come partly or wholly from the native peoples of the Americas. For some, the immigrant generation of their family arrived before the Revolutionary War; for others, ancestors came as part of several waves during the 19th and early 20th centuries. However far back we must go, most of us eventually reach some ancestors who arrived here from outside our current borders. Because of this, American genealogists share an interest in understanding that aspect of family history. The significant spike in interest in genealogy during the past few decades stems partly from Americans' increasing desire to learn about those who crossed thousands of miles to get here. What was the experience like?

Two excellent publications help paint the picture of what travelers went through before, during, and after their journeys: John Philip Colletta's *They Came in Ships* (2002) and Mark Wyman's *Round-Trip to America* (1996). Whether they came by choice or by force, that ocean crossing was an experience like no other. For those who chose to make the journey, the quality of the experience depended primarily on two things: when they traveled and what type of ticket they had. Ocean voyages during the time of the earliest settlers took about two months (the *Mayflower* took sixty-six days to cross from Southampton, England, to Plymouth, Massachusetts). Conditions on board those early sailing ships were primitive and miserable; the ships were built to accommodate sailors, not families. By the mid-19th century, the steamship had replaced sailing vessels and cut crossing time dramatically. By the end of the 19th century, a transatlantic crossing might take as little as a week, though usually nine to fourteen days at sea could be expected. Shipboard conditions improved during the 19th century as the federal government passed laws relating to how passengers bound for the United States had to be accommodated.

Most people who came to America voluntarily during the hundred-plus years of the highest immigration levels (roughly 1820 to 1920) purchased the cheapest ticket available: third class, also known as steerage. Unlike the holders of first- and second-class tickets, who had cabins and could move about on deck, steerage passengers lived below-decks in what was essentially the cargo hold; shared bunks were the norm. In the last decade of the 1800s, Congress mandated that steerage passengers be given separate bunks and dictated how many toilets were required per hundred people, but there were still no private spaces. American immigration rules also spelled out how much food and water should be provided, but steamship companies sometimes offered only the minimum, the better to maximize their profits.

Legislation was enacted in the late 19th century requiring ship captains to allow steerage passengers a brief period on the top deck, but the rest of the day they were below, where the "bunks" might be just iron frames and thin blankets and the "toilets" only covered buckets that were emptied over the side each day by the crew (who were sometimes fellow passengers paying their way by working). Water for washing was a luxury reserved for the first- and second-class passengers. It wasn't so bad for the first day or two, but after that the steerage compartment could be smelled throughout the ship.

In addition to their body odor, travelers shared whatever germs and body lice they carried. It's not a pleasant thought, but that was their reality. For the women, the primitive conditions and lack of privacy during this claustrophobic and unhygienic voyage made dealing with babies, pregnancy, and menstruation an added challenge. And women who were sexually assaulted by a fellow passenger or crew member had no way of filing a complaint or receiving justice. In short, conditions in steerage ranged from tolerable to miserable, and what an individual got depended on luck alone. These people did not decide which shipping line to use based on TripAdvisor.com; they did not have a Passenger's Bill of Rights to wave at the ship's crew. The steerage passengers took what they were offered and suffered through it.

Although it was not the only port in America that received massive numbers of immigrants, the facility at Ellis Island has become the best-known processing point for the late 19th and early 20th centuries, when

America received the greatest number of immigrants. Today, you can walk through the buildings and learn, through audio and images, what happened there all those years ago. The immigrants who reached New York Harbor docked in the shadow of the Statue of Liberty, but disembarking at Ellis Island did not end their ordeal. Having crossed the ocean and reached port was no guarantee that they would set foot in America proper. With their clothing deteriorated and their emotions similarly ragged, new arrivals at Ellis Island and the other ports were subjected to more hours of packed spaces, to sitting with nothing to do until called, and to mental and physical examinations.

In those crowded, chaotic rooms, many people must have feared the officials shouting orders at them, pushing them into lines. Back in Europe, the government's agents usually meant trouble; it was the priests and rabbis whom the people trusted. But there were no friendly religious leaders here, just overworked men in uniform trying to get everyone moved along. At Ellis Island, the first barrier that the immigrants faced inside the processing facility was a line of officers sitting at high desks. On these desks were the ship manifests, divided into groups of pages and coordinated with cards held by the passengers or pinned to their clothing. As each man or woman stepped up, the officer asked a series of questions that were translated (if necessary) into that person's language, and the answers were translated back. The answers had to match the information recorded on the manifest, which had been taken down when the ticket was purchased. If a name was not on the list or the information did not match, the person was put into detention to await further inquiry.

The bewildered, frightened people were pushed from room to room, questioned repeatedly, and subjected to invasive tests; doctors and nurses examined every orifice of their bodies for signs of venereal disease. Their eyelids were grasped with a pinching tool and yanked back so the medical examiner could verify they did not have any contagious eye diseases, such as trachoma. Those individuals with any suspicious condition had their clothing marked with chalk and were then detained in a separate area for further testing. If, after that second examination, the traveler was confirmed as deaf, senile, lame, or infected with syphilis, tuberculosis, or any other contagious disease, the process of returning that person to his or her homeland began. Officers knew that marking someone might mean ultimate deportation and the splitting up of a family, but they had no choice; federal law spelled out exactly which defects would keep a person from entering the country legally.

In short, America welcomed only those immigrants who would not become a burden on the government. Anyone who didn't meet these standards was sent back (at shipping company expense), regardless of whether he or she had any place to go or the means to get there. The words from Emma Lazarus's 1883 poem "The New Colossus," inscribed on the pedestal of the Statue of Liberty ("Give me your tired, your poor / Your huddled masses yearning to breathe free / The wretched refuse of your teeming shore"), convey a nice sentiment, but the reality was quite different. The federal government did not want Europe's refuse; it wanted strong, healthy individuals who were able to work and support themselves. The rest of the huddled masses were returned to sender.

At Ellis Island, once the examinations were completed, the immigrants who passed were put on the ferry to Manhattan. Docking at what is today Battery Park, the travelers met a new set of officials who helped them exchange their money for dollars and, if they were not staying in New York, find the correct transportation for the remainder of their journey. Lucky ones were assisted by charitable organizations in obtaining provisions and dealing with children's needs; unlucky ones had their money and possessions stolen. But at long last, the journey *to* America had ended and the journey *inside* America had begun. What became of them from that point on would depend on luck and their own strength.

The Ellis Island facility closed in 1954; it has since been renovated and turned into a museum. Millions of immigrants came through the main hall, including bodybuilder Charles Atlas (Italy), composer Irving Berlin (Belarus), film director Frank Capra (Italy), bandleader Xavier Cugat (Spain), cosmetologist Max Factor (Poland), comedian Bob Hope (England), actor Cary Grant (England), singer Al Jolson (Lithuania), actor Béla Lugosi (Hungary), dance studio owner Arthur Murray (Austria), football coach Knute Rockne (Norway), and even the man who became "Chef Boyardee," Ettore Boiardi (Italy). Tourists today can rent an audio tour headset and follow the steps that their ancestors took, climbing up a set of wide stairs (the first test of mobility) and then standing in the great hall, imagining all those people inching their way down the length of it, praying that they would be allowed to go beyond the far end and into America.

The name *Ellis Island* has come to stand in for the typical immigrant experience that began overseas and ended on the shores of North America. Obviously, not every immigrant came through that facility, which was one of many ports. But it is the best preserved and most accessible of the processing stations, and its records, now held at the National Archives, are essential for many genealogists.

FAMILY NAMES

Most Americans are familiar with the idea that immigrants to the United States during the Ellis Island years (1892–1954) had their surnames altered by the processing officials, either deliberately or through ignorance of the correct spelling.[5] An Internet search of the phrase *name was changed at Ellis Island* yields over three hundred thousand hits; variations on the phrase yield even more. Here is a sampling of recent statements in an online forum[6] asking people whether they believe that such a thing happened:

"My family name was probably shortened from something Eastern European to something German, certainly at Ellis Island."

"My great-grandfather came through and the name was shortened and changed by the worker."

"Some of my relatives' surnames were recorded incorrectly on arrival."

"My great-grandfather and his two brothers came over together from Lithuania and left Ellis Island with three different last names."

"Our Italian surname was changed at Ellis Island when my great-grandparents came over."

If one believes these earnest posters, the surnames of immigrants to the United States were routinely treated in a shoddy, unprofessional manner by the government representatives at American ports.

They are wrong. No one's family name was changed, altered, shortened, butchered, or "written down wrong" at Ellis Island or any American port. That idea is an urban legend.

Names did get changed as immigrants settled into their new American lives, but those changes were made several years after arrival by the immigrants themselves. The belief persists, however, that names were changed by someone at the entry point and that the immigrants were unwilling participants in the modifications. Experienced family history researchers have long rolled their eyes at this "Ellis Island name change" idea. In genealogy blogs and online publications, the correction is wearily repeated: names were *not* changed at Ellis Island; immigrants changed their own names, usually during the citizenship process. But the belief persists, perhaps because people need to explain surname changes in a way that satisfies them (thinking that their immigrant ancestors made the changes themselves apparently does not do so).

Why is this myth so persistent? Malcolm Gladwell, in his book *The Tipping Point*, explains his concept of "stickiness," the elusive quality that some ideas and concepts have: they catch on and don't let go.[7] Since Gladwell's book was published in 2000, social science and behavioral researchers have explored the nature of "sticky" ideas, concluding that "when we have a gap in our knowledge, we strive to resolve it."[8] Across America today, people descended from 19th- and 20th-century European immigrants strive to resolve why their family's surname is different from the (presumed) original. In addressing this gap, however, many seekers have reached the wrong conclusion. Unfortunately, their incorrect conclusion has proved quite "sticky."

Other writers have dealt with why and how surnames evolved or were altered as immigrants settled into U.S. cities to begin their lives as Americans;[9] the focus here is on what the clerks at Ellis Island and other immigration points during the 19th and early 20th centuries did when they encountered (primarily) European surnames. These federal employees have been accused of, at best, carelessness, and at worst, racial prejudice. What does the historical record tell us about these immigration officials and about the U.S. government's policies and procedures relating to immigrants? That record begins with the inception of America itself: everyone who came here, or who was brought here, after the official founding of the nation was an immigrant. Until 1819, people coming to the United States were dealt with according to state laws. In 1819, the federal government took over, and immigration law and policy as we know it today began.

Tempting as it is to blame the government, federal officials at American ports can be cleared of all charges of changing immigrants' names. If we look at federal laws relating to immigrants, at the copious paperwork from the period, and at contemporary writings and imagery, we can see for ourselves that the accusation is false: not only didn't those officials change names—they *couldn't* have. Abundant evidence from the period shows conclusively that American officials did not write down passenger names.

It's difficult to say when the urban legend about names being altered at Ellis Island began, but we do know when the notion spread to the popular imagination. In the 1974 film *The Godfather II*, which closely follows events described in the novel *The Godfather* by Mario Puzo, little Vito Andolini is sent away from his violent hometown of Corleone, Sicily. He arrives at the Ellis Island processing station and, overwhelmed by the noise and the people, finds himself unable to speak. The immigration official asks the boy his name, and the question is repeated in Italian by a translator. The frightened boy stays mute, so the translator looks at the card pinned to Vito's clothing. He clearly says, "Vito Andolini, from Corleone," but the clerk misunderstands and mutters, "Vito Corleone" (for some reason, the translator does not correct him). The clerk then appears to record "Vito Corleone" on the paper in front of him, and little Vito is sent on his way. And that, we are clearly expected to conclude, is how the Godfather got his name.[10]

It's a powerful, but ridiculous, scene. The idea is based on a misunderstanding of what really happened when someone was asked, "Name?" Though the film otherwise captures the crowded, noisy process at Ellis Island effectively, an egregious historical inaccuracy occurs the moment the clerk writes down Vito's name incorrectly. In reality, immigration officials did not write names down; they checked them off on a list. In other words, the names were *already written down*. The officials were not working with blank sheets of paper on which they created lists of newly arrived passengers but rather with ship manifests, official lists of passengers who had disembarked. These manifests were required by U.S. federal law as of March 2, 1819. Beginning on that date (when the federal government assumed control over immigration), ship captains were required to report a list of all passengers brought to U.S. shores from foreign countries; information required included name, sex, age, and occupation.[11]

Several decades later, in 1893 (just after Ellis Island opened), the requirements for manifests became even more specific: the shipping company clerks were required to obtain contact information and to ask each passenger a series of questions about their health and political views. Furthermore, the clerks who created the manifests were told that "immigrants shall be listed in convenient groups . . . and no [list] shall contain more than 30 names."[12] These instructions are precise and clear; they are published in the *U.S. Statutes at Large*, which contain federal laws as they are passed by Congress. Any captain who didn't turn over a list of names when he dropped off his passengers faced a displeased federal official and some steep fines.

As the *U.S. Statutes at Large* make clear, the passengers' names were recorded long before they arrived, usually as part of the ticket-buying transaction—the same way we arrange travel today. And just like today, before they boarded, each traveler's name and ID was checked against the list of people who had purchased tickets. Today we don't also give our names at the arrival point, but this additional step was part of the processing during the height of immigration to America—hence the misunderstanding promoted by *The Godfather* films.

It's vital to remember that the people coming over from Europe and other places were paying passengers, not cattle. They weren't shoved onto ships and then dumped onto American shores to be newly cataloged by harried immigration officials. The shipping companies were running a business, much as airlines do today; they sold tickets to people who could afford to purchase them (even a steerage-class ticket cost almost $1,000 in today's currency). These companies aggressively advertised, and their agents crisscrossed Europe in search of customers. Someone wanting to book passage to the United States, Canada, Australia, or South America would have had little difficulty locating an agent. Agents quoted ticket prices to the would-be traveler, accepted payment, and then recorded each traveler's name and other identifying information (the specific information collected varied over the years). The information taken down by the agents was sent to the home office, where it was transferred by shipping company clerks onto large preprinted forms provided by the U.S. government. Those sheets became the passenger lists that were eventually used by American port officials to process arrivals.

After all the tickets for a particular voyage had been sold and the manifest was complete, it was turned over to the ship's captain. On departure day, crew members checked people's names against the list as they came on board. The crew allowed past them only those people whose names were on the list (i.e., those who had paid for a ticket). If a person had paid but did not board, his or her name was crossed out on the manifest. If someone was transferred to the vessel after the official manifest had been handed to the captain, that name was added to the list. If a passenger died en route, a notation was made.

Thus, the captain had an accurate, up-to-date list of who was on board when the ship left its home port and who was on board when it docked at the end of the journey. This carefully delineated process explains why there can never be an accurate list of *Titanic* passengers. There were undoubtedly people listed on the manifest who did not board and others whose names were added after the manifest was delivered to the captain (people who missed their departure on another ship and had to be reassigned). Alterations made by the ship's crew existed only on that single copy of the manifest, and that document, like the captain of the *Titanic* himself, went down with the ship. Any list of *Titanic* passengers published today is a reconstruction made with shipping company notes and earlier drafts of the manifest.

Captains were required by the 1819 Steerage Act mentioned above to sign a statement printed on the manifest verifying that the names on each list matched the names of those people disembarking.[13] Any discrepancies resulted in fines for the shipping company. Thus, it was in the shipping company's interest to make sure no one stepped onto American soil whose name was not already on a manifest.

When the ship arrived at an American port, the captain signed the manifest and delivered it to the chief immigration official. That official checked it over and then gave the manifest to officers called registry clerks who questioned each traveler and verified the information recorded on the lists. Figure 1.1 shows immigration officials at Ellis Island. On the left, officials work with completed manifest pages; on the right, travelers (with clothing tags) wait in line and a translator (seated) waits to be needed.

Each official at the high desks worked with a subset of pages from the manifest of a particular voyage. The pages given to each corresponded to the numbers on the clothing tags issued to passengers.

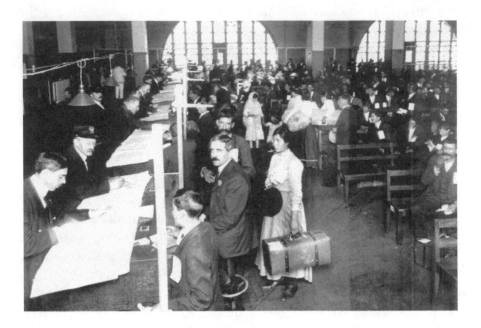

Figure 1.1. **Immigration officials at Ellis Island processing arrivals (ca. 1910).**
Courtesy of Statue of Liberty N.M. and Ellis Island, National Park Service.

These tags, which you can see in the photograph and which play a prominent role in the *Godfather II* scene, usually included the individual's name, home address, and numbers that corresponded with a page in the manifest. A quick glance at a traveler's card told the officials charged with moving people along which line each person needed to stand in.

Obviously then, despite what the *Godfather* film conveys, the officials at Ellis Island did not record travelers' names because they had pages with the names *already filled in*. The task of the registry clerks was to do the same thing the ship's crew had done: check each person's stated name against the name recorded on the manifest. If they didn't match, the newly arrived passenger was sent to detention so his or her case could be reviewed by a board of inquiry. Anyone who could not prove he or she had paid for a ticket (i.e., whose name was not already written down on the manifest) was sent back to the point of embarkation. Those people were (and still are) called "stowaways."

Multiple contemporary films and photographs show officials working with already completed lists, making only checks and tick marks rather than recording the information each time.[14] As you can see in figure 1.2, the manifests were marked on repeatedly.

In addition to the tick marks, a name has been crossed out, indicating that although a ticket was purchased, the passenger did not board. Every manifest page looks like this—full of names written out in Europe or wherever the immigrant originated with a series of marks over numerous columns and some names crossed out. The manifests did not even have blank lines by the time they reached the registry clerks; those blank spaces were lined through by the captain once the ship sailed to prevent any unsanctioned additions. Remember that these manifests

Figure 1.2.   Typical manifest page, with names recorded at origin point and checked off as the immigrant proceeded through the various stages of the journey. *Courtesy of the National Archives.*

became U.S. federal property from the moment the captain passed them on; any alterations had to be made according to federal law. Had the officials at Ellis Island done what they are routinely accused of doing, they would have put their jobs in jeopardy. The manifests, after serving their official purpose, were boxed up and saved; later they were completely microfilmed. Details on this record set are given in chapter 4.

So no one's name was changed at Ellis Island. Though denizens of the Internet will continue to state the myth as if it were truth, their immigrant ancestors without a doubt carried away from Ellis Island and other ports the same name they arrived with. Many immigrants chose to change their names later on. In 1906, federal law made it easy to do so during the citizenship process and still does today.[15] The travelers themselves, then, were responsible for the name shortening and changing that so bothers many people trying to figure out their family history.

Even this brief examination of the procedures involved in traveling and processing makes clear that no federal officer at an American port ever carelessly or maliciously altered an immigrant's name because it was too difficult to spell or sounded too foreign. As a side note, the belief that immigration officials changed names to make them less "foreign" presumes that the Ellis Island officials were of different ethnicities than the immigrants and were openly hostile to them. In fact, officials were often hired because they spoke multiple languages. New York mayor Fiorello LaGuardia began his career as a translator at Ellis Island. The child of European immigrants, he spoke Italian and Yiddish in addition to English.

The memoir of one Ellis Island official provides a fascinating look at the process from within. Victor Safford began working at Ellis Island in 1895. In his 1925 book, *Immigration Problems: Personal Experiences of an Official*,[16] Safford describes encountering crowds of passengers on the day of his job interview. He notes the conversations he overheard between people who spoke a variety of languages, including German, Norwegian, Yiddish, Italian, Croatian, and Hungarian. He says this casually, as if a working knowledge of several languages is not unusual— and it wasn't, for someone being interviewed to work with foreign-born travelers. Safford was not an outlier in this fluency. He notes that at his interview, officials and government employees were conversing among themselves in various languages other than English. And if the official did not speak a traveler's language, translators were available to assist, as the photograph shown in figure 1.1 makes clear.

Mario Puzo's famous novel was published in 1969; unlike the later film director, Puzo says that Vito Andolini changed his own name later on to honor his hometown of Corleone. Perhaps Francis Ford Coppola, director of *The Godfather* (1972), *The Godfather II* (1974), and *The Godfather III* (1990), did not know this or did not know how the immigrants were actually processed. After all, his film was completed long before today's relatively easy access to the passenger manifests, federal documents, and contemporary video and photography that show that processing. But the time when such ignorance of historical reality can be excused has long passed.

SUMMING IT UP

Genealogy has been around for many years but has never been more popular. It is both easier and harder to do today, both for the same reason—the availability of records. But connecting people to records is only the beginning; real understanding of the past takes time, patience, and dedicated effort. Remember:

- The best place to start a family history is with yourself, with what you already know.
- All families have secrets; if you research your family enough, you will uncover some.
- If your family's original surname was changed, it was almost certainly done intentionally by someone in the family.

Next: The best first steps for a beginner.

2

THE BEST FIRST STEPS FOR A RESEARCHER

This chapter addresses:

- Recording what you and your family members know
- Finding family pictures and documents
- Conducting online and offline research
- Best research practices

What does the potential genealogist need to know to get started? Well, it helps to get a sense of the big picture.[1] Ideally, a genealogist does three things: (1) preserves the memories of living family members through interviews and recordings, (2) preserves family photos and other artifacts by scanning and safely housing them, and (3) researches the movements and connections of people through a variety of online and offline sources.

Family historians are driven by a sense that future generations deserve to and will want to know about the people who came before. Serious genealogists put in countless hours piecing together a history, and that hard work pays off in at least three significant ways. First, it satisfies the researcher's own curiosity. Second, it helps living people become better informed about their family's movements, connections, and stories. Third, it preserves the information and artifacts for future generations. Because of the nature of the process, genealogists also play a role in bringing family members together.

Genealogy can be many things: an interesting subject at family reunions, a way to connect people over shared memories, but also a time-devouring, never-ending project with notes that take up every available surface in a home office. Wherever you are in the process, there is always more to learn—family members turn up, record collections expand, and search strategies improve. It's easy to get overwhelmed. Each new bit of information can lead to a new avenue to explore, new people to call, and new data to enter.

We've all seen those Ancestry commercials that make doing family history seem easy (Oh, look—a leaf!). But complex research projects are never easy. Researching and recording a family history involves commitment of resources (time, energy, and money), plus large amounts of patience and creativity. Many people who enthusiastically start a genealogy project give up in frustration after a short time. If that's happened to you, this book can help you get past that frustration and achieve satisfying results from your efforts.

You already know doing family history involves research—lots of it. But you should start with something more important: preserving your own memories and those of your still-living family members. After that, it's more important to preserve family documents, photos, and other artifacts than it is to do records research. The records will be there long after the living people are gone, and your precious family artifacts need your protection as soon as possible.

Here is a recommended five-step plan for approaching and succeeding at a family history research project:

Step 1. Obtain and record the most easily accessed information about your family.

- Write what you already know onto an ancestral chart and on family group sheets.
- Make calls to family members to fill in the gaps. Ask questions that elicit hard data.
- Jot down the questions not yet answered. Conduct more interviews to get answers.

Step 2. Record interviews with family members using a detailed questionnaire.

- Select a high-quality audio recording device and learn how to use it.
- Learn good interview techniques and use the questionnaire in the appendix.
- Use pictures to prompt memories and stories.
- Transcribe the interviews into a Word document and edit the audio files with Audacity.

Step 3. Find and scan all the family papers and pictures that you can access.

- Use a flatbed scanner, not your phone or a "wand" scanner.
- Scan photographs at 600 dpi and documents at 300 dpi.
- Label scans as soon as possible, using a consistent system.
- Preserve family papers and pictures using plastic sleeves.
- Use a consistent system for labeling digital files.
- Make multiple backups or use an online service that automatically backs up your data.

Step 4. Do online research to document the information already obtained and get new information.

- Aim to create an *evidence-based* family tree.
- Use the gold standard as your guide: information is the currency, and documents are the gold.
- Download, label, and save every document that contributes information to your family history.
- Use free resources as much as possible, but be ready to spend some money on the project.

Step 5. Share your findings.

- Use a family-tree program to record information as you collect it; be sure to note sources.
- Upload and tag pictures on Facebook and other sites.
- Create a YouTube video using pictures and audio clips from your interviews.

START WITH YOURSELF

The classic advice for aspiring writers has always been to "write what you know." The same advice applies for the novice genealogist. The best place to start a family history is with *you*. A pen and a piece of paper are all you need to begin recording the names, dates, and other relevant information about the people to whom you are related. Sketch it out in tree form on a big piece of paper, with yourself and your siblings in one row; then add earlier and later generations above and below that line. You can also use a writeable PDF (available online). To prompt your memory, use the questionnaire included in the appendix.

To take this step further, you might get a workbook (there are several available through Amazon) wherein you can record your personal information and memories in a systematic, logical way. These books are widely available but vary in usefulness, so check reviews first.

After your own information is captured, it is time for the real work of genealogy to start: interviewing people, preserving information and artifacts, and researching with available online and offline resources. As you move along in the process, keep a higher goal in mind than simply making a family tree. You are doing historical research—creating a history where none existed before. The tree is nice, but it's only a convenient way to look at the information you collect, not the ultimate goal of the project.

CHOOSE A FAMILY TREE SOFTWARE PROGRAM

Before you start your calls and interviews, think about how you are going to capture and display the information you obtain. The choice of family tree software program is crucial; it will be your constant companion on this journey, so take the time to choose wisely. The program will represent your family's history in visual and graphic form; the best ones allow you to share the information easily in the form of charts and reports. Options and products abound; a Google search of *genealogy software review* should pull up plenty. But don't stop there; ask experienced family history researchers which programs they use and are satisfied with. A genealogy software program does far more than make a "tree"; it is an essential, data-intensive storage mechanism for records, abstracts, analyses, and conclusions. Whichever program you choose, be sure that it allows you to export your tree as a *.ged* file. Also, make sure that if your work is shared online, it does not disclose names and dates for living people.

CONNECTING WITH THE LIVING

After you've set up your genealogy software program, enter the data from your own recollections. It's tempting to plunge into some online research at this point, but resist the temptation for a while. Historical records and indexes are vital to family history research, of course, but the most valuable resource you have right now is living people, so the next step is to interview and record the oldest generation still around.

Start calling or visiting elderly relations as soon as possible. Begin by telling your subjects that you are compiling the family history and that you welcome their participation. Show them the "tree" you have created thus far, and ask permission to record their answers to questions like the ones given in the appendix. Try to obtain specific information: names; dates and places of births, deaths, marriages, and divorces; locality and street names; churches and schools attended; military branches served in; and any unusual facts, such as nicknames or whether someone was in an unusual profession or lived somewhere the others did not. Above all, frame your questions to make remembering easier for your subjects: "How old were you when your grandfather died?" is easier to answer than "What year did your grandfather die?" For now, avoid questions that are open-ended invitations to reminisce ("Tell me about your grandfather"). Plan on multiple sessions, because your subjects will run out of energy before you run out of questions. Also, as you dig for documents to prove or disprove what you have heard, you will have some follow-up questions. End each interview session by asking if you can come back later.

Keep in mind that interview subjects are sometimes justifiably concerned about disclosing personal information, especially birth dates. If you have chosen the right database program, it will not reveal that information about living people when uploaded or shared as a .ged file. The highest-rated programs display only a blank square with the words *living person*—nothing more.

If you are lucky, your interview subjects will let you handle documents and other artifacts they possess. If they do not possess such family records, ask them who in the family does; that's the next person to talk to. Every family has a member who saves everything, especially papers and pictures. Keep asking until you find the person who has that stash of papers, books, and other objects. You will need to scan these items so that you can access them long after your visit to the person who holds them, so bring a laptop and scanner or a digital camera/phone that takes high-resolution photos to your interviews. Whichever technology you choose, your aim is to end up with quality images that you can view repeatedly as the months and years pass. See chapter 3 for advice on managing digital files.

In addition to these formal interviews, it's a good idea to establish regular contact with the person in the family who tends to know everyone else's business; every family has somebody like this. In sociological terms, this person is the "maven"—the one most plugged in to the family's activities. That person will not only give you clues to follow multiple trails but also will often help you connect with previously unknown relations. Mavens are often keepers of family pictures, documents, and other treasures, so spending time with them is doubly rewarding. Photographs are especially valuable when used in conjunction with interviews and conversations. People's memories improve dramatically when they look at photographs; suddenly, the past is visual in the present, and the words come more easily.

Obtaining precise information from living people is not easy. In today's media-saturated world, we are all mentally fixed in the present by what we see and hear, and the past can seem remote and uninteresting to those not immersed in a historical research project. Be patient with the process.

FINDING FAMILY PAPERS, PHOTOS, AND ARTIFACTS

People save all sorts of papers, but usually the saved material has some special significance, whether personal, social, legal, or otherwise. Papers whose value is not immediately obvious to the holder tend to be discarded, but sometimes you will luck upon a trove of papers kept by someone "just in case." Photographs are more predictably saved, no matter the quality, so they present a different problem (more on that in chapter 3). If you own any of these items yourself, take steps to protect them from natural enemies such as dirt, moisture, light, and insects. And then do the same for the pictures and papers you have access to at the homes of family members.

These papers and pictures are vital to your work as family historian. Certificates, deeds, invitations, memorial cards, and even pictures all potentially contain important facts, such as names and dates, and sometimes they provide essential links among people, making clear who is related and how. When you scan pictures, be sure to scan the back of the photograph as well if it has handwritten words identifying the picture or event. When you label your scans later, indicate in the file name or notes who wrote the picture info.

Accessing these family papers usually costs nothing, and the payoff from them is immense. Before you spend money and time obtaining records from genealogy subscription sites, mine your family's own collection.

It's important to keep a mental list of what documents are often found among family papers and to keep asking about them until you find them. Following is a working list of categories.

Birth

Birth documents include not only the certificate issued by the county or city where the birth occurred but also such items as memorial certificates issued by hospitals. Look closely at the certificates to establish whether they are original or extract (a later version giving the information) and what date they were issued. Also in this category are copies of hospital bills, newspaper clippings and mailed cards announcing a birth, and, in many religious denominations, baptism records. Baby books are always a wonderful find because they often state the exact time and place of birth and mention not only the parents but also the baby's siblings and godparents. Baby books often contain loose or glued-in papers, so handle them carefully.

Marriage

This category includes newspaper clippings announcing an engagement or marriage, wedding invitations and programs, lists of shower attendees and gifts, and notes about the wedding party. It also includes any legal paperwork relating to divorce proceedings, which tend to be saved alongside the happier things, as well as later marriage-related items, such as anniversary party invitations and pictures (e.g., a dated picture showing a cake with "Happy 50th, Mom and Dad!" on it). Rarely do marriage documents in family papers include a copy of the marriage license (that's usually on file at the county archives), but people do as a rule preserve the official certificate issued by the religious institution that married them.

Death

Many families today obtain copies of death certificates as a matter of course, but in the past, this rarely happened. Instead, you might find among family papers obituaries clipped from a newspaper (ideally with the paper's name and date written in), small memorial cards and sign-in books from funerals, and bills or receipts for funeral expenses, including the purchase of engraved headstones. Families usually save the paperwork relating to the purchase of burial plots; the purchaser was buying real estate, after all, so an official-looking deed is issued. Also included in this category are photographs of gravestones. The funeral sign-in books, by the way, are an excellent source of names of other family members you can find and interview. If they attended the funeral, they knew something about the deceased.

Travel

The federal law requiring all American citizens to have a passport to reenter the country dates back only to 1941, but passports have been available since the earliest days of the nation, and sometimes these have been preserved. Additionally, many other nations had passport requirements for their citizens, and these documents were typically brought over by immigrants. Travel documentation apart from passports is rare among family papers, but occasionally you will discover receipts, itineraries, or maps. The best travel-related documentation—incoming passenger lists—comes from a federal source and is not found among family papers.

Organizations

Almost every adult has belonged to some organization, and sometimes you will find membership cards, receipts for payments, and printed materials describing the organization and the benefits of membership. In the past, many social organizations offered life insurance or savings plans, and families sometimes still have the record books for these accounts. Accessing the archives of these organizations is usually not possible, but the mere evidence that your family members belonged can potentially help you later.

Social Security

The familiar blue-and-white cards Social Security cards, first issued by the federal government in 1937, sometimes appear among preserved family papers, along with letters and benefit statements from the Social Security Administration. What you will not find among the family papers but can easily order is any deceased person's original application for a Social Security number. See chapter 4 for details on this important resource.

Medical

The medical category contains documents available exclusively within the family; medical records are almost never available online. Ephemera such as an ancestor or family member's immunization, vision, and dental records often contain the patient's address at the time of service and the name and address of the medical service provider, among other clues, so are always worth examining. Insurance cards and statements (also with addresses) are sometimes saved for future reference, although they might be buried in files and not kept in a strongbox or other more protected environment.

Photographs

Much of a family's history can be traced through its photographs. Pictures show aspects of a family that are rarely written down: clothing, vehicles, home furnishings, party attendees, affection between friends, and cherished pets. Sometimes we forget that the lives of our ancestors took place outside those moments when they were creating another stop on the paper trail we are following. The pictures, if someone has been diligent about labeling them, can provide good leads for how people were connected and where they were on particular dates. In one case, a researcher ran across a series of unlabeled photographs showing his city-dwelling relatives posing with farm equipment and feeding farm animals. But they lived a long way from any farm, and no one in the family knew of a connection to farming. Those photographs remained an unexplained oddity until a subsequently discovered newspaper clipping noted that a distant cousin had purchased a farm in another state. No one alive today remembers the road trip that produced the pictures, but those pictures provide evidence that it occurred and who was involved.

Old film and video can also provide vital clues to an ancestor's activities. Moving images are less useful, however, because they cannot be labeled as effectively as photographs, nor can they be easily enlarged for close inspection. Even worse, the material that composes film and videotape has a short life span; it deteriorates much faster than photo paper.

Newspapers

People of the past were consumers of newspapers in a way that today's media consumers are not. They read their papers thoroughly and often clipped out notable items, such as recipes, book reviews, and advice columns. They also clipped birth and marriage announcements, obituaries, news of performances by family members, workplace or organizational awards, and other social activities. The smaller the town, the more likely that such items would appear. Small towns printed "news" that was ignored by large city papers: hospital admissions and discharges, police activity, and farm reports. Many times, someone has cut these stories out and put them in a scrapbook.

Unfortunately, the quality of the paper used for almost every news publication since about the mid-19th century is poor: Called *newsprint*, this cheap paper made from wood pulp is thin and highly acidic. The ink tends to smear, and as the years pass, the paper will turn yellow and crumble. Most people have seen the effect of a clipped newspaper column tucked into the pages of a book—the adjacent pages are stained in the exact shape of the clipping. Newsprint was not designed for the future but for immediate use. If you find saved newsprint among your family papers, take the time to enclose the clippings in plastic (a resealable baggie works fine) so that the acid in them does not affect other papers.

School

The subscription site Ancestry makes available the scanned pages of many high school and college yearbooks. Before this addition to their resources, school records were found only among family papers. But you can still find much among private papers that connects to schools: grade report cards, test results, diplomas and certificates of completion, performance and graduation programs, medals and other awards, letters from school administrators. Every student brought home some of these items, and most parents saved them.

Correspondence

Family letters and postcards can be the most precious of treasures because, unlike the other paperwork, they usually give a sense of someone's personality, and they are almost never found outside of private collections. Make careful scans of each page and envelope you find, front and back; later you can create a PDF so you have a single file with all the images pertaining to a single letter (see chapter 3 for details on how to do this).

Today's genealogists are lucky: they are likely to find handwritten letters. But what of the genealogists a hundred years from now? How will they find correspondence that now exists only in digital form?

Bibles and Religious Books

The tradition of recording pertinent family information in religious books has not died away, and the further back the family's religious book goes, the more likely that it will contain lists of births, marriages, and deaths. People often tuck into Bibles things like memorial cards and notices about baptisms, weddings, and funerals.

Other Records

Into this category fall the rest of the items potentially to be found among boxed-up family treasures: award or recognition plaques, trophies, scrapbooks, expired driver's licenses, and old address books, among other things. All provide evidence of activity that cannot be found online or through research in archives. Scrapbooks, if they were maintained over a stretch of time, can reveal a context that you could not re-create from documents alone.

Things to Keep in Mind about Family Records

It is tempting to move quickly through the papers found within your family's collections, mining each one for pertinent data and then dumping the lot back into the cardboard box that it came in. But that is the wrong approach. See chapter 3 for details on managing paper genealogy records safely and effectively.

Once you have interviewed relatives and scanned available documents from family collections, you should have a good idea of what information in your history still needs verification or is missing. Remember that, ideally, all the data entered into your software program should have reliable documentary evidence behind it. Think of the information in your tree like paper money used to be when we were on the gold standard—merely a representation of the real value. Your growing digital archive of scanned documents is the gold that backs up the representation.

CONDUCTING RESEARCH

Moving on to the research phase of family history work is a big step. Research can be exciting, rewarding, and challenging all at the same time. Usually, we think about genealogy research as something done online, but that's only partly true. Thorough family history research involves both online and offline resources. Conducting online research is, of course, a big part of what family historians do, and as such it will be the subject of two chapters (5 and 6) in this book. For now, here is an overview of the research angle of your genealogy project.

Gathering documentary evidence from family sources is an essential step. To go further, you will need records from federal, state, county, and city record archives, as well as from nongovernment sources such as newspapers. Fortunately for the 21st-century genealogist, access to these resources is easier than it has ever been before, thanks to digitizing projects at all levels. The goal of your research at this stage is to collect *records*. A record is anything with information that helps you place people in connection to other people, places, times, and activities.

For the last century or so, every person born has caused some paperwork to be generated. Beginning with birth, the paperwork generation process continues, mostly out of our sight, until death. This has not always been the case. In general, the further back in time you go, the fewer paper records there are to find because fewer were created than is customary today; even more significant, the passage of time has led to the disappearance of records. Every year that a paper record must survive is another year that it could be damaged or lost. But millions of paper records remain, and almost everyone who has some basic information to begin with can find family-relevant federal, state, or county records.

Begin the process of searching for records outside the family by making a list of which ones *should* exist for each person. If you are researching someone born in the 20th century, a birth certificate for that person likely exists somewhere, as do the death certificates for those no longer living. A county marriage record was created regardless of whether the marriage took place in a church; churches, synagogues, and mosques kept their own records. And if a marriage ended in divorce, a court record was created. If your relative served in the military, there is a paper record to document that. And if your ancestor was born outside the United States and became a citizen, you stand a good chance of finding immigration and naturalization records.

Tip: Before you plunge into online searching and certainly before you commit any money, you should weigh the advantages and disadvantages of having one username and password for all your genealogy-related research. Having the same password for multiple sites is not usually recommended, but in this case you might want to consider it just for this project.

There are many free genealogy sites, but to do quality research you will need the subscription service called Ancestry, which is available as a personal subscription and through public libraries. But Ancestry alone isn't enough; you will need others, some free and some not. You should make extensive use of free sites and the subscription databases available at the public library, but the most powerful tool you have apart from Ancestry is called FamilySearch (familysearch.org), a site run by the LDS church. FamilySearch offers free access to indexes and download-able records from an incredible variety of sources. At FamilySearch, you can download original birth and death certificates that otherwise would come with a fee if ordered from the relevant county vital records office. No genealogist can do without this site. See chapter 5 for details.

So what records are you looking for? If you do a search in either Ancestry or FamilySearch, you will notice that the U.S. federal census record set appears first in the list of results for both. That is with good reason. The federal census is the best verification for family groups— who went together and (since 1880) what relation they had to the head of the family. As you find census records for various branches of your family, you will learn a great deal about the people involved, including where they lived and, if relevant, what type of work they did. You simply cannot compile an extensive family history without census records. Fortunately, they are not difficult to work with.

If you have relatives who came to the United States from another country, you will want to make use of the immigration and naturaliza-tion records available for download through Ancestry and Family-Search, among other places. These sites are essential for all genealo-gists. Although they do overlap some, their differences are important, and the sites should always be used in tandem.

There is a downside to using your library's Ancestry subscription: it is usually restricted to in-house use only, which means that you must use one of the library's public computer stations. If you decide on a personal subscription, remember that Ancestry offers a U.S. records–only plan and an international plan. Before you choose the latter, be sure that you need the specific international records that it offers. You can access many international records through Family-Search for no cost at all.

Immigration records, which include the passenger lists of people arriving at Ellis Island and other ports, are held by the federal government and are made available through the National Archives in partnership with genealogy sites. Naturalization records, however, are not always federal; these records are often held at the county level (see chapter 4 for details).

Some records will not be so easily obtained, but it is possible to get them if you have the know-how. There is no online source for religious institution records, but between them, Ancestry and FamilySearch have covered a lot of ground here. Most military records are available upon request, but you will find no comprehensive index for them. Legal records—such as those pertaining to divorce, probate, adoption, criminal proceedings, and court-ordered institutionalizations—are often available but usually not online, so you must work at the county level to access them. Many counties and states allow you to search a records portal, from which you can obtain document numbers; the documents themselves can then be ordered with that reference number. Municipal sites often make property value and tax assessment data available for free, whether online or in person.

Digital Problems

When your research is just getting started online, the records come easily. But then the day arrives when no more records are revealed by searching a surname in its correct form; you have hit the inevitable brick wall that genealogists are so fond of referring to (some bloggers mix up their metaphors and speak of the need to "tackle those brick walls"). Whatever the metaphor, you will need to learn how to search creatively if you want more records. Searching creatively requires time and patience, plus a basic understanding of how the search function works and how the information you are searching was created.

Several decades ago, all researchers operated without digitized information. They consulted printed indexes that pointed them to text sources that had to be examined in print or microfilm form. There were no indexes that had the articles themselves attached, as you can find today. It took these first-wave genealogists years to track down information that can now be obtained in days.

No longer do people looking for journal articles need to consult heavy index volumes with tiny print. With the advent of computerized databases such as InfoTrac, WilsonWeb, and EBSCOhost in the 1980s, the procedures for all academic research, including genealogy, were changed radically. While the underlying nature of research did not change—you still needed to find data, analyze evidence, draw conclusions, and cite sources—searches that the first wavers could not have dreamed of became possible overnight. You could do a search in a library catalog, for example, that combined a keyword in the title field with another keyword anywhere in the record and that limited the results by date. That kind of flexibility was brand new, and genealogists took full advantage. Soon, not only were the hefty indexes being digitized but so were the texts themselves. Digitization projects began across North America, and by the end of the 20th century, digitized images were part of every researcher's life. Travel is still necessary, of course, when the material you need has not been digitized or made available through interlibrary loan (a system that allows one library to borrow from another).

What we sometimes forget, however, is that for genealogy-relevant record sets, those computerized databases—the indexes and extracts—were sometimes created by, or at least sponsored by, for-profit companies. The highest goal of those companies was to create a product (searchable indexes) that could be sold in the form of subscription access. And they wanted those products created quickly, because the sooner the information became available, the sooner access could be sold. The business model works; Ancestry, Fold3, and other companies like them are hugely successful, and no one questions the value of their products to genealogy research. But that particular business mode, based on maximizing the profit from selling access to information, is not necessarily the best one for creating an accurate index to a database.

Libraries, archives, and municipal offices are awash in a sea of paper records, almost none of which are findable until they are indexed, with the basic information extracted into searchable form. A list of Civil War casualties from one small town in New York is a wonderful thing if you are researching families in that town, but if the only copy of it resides in a distant or inaccessible archive, it cannot easily become part of your data. Someone must input the information contained in that list into a database so you can connect to it, and that someone is a particularly weak link in the chain.

Data entry work has never been glamorous or well paid, and yet the entire paradigm of searching online and in electronic indexes today rests on the work of individuals who entered, one character at a time, all those names and dates. In more recent years, the digitization has been done partly by optical character recognition, which has somewhat eliminated the need for data entry, but even that still requires a human eye to correct the resulting digital text. Whether they were being paid or were volunteering for a library, archive, museum, or not-for-profit organization (e.g., the LDS church's Family History Library), the individuals who indexed and copied were only human, with all-too-fallible connections among their eyes, brains, and hands.

Western culture has a five-thousand-year history of people copying written texts. Beginning with the earliest clay tablets written on with a sharp stick (the resulting script is called cuneiform) and lasting until the 15th-century advent of the printing press in Germany, people produced texts by hand. If a copy was desired, that also had to be created by hand. Gutenberg's press made large-scale copying jobs (e.g., entire books) obsolete, but it did not eliminate the need for handwriting and hand copying. Well into the 19th century, until the widespread use of the typewriter, businesses and individuals who wanted a second copy of something (say a legal document) had to engage a *scrivener* (like the famous Bartleby of Melville's story), a person who would copy an original text onto a fresh sheet of paper. These scriveners, or professional copyists, followed the same procedure established thousands of years before by their copyist brethren: they transferred the words by glancing first at the original, then at the copy being created as they inscribed the remembered words onto it. The work of scriveners was eventually taken over by typists, who do the same thing when copying.

Rather than looking at two pieces of paper simultaneously, copyists and typists transfer bits of data from one document into their brains for a few microseconds before completing the transfer to another document (on paper or screen) via movement of the hands (i.e., either writing or typing). That's why the possibility of error is always present. A tired copyist might write out the same line twice, might skip a line entirely, or might replace an unfamiliar word with one that is more common (e.g., *indicate* instead of *indict* in a legal document). These errors have always been part of the copying process; they result from the limitations of human perception and the reality of how eyes, minds, and hands do not always work together perfectly.

The errors of early copyists are well known by historians who study ancient and medieval documents. Those long-ago scribes were, like later data-entry personnel, often overworked and underpaid, and yet they were doing work that later generations would base research, even careers, on. If those scribes made errors (which they certainly did), we cannot doubt that the later scriveners, typists, and copyists did as well. The people who did the indexing for the major record sets commonly used by genealogists operated within the same perceptual limitations as those earlier copyists and were thus prone to making the same errors.

Yet the problems with the indexes are rarely mentioned by the organizations that sell or provide access to the databases. Some, such as Ancestry, do offer subscribers an easy way to submit corrections; most others, even the massive Ellis Island database (www.libertyellis foundation.org) and FamilySearch, do not. This silence leads to the mistaken impression that the indexed names are an accurate representation of the names in the original records. In reality, just about every page of vital record sets such as the federal census and the ships' passenger lists is replete with copying errors serious enough to prevent you from finding those documents.

In addition to the built-in tendency toward error when human beings are copying, genealogy data banks have a second problem: the speed at which the extracting or indexing was done. When the pages of the 1940 census were released in 2012, a call went out across the Internet for volunteers to extract the documents quickly so that genealogists could get online access to the information that those records contained. Everyone doing family history research waited impatiently for that data, and many joined in the extracting efforts.

Here was a newly available record set of unparalleled significance for genealogy, one destined to be used by countless researchers in the future, and the highest priority when it was released by the National

Archives was that the data be indexed *as soon as possible*. Companies that sold access to the census posted regular updates on when it would be available; they wanted that data for their subscribers and attracted new subscribers by promising access. No one, it seems, was wondering if making speed the highest goal for that set of extractions was the best approach.

Whether the indexers were being paid or were working as volunteers, they were usually given the same set of instructions: copy accurately—that is, "write what you see." They were asked *not* to think about what they saw but merely to reproduce it. That is not a bad set of instructions for copyists, but it creates a problem when the information in the document is incorrect or the indexer cannot read the handwriting of the original. It is difficult enough to read the handwriting of contemporaries; indexers usually did not get training in the handwriting conventions of people decades ago. Their goal was to copy what they saw. If they saw gibberish because they did not recognize the names and words in someone else's cursive script, they wrote gibberish.

Do an index search on any common surname in the census or passenger records on Ancestry or FamilySearch and you will see that this is the case—nonsensical names instead of people's actual names, simply because the indexers could not read the handwriting and were working under pressure of a deadline. They can be forgiven for following orders to write what they saw, but those orders did not preclude them from recording an additional entry—the one that their common sense should have told them was correct.

Apart from the future release of the decennial census pages, the major record sets used by genealogists have already been indexed and extracted, and the errors are in the databases to stay. Over time, perhaps, at least with Ancestry, user corrections will create a more accurate index. For now, the most practical thing that a genealogist can do with these error-filled indexes and databases is to learn what sort of mistakes were typical, why those particular mistakes were made, and how to work around them. Chapter 5 gives helpful search strategies for finding online records.

Doing genealogy research is easier today because of the abundance of digitized information, but it is not easy and never will be. Working with these databases can be immensely rewarding and exciting, but that work can also be frustrating because of the errors that permeate them.

The mistakes typical to one record set are different in another one, so it is a good idea to become familiar with which documents invited certain mistakes.

Cluster Research and Negative Results

Searching for records can be a challenge if you stay focused on a single person. If you have no luck finding someone, expand your search to the known siblings, friends, and neighbors of the person to generate clues for finding the real target. Genealogists call this *cluster research*. For example, go back to the family photo collection—how near is your targeted person to other people in the pictures, perhaps posed in a way that indicates a close relationship? Who is buried next to your family members? Check the census pages—who lived next door? Look at the death certificates you have obtained—who provided the information and signed as the informant? If you are lucky enough to have access to family correspondence, look up the people who sent letters to your relatives.

Sherlock Holmes, in the Arthur Conan Doyle story "The Silver Blaze," famously drew Watson's attention to "the curious incident of the dog in the night-time." When Watson pointed out that the dog did nothing—that is, it did not bark—Holmes pointed out that the absence of something can be used as evidence: the criminal was someone the dog knew well, so the dog didn't bark. The lesson for genealogists here: pay close attention to what you *don't* find. For example, imagine that you are looking up a family in the 1940 census. You know that by 1940, the family consisted of two parents and three children; yet, when you find the census record, only two of the three children are listed; the youngest, age nine, is missing. You are certain that child lived well past 1940, but he is not there with his family. You should not ignore that fact but instead start looking for the child somewhere else; he must have been living with relatives or perhaps as a patient in a hospital. Remember that the census is a snapshot of one day in the life of people across the nation. A child born the day after will not be represented, even though the birth occurred in the same year as the census.

Recognizing and dealing with information you do not see when it should be there will help you solve some of your family mysteries. But the biggest questions of all will likely remain unanswered. As you research, you will find yourself asking over and over, "But *why*?" Why did the child live with a relative? Why did this person die in a place where she did not reside? Why did this family end up living in a faraway state? Why did your ancestor bring a certain artifact from his home country? Finding records will not usually supply you with answers that get at motivations and explanations for events. You will have to be content with noting that these things happened.

You'll find lots more about doing online research in later chapters of this book.

Making a Research Plan

After you have spent some time searching online, you will reach the point where you have downloaded all the easily accessed documents. Ancestry does make the initial process easy and exciting with its sidebar suggestions for records to look at. But eventually you will reach the end of the easy part. When that happens, consider making a more formalized research plan. Start by drafting a list or description of what information you already have for each person you are researching, and then make a list of the documents and information you do not have but that should be available. For example, if you are researching a male relative who was of the right age to register during one of the draft calls but that record didn't turn up right away, keep digging; perhaps the name was misspelled by the indexer. If you know a record should exist, don't be put off by not finding it immediately. Searching creatively will eventually yield some of the records you weren't able to find right away, and those will lead you to others. With family history research, persistence inevitably pays off, even if you don't always find exactly what you're looking for.

Most important of all, do not get so caught up in the thrill and challenge of online searching that you forget to keep talking to and interviewing elderly relatives; they are your most important source for the full picture of a family's history, the ones who can supply the information not contained in the documentary record. The documents will still be available when the living people are gone.

Local History Files

Your local library probably has a special section devoted to material pertaining to the place you live, much of it not duplicated elsewhere. In the past, public and school libraries maintained what were called *vertical files*, folders containing miscellaneous articles, clippings, pamphlets, and fact sheets on a wide variety of subjects. Though not on public display, these materials often still reside in libraries; you just have to ask. What you're after is a collection of local history books and newspapers, whether in original form, microfilmed, or digitized. What's in those books and papers isn't of tremendous interest outside of a certain locality, but it is of great interest to historians who work within it. Many towns and cities also have a local history organization that maintains records and files.

If you grew up in a small town, you know that the local town newspaper regularly published newsy items relating to people who lived in the area. Not just engagements and marriages but also parties, hospital stays, visits from relatives, school awards, and social events were (and in many cases still are) routinely reported. But even if you grew up in a city, you probably know about neighborhood-specific papers. Large cities have one or two publications that focus on national, international, and city-specific news, of course, but those cities are divided into neighborhoods and usually have suburbs. For city dwellers, neighborhood or suburb identification can mean more than their affiliation with the city. A person who grew up in Chicago will most likely say "Chicago" to the question "Where are you from?"—but only if asked by someone not from that city. Another Chicago resident asking the question will elicit a more precise response, identifying a quadrant of the city, specific neighborhood, or suburb.

Neighborhood and small-town papers vary widely in quality and quantity but are always worth pursuing. Many of these repositories of local doings are not digitized, and they are likely to be in a fragile state so might not be available for handling. Keep digging though; they are out there and ready to play a part in your family history research.

Cemetery Research

Most people today rarely visit cemeteries, but for many families, such visits were once a normal part of their routine, especially on holidays. Decades ago, people tended to make a day of it, bringing a picnic lunch along with their sun hats and floral arrangements.

Cemeteries have always attracted genealogists because the stones are lasting testimonials to those who have passed. Some family historians and hobbyists in the past did *gravestone rubbing*—making an image on paper of something carved into stone by rubbing charcoal, wax, or graphite over the paper while it is pressed against a stone. However, this practice has largely been abandoned and is discouraged because it can cause damage to the stones. The advent of digital photography has made stone rubbing unnecessary, because you can take multiple shots of each stone and enlarge them later for closer study.

Working in cemeteries is inevitable for the genealogist who desires to be thorough, but it requires some preparation. Remember that cemeteries were created to be places of eternal rest and were not set up to facilitate genealogy research. Furthermore, most cemeteries are not managed by the government, so their records are not public; you have no citizen's right to see them.

To prepare for your visit to a cemetery, check to see if the place has a website or is part of a site that lists the area's burial grounds. If you find online information, note the cemetery's hours, parking availability, the nearest entrance to the office building, and where the nearest restrooms are. Make a printed list of names that you want to look up and bring along some additional note-taking materials. Wear sturdy shoes. Most cemeteries do not have walkways and smooth paths along the rows, and the ground can be treacherously uneven. Also, bring a hat and sunscreen and, of course, your camera. If you are looking for older graves, carry some gardening gloves and a tool to trim away the grass that has most likely overgrown the flat stones. Most cemeteries close well before dark, so plan accordingly.

Cemeteries' grounds are usually organized by section, then by block (or row), and then by grave. Ideally, the burial records held by the cemetery office are precise and match the labeling out on the grounds. The older a cemetery is, however, the less likely it is that the blocks and graves will be labeled accurately. Finding crypts and mausoleum burials (as opposed to in-ground burials) is usually much easier.

Your first stop on-site should be the cemetery office. If you are lucky, you'll find a search kiosk that allows you to look up multiple gravesites from your list. Otherwise, you'll have to ask the desk clerk to conduct your searches. Responses from cemetery personnel vary widely. Some are accustomed to people searching multiple names, but others are willing to look up only a few names at a time. To get accurate burial information, approach the counter, politely make your request, and then watch, if you're lucky, as the clerk flips through heavy, interesting-looking volumes called *plat books*. That term comes from geographical mapping and is connected to the fact that burial plots are sold as real estate (an exact map of the boundaries for real estate plots is required by law). Ask the clerk to note the location on a map of the cemetery, but do not forget to obtain a blank map as well so that you can scan it and add the image to your digital files. The scanned map will come in handy later if you want to create a customized map of all the burials for a particular family. Of course, many cemeteries are small and have neither offices nor maps.

Cemetery searching can be both frustrating and rewarding. You can spend hours searching for graves without success and then find one unexpectedly. If you stick with it, cemetery research will reward you with not only data for your family history but also a sense of connection with long-gone family members, and you will almost certainly find relatives you never knew about before. Take pictures or make notes about the graves in the immediate vicinity to your special people; sometimes they turn out to contain people connected to your family.

DOING QUALITY RESEARCH

In the mid-1840s, a newly hired Hungarian obstetrician working at the Vienna General Hospital noticed something strange about the hospital's two free maternity clinics: women were dying from "childbed fever" in Clinic 1 at twice the rate of those in Clinic 2. Childbed fever (now known as *puerperal fever*) was, in the mid-19th century, a mystery to doctors, but Ignaz Semmelweis was intrigued by the disparity in mortality rates within two parts of the same hospital. As he tended his patients,

Semmelweis discovered that the doctors examining patients in Clinic 1 were primarily medical students who, as part of their studies, also performed autopsies, which the doctors in Clinic 2 did not do. He hypothesized that invisible and unidentified disease vectors (which he called *cadaverous particles*) got stuck to the hands of doctors during autopsies, survived the normal quick wash with soap, and were then transferred into the bodies of women during obstetric examinations. His colleagues laughed at him. How could they, the doctors, be responsible for the very illnesses they strove to cure?

To test his hypothesis, Semmelweis convinced the doctors of Clinic 1 to soak their hands in a chlorinated lime solution after contacting cadavers and between examinations of their pregnant patients. The lime, an antiseptic, proved effective, and Semmelweis observed a dramatic drop in Clinic 1's incidence of mortality due to childbed fever. The young doctor described the affliction as *iatrogenic* (i.e., caused by the medical process itself)—a conclusion supported by his evidence. Unfortunately for Semmelweis, his colleagues disliked his conclusions and would not change their practices. He left Vienna a few years later, ostracized by the medical community and unheralded as the pioneer we now recognize him to be. Only later, after his death, would Semmelweis be vindicated.

Today, we consider it obvious that doctors should don latex gloves before conducting an obstetric exam, but in that time—before the germ research of Louis Pasteur and Joseph Lister and before the development of a germ-based theory of disease—doctors typically did autopsies and cervical examinations barehanded, with nothing but a superficial soap washing between activities. How did the truth about antiseptic cleansing come to be so obvious and universally accepted? Ignaz Semmelweis followed a procedure quite familiar to lab researchers and problem analysts of later centuries: After identifying a problem, he hypothesized a reason for it. Then he carried out an experiment designed to prove or disprove his hypothesis. During the experiment, he gathered and collated results. Finally, he analyzed his results and announced his conclusions.

Creating evidence-based conclusions by following the scientific method forms the basis of not only all scientific research today but all research projects, including genealogical ones. The scientific method of *hypothesis, experiment and data collection, data analysis,* and *conclu-*

sions has been the way that human beings have created knowledge not obtainable by simple observation (i.e., nonempirical knowledge).

The Connection to Genealogy

So what connects the scientific research method demonstrated by Semmelweis with genealogy being done today? Plenty! Creating a documented family history is a research project, and you can do it either the right way or the wrong way.

The right way is well established within the professional genealogy community; it is based on the best practices for academic research, which demand verifiability for any conclusions. *Verifiability* means being able to produce the evidence that contributed to a conclusion. For the information in a family history to be considered valid by other researchers, all the evidence must be documented, just like the sources that students use in their research papers. Valid genealogical conclusions can be established only by following the scientific method, which many people learn as undergraduates (whether they realize it or not). One difference: genealogists generally ask questions first rather than forming hypotheses. A hypothesis should be proposed only when research is mostly complete; then it can be tested with additional research.

Usually people start a genealogy project by browsing the Internet and searching Ancestry. They download records and copy information without understanding the importance of using established research methods from the start. Novices would be better off slowing down and proceeding carefully, documenting every bit of information they pin to their developing family tree. If you enter data without paying attention to where it came from or whether it was valid, you will probably have to "re-source" it later: go back and figure out where each piece came from. Re-sourcing is a pain; better to begin the right way, by documenting sources and following the genealogical rules for the analysis of evidence.

Facts are not the simple pieces of information they seem to be. The relative truth of facts must be examined, and the evidence must be weighed and assessed. Just as data in scientific research does not speak for itself, neither do deceptively simple facts. Sometimes the thrill of getting a new document can overshadow the differences among the pieces of information on that document. For example, imagine that you obtain a relative's death certificate. That's great, because a death certificate is an excellent attestation for the date, place, and cause of death and for the name of the attending doctor and interment details. It is not, however, an excellent source for the other details usually found on a death certificate—the deceased's full name, birth date, birthplace, occupation, Social Security number, parents' names, and length of residence in the county where death occurred. The difference is between primary and secondary information (i.e., firsthand versus secondhand knowledge); learning to identify this difference is one part of the larger issue of considering evidence.

It has already become a truism for genealogists that "without proof, it isn't truth," and the sooner you absorb this golden rule for genealogy and let it guide your research practices, the better. Historical records need interpretation; the information they contain must be assessed for its evidence value. Then that evidence must be examined in light of other evidence before legitimate conclusions can be drawn.

When Does Evidence Equal Proof?

Realtors say that the key to selling your house is location, location, location. For genealogists, the key to creating a legitimate, shareable family history is evidence, evidence, evidence. Just as in a court trial, the evidence produced and the nature of that evidence make all the difference.

On the subject of evidence, the name you should know is Elizabeth Shown Mills, longtime editor of the *National Genealogical Society Quarterly* and past president of the American Society of Genealogists and the Board for Certification of Genealogists. Mills has no equal voice in the genealogy community. Her book *Evidence Explained* (3rd edition, 2017) is the "bible" of evidence-based genealogy research, especially if you want to share your information on a professional level. The issue of evidence analysis and citation grows in importance with each new generation of genealogists.

In an online essay expanding upon *Evidence Explained* called "Sources vs. Information vs. Evidence vs. Proof,"[2] Mills explains the relative relationships among sources, information, evidence, and proof. *Sources*, she says, are "artifacts, books, documents, film, people, photographs, recordings, websites, databases, etc." In other words, a source can be just about anything that contains information. Evaluation of a source, she says, "begins with its physical form"; that is, whether it is an *original* (firsthand) or *derivative* (secondhand) source. The traditional division into "primary" and "secondary" sources is illogical—after all, even a primary (original) document might have information that is hearsay. A source can also be classed as an *authored work. Information* refers to what the source contains—"its factual statements or its raw data." The pieces of information you find in a source are not necessarily "facts" but assertions that must be verified or interpreted. Information can be classed as *primary* (firsthand), *secondary* (secondhand), or *undetermined. Evidence* is the researcher's interpretation of information as applied to a research problem. It can be classed as *direct*, *indirect*, or *negative*. The body of evidence assembled can be seen as the *proof* needed to support a conclusion. Sound conclusions, says Mills, reflect these four things: thorough research and documentation, accurate interpretations of the information, careful correlation of all the evidence, and a well-reasoned, well-explained analysis or proof argument.

In "Sources vs. Information vs. Evidence vs. Proof," Mills sums up her distinctions in this neat formula: "*Sources* give us information from which we select *evidence*. If our research is thorough and we have soundly analyzed our findings, we might reach a conclusion. The *body of evidence* on which we base that conclusion is our *proof*" (emphasis in original).

You will eventually run into the distinction between source and information when you share your findings with family. Someday, you'll be sitting with your laptop eagerly showing someone original records, and you'll realize they are not interested. Most nonresearchers just want the information, not the sources.

Part of Mills's work with the Board for Certification of Genealogists involved creating the genealogical proof standard, which defines the process by which proof is achieved. Briefly, to be accepted as proved, a researcher's conclusions must meet the genealogical proof standard. To prove a piece of evidence, in the words of the board's *Genealogy Standards* (2nd edition, 2019), "the researcher must conduct reasonably exhaustive research in the best quality sources, supply complete and accurate citations, skillfully analyze and correlate the collected information, resolve any conflicting evidence, and create a soundly reasoned, coherently written conclusion based on the strongest evidence available."

Remember that the aim is not to obtain 100 percent infallible proof (an impossible task) but to establish a reasonable conclusion based on evidence. Evaluation of material is crucial for the genealogy process. Errors made and perpetuated can potentially have major consequences for the work of others, so evaluation must be rigorous and explicit. Those wishing to pursue this subject further are advised to obtain a copy of *Mastering Genealogical Proof* by Thomas W. Jones (2013).

A Bit More about Sources

It is not enough simply to decide what is primary and what is secondary information; you also must determine whether the source is *original* or *derivative*. Even the word *original* does not mean what it looks like. An original source could be the "true original" or an exact image copy made by a reliable authority. Those reproductions, though not the exact documents, are treated as originals. A derivative source, unlike an original, is a record that has undergone processing of its content; for example, an abstract, extract, or transcription, or an index/database entry.

A *transcription* is an exact written or typed copy of an original source document. If the source document is a letter, a transcription preserves the spelling, spacing, and even the mistakes of the original. Comments by the transcriber usually appear in brackets to distinguish them from the text of the original. Transcriptions are quite useful to make and can save time later. For example, let's say that you have worked extensively with microfilmed images of records from some 19th-century villages in Germany. The time and effort you spent learning to decipher the handwriting for each place gives you the ability to read the records easily now. But will that knowledge be available to you in two or ten years? Unlikely. A transcription of the records will help preserve the information and reduce the need for you to relearn the script later.

However, a transcription can contain errors. Anytime someone transfers data from one form to another, that possibility exists. For this reason, transcriptions are not as valuable as originals and should be used with caution. If you rely on a transcription without verifying the original source, you risk absorbing inaccurate data into your family history; as such, it is important to seek out corroborating originals. If you do make transcriptions, take the utmost care to copy exactly.

An *extract* is a partial transcription—still exact but constituting only a part of a longer original. Copying down passages from source materials is considered extracting as long as the accuracy of the original is preserved. Creating an extract allows you to omit extraneous information and move quickly through a note-taking session. However, errors can occur during any copying effort, so extracts must be used with caution. If you are making a transcription or extraction that you intend to share later, remember to label it with your name and the date.

An *abstract* is another type of derivative source. But unlike an extraction or transcription, an abstract is a summary or description of the contents of an original source. It contains less detail and represents the note taker's interpretation of the original because decisions were made about what would be left out. As with transcription and extraction, errors can creep in.

In short, it's important to avoid relying on derivative sources and to obtain a full copy of original documents if possible. Derivative sources should always be seen as clues and pointers, never as the final word. Information posted in other people's family trees falls into this category, as do family stories, even if told by someone who was present at an event. The key thing to focus on is the timing of the source—that is, if the document, story, or data construction was created long after the event, it may not be the best evidence. Sometimes people defend a family story just because the person telling it was a participant—they believe that it *must* be true—but a story told forty years after the fact is less reliable than something like a diary kept at the time of the events by someone personally involved in an event. Then again, an account written by a participant forty years later, who has a good memory and no bias, might well be more reliable than a contemporary account by a biased participant.

Best Practice for Establishing Dates

Professional genealogists follow a prescribed methodology for establishing accurate dates within a family history. If an original source is unobtainable (e.g., a long-form birth record to establish a birth date), then the best derivative source is usually (though not always) the one closest to the event. For example, let's say that someone's great-grandfather immigrated to North America from Serbia around 1900. Although many vital records (birth, death, marriage) are available online through FamilySearch (a resource discussed in chapter 5), they are not available for many places. If the birth records from a specific Serbian town are unavailable, the researcher should use the best available derivative source to establish the birth year. Sometimes the next available record is many years after the birth, but it might be all there is to work with. Of course, there are exceptions, but in general, the closer to the original event, the better. If you can't prove a date or kinship with primary information gathered from multiple, independently created original sources, you may be able to build a case with multiple pieces of evidence derived from independently created derivative sources. According to current genealogical standards, even if we have an original source with primary (firsthand) information, we are still obliged to gather multiple sources in order to test the validity of what we already have. One record, or even a few, would not meet the standard of a "reasonably exhaustive" search.

SUMMING IT UP

Here are the best first steps you can take as a beginning family historian:

- Write what you know onto a paper chart.
- Interview (and record) family members using focused questions.
- Find, scan, and preserve family papers and photos.
- Select a family tree program and enter your data.
- Create lists of what records should exist for each individual you are researching.
- Do an initial search online for records.
- Make use of local records repositories and local newspapers.
- Conduct cemetery research.
- Follow the established best practices in the field.

Next: managing genealogy records, both physical and digital.

3

MANAGING GENEALOGY RECORDS

This chapter addresses:

- Organizing and preserving paper records, photos, and digital files
- Keeping research organized and citing sources
- Working with audio and visual recordings

Keeping your research and files (both paper and digital) organized is an essential part of being an effective genealogist, but this task can be the most tedious part of the process. Paper records and digital files both need a dedicated organizational scheme maintained consistently over time. Such schemes inevitably get refined, but then all files must retroactively be renamed in compliance with the new approach (that's where the "tedious" part comes in). Both paper and digital files require time and effort to make sure they are protected and accessible in the future.

PAPER RECORDS

In the past (i.e., before Ancestry), family historians worked primarily on paper. They kept their research notes on paper, wrote out the family tree on paper, and made photocopies or printouts of records they found. Things have really changed. If you have family papers, by all means preserve and store those appropriately so they can be passed down, but for your research project, the best advice an experienced researcher can give is *go digital*. But first, let's focus on those paper records—how to preserve, digitize, and store them.

Your work as a family historian will inevitably involve you handling paper records. You might already have inherited your parents' or grandparents' collection of preserved documents—certificates, diaries, yearbooks, baby books, burial deeds, school programs, clipped articles, entire magazines, bank books, passports, small wallet cards, and so on. These items get saved for a variety of reasons, and most of the time when someone passes away, that person leaves behind boxes of such things. Your goal as a family historian, as explained in the previous chapter, is to find these records and make use of them as one of the earliest steps in the project. Because these are private papers, they are for the most part not available anywhere else, so it's especially important to treat them carefully.

Many older paper records can be fragile or damaged. When you encounter something in that state, take immediate steps to prevent further damage before any more handling occurs. Professional-level preservation is not the goal; you just want to protect the papers from further damage and help ensure they are around for future generations.

First, assess each item to determine whether it needs special care or repair. Poor-quality paper that is flaking or crumbling should be handled as little as possible. It is always best to store paper unfolded, but be careful—the crease where a fold was made can easily become the line along which the paper tears. If a document was repaired with cellophane (Scotch) tape years ago, the tape has probably begun to separate from the paper. If you can remove the tape without affecting the paper, do so; if not, carefully trim away the tape no longer adhering to the paper and leave the rest. You will find that the pulled-away tape has left behind both a residue and a stain; that is the disintegrated adhesive, which was originally a coating on the underside of the cellophane strip. Like newsprint, cellophane tape was not designed with the future in mind; it provides a quick fix and adheres satisfactorily to most paper surfaces. But it inevitably degrades, and its use is not recommended for repairing documents. If you need to repair documents cheaply, get some archive-quality repair tape; an online search for *archive supplies* should bring up your options.

After you have unfolded everything that can be safely unfolded and removed any tape strips that have already detached, place the documents into appropriate protective coverings. Office supply stores sell packs of letter-sized plastic sleeves that will work for most of what you have. You can insert each paper, letter, news clipping, and so forth into a separate sleeve, then put all the sleeves into three-ring binders. For more important and precious documents, you can purchase specially designed document holders (made in multiple sizes) from the same companies that sell archive repair tape. If you have large certificates, this option is best because the inexpensive plastic sleeves that come in a pack are not big enough to hold them.

Once the most important papers have been contained in sleeves, take a hard look at the box they have been stored in. Family papers are almost never stored in the best available containers. Often they are crammed into cardboard, which is probably the worst container for paper in common use because cardboard is itself paper. Cardboard boxes were not designed for long-term storage; they briefly serve a purpose and then, like cellophane tape, begin to disintegrate. Because it is just reinforced paper, cardboard will not protect paper from two of its greatest enemies: moisture and insects. Insects, in fact, are drawn to the glue that holds the box flaps together. Additionally, the cardboard material itself disintegrates over time, becoming a coarse dust that can damage stored materials.

Get rid of all the cardboard boxes holding your family papers and replace them with plastic bins. Some archivists will tell you that plastic is not a perfect container either, but again, the goal here is not archival-quality storage but merely an inexpensive, easy way to preserve family papers. If your family's collection contains something truly valuable, such as a signed letter from a famous person, consider having professional conservation work done. For the rest of it, the plastic sleeves and bins from an office supply store will do nicely. Look for bins that have locking handles (Sterilite is an excellent brand).

If you have a large number of paper records, you might have to prioritize your "individual plastic sleeve" storage approach. Documents that are especially valuable to you as a researcher or that have value as a historical artifact within your family should be so preserved, such as birth, death, and marriage certificates. But also be sure to separate newspaper clippings, because the acid in them can bleed into whatever they touch. Inserting each item in a simple Ziploc-style bag can keep that from happening.

Don't stop at plastic protection for individual sheets of paper and certificates. Do you possess your grandfather's business ledger or your mother's high school yearbook? How about your own baby book? Those things need protective storage too. They can be encased in sturdy, zip-top plastic envelopes; get the clear kind so you can tell at a glance what's inside. These heavier plastic envelopes are available at any office supply store for a few dollars—well worth the investment to protect multipage artifacts like yearbooks and diaries. Once encased, they can be stored together in a large plastic bin without fear of further damage.

As you work with collections of family papers, get rid of any metal paper clips and rubber bands that you find. Invest in some nonharmful fasteners (plastic clips are one option) before you start handling the papers and replace the damaging ones as you go. Metal paper clips can rust and leave an impression on the page. Rubber bands, like cardboard and cellophane tape, were designed for short-term use and over time will inevitably disintegrate. Most of us have had the experience of en-countering a rubber band that has turned to goo and stuck to whatever it was holding.

Finally, for the most precious documents and your other important papers (birth certificates of living people, passports, car titles, savings bonds, Social Security cards), you might want to invest in a document safe. These are available for around $60 to $70 at most office supply stores and at large hardware stores. Document safes come in a variety of sizes. The best ones for storing your paper records allow you to lay everything flat. The safe, even if left unlocked, will protect these papers from fire as well as water and insects.

Before you put the paper records away, however, take the time to scan everything and then label the resulting digital files. See the next section for scanning information and advice.

PHOTOGRAPHS

Photos can be difficult to deal with. We used to keep them in albums, or at least that was the goal, but almost no one does that now. Instead, our personal devices are flooded with digitized pictures that need to be purged, organized, and labeled. Printed photographs are fairly hardy; they were intended to be stacked, flipped through, passed around, and stuck into albums. At the same time, they are vulnerable to the same enemies that can harm paper, because photographs are just glossy images printed on reinforced paper.

Although they have many of the same properties as paper documents, photographs require a slightly different approach to organizing and preserving. Most people throw out paper records that are not useful or valuable so that what remains is the good stuff. However, many people are simply unable to throw away a photograph no matter how bad it is. Photos conjure an emotional response that paper records do not, because they show people—often people who are known to the photo holder. Chapter 2 covered using photographs to prompt memories and stories in interview subjects; the power they have to connect someone to the past is simply remarkable, but it also explains why throwing photos away is so difficult.

Ultimately, photographs fulfil their function when they are *seen*. The best ones can be framed and put on the wall, but what about the rest? What is the best way to manage a photo collection today, usually an unwieldy combination of printed photos stored in boxes and many digital photos stored on various devices in the household? If you are ready to start taming your photo collection, following are six recommended steps.

Step 1. Purge

Go through every picture and separate out the duplicates and the bad shots (the lighting is poor, the framing is awkward, the focus is blurry, everyone's got their eyes shut, you hate the way you look, etc.). If you think it appropriate, give the duplicates to other people, but just toss the rest into the trash. This step is difficult for many people; throwing photos away seems almost sacrilegious. It is not. Why keep bad pictures or shots that you dislike? Why keep six or seven shots of the same thing? Pick the best one or two and let the rest go. And why keep old pictures of Christmas trees, lakes, food dishes, and the like that you no longer remember the significance of? Those can go in the trash as well. Anything damaged with transferable material like mold or sticky residue should also be tossed after scanning.

And while you're tossing those bad pictures, go ahead and pitch all those old negatives too; scanning technology has made them obsolete.

All this disposing will be painful, but a well-curated photo collection will ultimately be far more useful and valuable than one that contains every single shot ever taken and developed. By purging your photo collection before you do anything else, you will make the subsequent steps easier.

Step 2. Sort

Most people have both loose photographs and albums. Loose photographs are easier to sort, but before you remove photos from original albums, consider the following questions:

1. Does the album contain pictures in chronological or thematic order? If so, consider leaving the album intact to preserve that order. You can scan the page and crop the images into separate files.
2. Does the album contain labels and notes? If so, consider leaving it intact. If you really want to remove the pictures, transfer the information in the notes to the backs of the photos.
3. Are the photos at risk of being damaged by tape, acidic backing, or glue? If so, consider removing the photos after making a scan of the entire page to preserve the order and notes.

If you decide to remove pictures from albums, do so carefully, especially if the pictures are adhered to the page. A popular type of album decades ago had stiff cardboard pages with adhesive covered with a peelable plastic film. You placed the photos onto the sticky page, then covered them with the plastic. That approach seemed fine until people discovered that often the adhesive would not let go of the picture. If you've got albums like this and want to remove the photos, use dental floss; it's more likely to allow safe removal than tugging on the pictures. Slide a string of floss between the picture and the surface and pull it back and forth while gently pulling it toward you.

To sort effectively, work in a large space like the floor of an empty room where you can make stacks. Sort first by decade—put everything from the 1990s into one pile, 2000s into another, and so on (older family pictures from before you were born can go together in one stack for now). Then, sort chronologically within each decade. Do your best to determine dates by looking at evidence in the photos themselves. Clothing and hairstyles are often a reliable indicator for dating, as is the photo technology and paper itself. Many early digital cameras printed the date right on the image, and before that developing agencies often printed the date on the side or back. Keep in mind that the date of the latter is for film development, not when the image was taken.

Once you've gotten the pictures in chronological order as well as you can, put the photos from the same event together. And then do another purge. Do you have multiple shots of the same people at the same event? Choose the best pictures to keep and let the rest go.

Step 3. Label

The purging and sorting process is time-consuming, but it makes the next step, labeling, much easier. Creating accurate labels for the pictures you possess will benefit the family members who eventually inherit the photos and will also help you when you get to the scanning phase.

Printed photos were designed to be written on. But be careful what writing instrument you choose. Ballpoint and pencil can make an impression on the backing paper, and some markers can smear. It's best to use an archival safe pen for the purpose (for sale at any office supply store). Ask for a special "photograph marking pen." These pens will write consistently on photo paper, and, when dried, will not smear.

When labeling your photos, write out (if you can) complete names, dates, places, and events for each one. You might need to make some phone calls or send scans to people who can help.

Step 4. Scan

Scanning is a big and somewhat monotonous job; most people avoid taking on the task for good reason. In fact, online services have sprung up offering to do the job for you; send them your photos and they will send them back to you along with digitized versions. But hiring out this step is far more expensive than investing in a small flatbed scanner and doing the work yourself.

Scanners come in a variety of styles; the best for turning your photo collection into shareable digitized images is a *flatbed* scanner rather than a wand or feeder type. Flatbed scanners can be found at all office and technology goods stores; look for one that that has a slide-scanning attachment. A flatbed scanner takes up space. It will need to be placed securely in the space next to your laptop or home computer and connected with a USB cord. The scanner should come with a dedicated free program that you install when you plug the scanner into a USB port; these programs are also downloadable from the scanner company.

Most programs allow you to preview your scan; in other words, the scanner does a quick view to let you see whether the paper or picture is laid out correctly (no edges cut off). Then you select your desired resolution and push the Scan button. The higher the resolution sought, the longer each scan will take. For photographs, scan each one at 600 dpi (dots per inch); for documents, you can use 300 dpi and still have perfectly usable images. Choose to scan everything in *color* rather than black and white or grayscale. The scans will take slightly longer, but the resulting images will be much better.

Once you've done this step, your photo collection that previously existed in boxes will be just like the digital photos on your phone and home computer. Scanning photos takes time and patience, but the rewards are worth the effort. The digitized photos can be shared easily, combined and cropped to create different effects, made into slide shows, and disseminated in myriad ways.

Step 5. Clean Up and Label Scans

Scanned images always require cleanup; they need to be cropped to eliminate unwanted background and edges and probably need the color or orientation adjusted as well. All these cleanup steps can be easily accomplished with free photo-editing software available online (search *free photo editing software*). One highly recommended program is Irfanview (www.irfanview.com). Use Irfanview to do everything you might think you need Photoshop to do, and for no cost. You can crop, clean up, combine, and even make notes on your photographs. Microsoft Paint is also a reliable free alternative.

Cropping and adjusting the color and/or orientation takes only seconds for each image and will result in images that are easier to work with on screen. Ideally, you should preserve the original image scan or photograph in a separate folder and make edits on copies only.

There is one additional step that you should consider if you are scanning documents or working with downloaded scanned documents: if your image contains multiple names (as on a census or city directory page), use the edit tool to draw a small star or arrow next to the pertinent names (that way, you won't have to hunt for it in the image later).

To label your scans effectively, work with the photos themselves. If you've done step 3 and labeled the backs of the photos prior to scanning, this step should be easy. First, choose a consistent labeling system that conveys everything in the file name you would need to retrieve the photos later. One reliable method is to start the file name with the year, then add the numerical month and day if known (e.g., 2019-06-16). After the date, write the full names of each person in the photo (abbreviations and nicknames will make finding the pictures later more difficult). If you've already written someone's surname, you can use just the first letter if the name repeats (e.g., Donna McKay, Carol M, Linda M). Figure 3.1 shows my method of labeling digitized photos.

File name characters are limited, so just put the date and the names. For additional information, such as the event and/or place, use the "comments" field in the file description that shows up when you choose the "details pane" view in Windows Explorer (Macs will have something similar).

Labeling documents requires a slightly different approach. With photographs, the essential information is the date and then the names of who is in the picture. With documents, you first want to know the document type, then the name of whom it concerns, followed by the date and other relevant info. Get as much information into each file name as you can. Down the line, when you have thousands of scanned

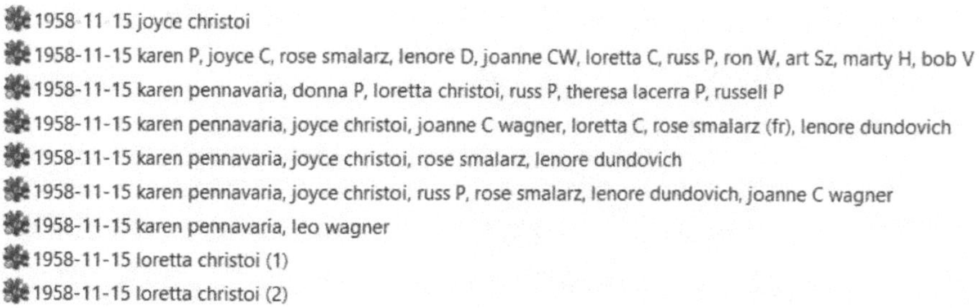

🌸 1958-11-15 joyce christoi
🌸 1958-11-15 karen P, joyce C, rose smalarz, lenore D, joanne CW, loretta C, russ P, ron W, art Sz, marty H, bob V
🌸 1958-11-15 karen pennavaria, donna P, loretta christoi, russ P, theresa lacerra P, russell P
🌸 1958-11-15 karen pennavaria, joyce christoi, joanne C wagner, loretta C, rose smalarz (fr), lenore dundovich
🌸 1958-11-15 karen pennavaria, joyce christoi, rose smalarz, lenore dundovich
🌸 1958-11-15 karen pennavaria, joyce christoi, russ P, rose smalarz, lenore dundovich, joanne C wagner
🌸 1958-11-15 karen pennavaria, leo wagner
🌸 1958-11-15 loretta christoi (1)
🌸 1958-11-15 loretta christoi (2)

Figure 3.1. My method of labeling digitized photos.

document images, you will be grateful to your past self for taking the time to label thoroughly.

Figure 3.2 shows my method of labeling digitized documents. Notice that the full name of each individual is given, including middle name. As you research a family, you will inevitably find that some repeat names. You can keep one William Long distinguished from the others by using middle names, or with Jr/Sr. It's important that each person represented in your document image files have a unique name, something that distinguishes him or her from others with similar names.

Sometimes the document that you want to scan is multiple pages. Wills, deeds, passports, baby books, and many other paper records like this should be scanned carefully, one page at a time. But rather than leaving the pages as separate images and labeling them numerically, create a single PDF file for the multipage document record. To do this, open Microsoft Word and paste each image in consecutively. Then save the whole thing as a PDF. Taking this step will eliminate multiple image files for the same document and make retrieval easier. Depending on your available storage space and time, you can save the original

D=galbraith, james nottman, 60y (1939-09-19) autopsy report

D=galbraith, james nottman, 60y (1939-09-19) cert [5547 baltimore]

D=galbraith, james nottman, 60y (1939-09-19) grave @arlington

D=galbraith, james nottman, 60y (1939-09-19) obit [no addr, phil]

D=galbraith, john barry, 62y (1977-10-22) grave @SPP

D=galbraith, john barry, 62y (1977-10-22) obit (DCDT, 10-24-1977)

D=galbraith, john, 50y (1920-09-28) cert [young, jefferson, PA]

D=galbraith, john, 50y (1920-09-28) grave @hopewell UM, frostburg

D=galbraith, john, 72y (1971) grave @hopewell UM, frostburg

D=galbraith, joseph d., 73y (1994-11-30) grave @SPP

D=galbraith, mary [gibson], 70y (1922-12-28) cert [1660 n. 55th st.]

D=galbraith, mary [gibson], 70y (1922-12-28) grave @arlington

D=galbraith, mary [gibson], 70y (1922-12-28) obit (PEPL, 12-29-1922)

Figure 3.2. My method of labeling digitized documents.

images in a separate folder in case you need to alter or add to the PDF someday.

Step 6. Store Photos Appropriately

If you have loose photographs, you can safely store them in a plastic "shoebox" holder after scanning. Intact albums can be laid flat and stacked in a secure bin such as Sterile containers with locking handles. The ones that have just lids that snap on tend to get misshapen over time, and then the lids don't fit well.

Remember that in addition to the usual enemies of paper (moisture and insects), photographs are also susceptible to light damage. Light shining directly onto a photograph will inevitably fade it over time. That's what will happen to those framed shots on the walls. Ideally, you can scan those framed images before the image degrades from light exposure. If possible, take them out of the frame before scanning.

For more information and helpful advice about managing family photos, check out the blog The Family Curator (thefamilycurator.com). The author of the blog, Denise May-Levenick, also has a book called *How to Archive Family Photos: A Step-by-Step Guide to Organize and Share Your Photos Digitally* (2015).

RESEARCH NOTES

You will help yourself out if you keep your notes and research organized from the beginning. It helps to keep digital and paper records organized according to the same principle so that someone else could easily figure it out. Labeling digital files thoroughly and consistently, while sometimes a chore, is essential.

In previous generations, genealogists had no digital files and no database to collate information collected. They kept track of data using paper records known as *pedigree charts* (which showed direct ancestors), plus family group and individual information sheets. These forms are still useful and are available for free download at many genealogy sites. Some researchers use them to create a hard-copy backup version of their family history database. Whatever strategy helps you ensure that your data, documentation, and conclusions will not be lost is the one you should pursue.

Before you scan documents and download records, take the time to decide on a labeling system. Many genealogists with extensive digital files organize them the way that you would organize paper files: by family, subdivided by document type. The organized file tree might look something like this:

Genealogy Research / [family surname] / Documents / Death
Genealogy Research / [family surname] / Documents / Marriage
Genealogy Research / [family surname] / Research in Progress

Whichever filing system you choose, make sure that your organizing strategy can be understood by someone later when you are not around.

To organize digital files so that they can be retrieved easily, you will need consistency and a commitment to labeling. Use individuals' full names rather than *Mom* or *Nana Jones*. Keep in mind that you are creating an archive that might be used by your own descendants a hundred years from now. Put as much detail into each file name as you can; later retrieval will depend on it. For example, the file name for a death-related record might look like this:

D [for death]—surname, first + middle names or initials (maiden name),
age at death (date, place of death) document type [associated address]

Translated into an actual file name, the template turns into this:

D—LaCerra, Angela (Mattucci), 53y (1940-04-21, Chicago) certificate [948 N. Trumbull]

That is a long file name, but it contains everything that you need to retrieve it quickly or to identify at a glance what the file contains and who it pertains to. Labeling downloaded and scanned files is not the exciting part of genealogy, but you will not regret taking the time to do it as you go, especially adding the addresses (or at least street number and name) to the file names. If you are lucky enough to have family members mentioned in small-town newspapers, you can search the on-line archives of those publications by address and pull up mentions of the family that match the addresses in your collection of documents.

It is also helpful to keep a research log to track what you have found—and *not* found—after searching and to write up research reports that give an account of a specific block of research done with a specific set of records. The report should identify the research goal, the sources used, the individuals searched in the block of records, all findings and problems that exist in that block of records (both positive and negative), and any interpretive or analytical comments necessary to understand the findings. These reports can be just for you or can be shared with other researchers. Many blank forms are available online to help you keep track of research.

RECORDING CITATIONS

As you uncover and save documents, note where each record or piece of data came from so that you or someone else can replicate your search. You can easily get caught up in following trails and in the excitement of a new trove of records, but no matter how good your memory is, you will not remember the details of where you found those records. Get in the habit of making yourself note, every time, where information came from.

You will sometimes find records that offer information that conflicts with other records; for example, you might have three records, each with a different birth year for the same person. Which one you settle on as the most likely birth year will depend on analyzing each piece of evidence. Set the stage for that later analysis by recording how you obtained each document. Remember that you have taken on a long-term project and will someday need to revisit documents gathered years before. Database programs usually give you a way to note the source for each bit of data you enter.

What is the best way to document sources? Any way that works easily enough so that you keep doing it. The best documentation is attached to the record itself. One way of achieving this: as you download images, use the editing tool in your image software (Irfanview, Microsoft Paint, Photoshop) to create a small blank margin on the edge of the image, and in that blank space record where the record came from. For example, if you download an image of an obituary from a city newspaper, you can write on the side both the paper's name and the date in much the same way that people used to write on actual clippings. By creating that margin and recording the source and summary information for the image, you lock the two pieces together (i.e., the document and the source information).

How much information you include in your source documentation depends on how much is required to re-create the search. The federal census is available from multiple sources, so you do not need to label a census image with the exact path you took to find it. If you have found an unusual or unexpected record, however, it is best to label it fully. Newspaper articles make excellent documentary evidence for your family history, but if you label an article with just the name of the paper, no one (not even your future self) will be able to find it easily again. Newspapers are usually daily publications, so an adequate citation for a newspaper record contains the complete date along with the name of the paper as well as the section and column (if available).

AUDIO AND VISUAL RECORDINGS

Many people who inherit boxes of family papers or find such stored materials at the homes of relatives discover among the papers old film reels, VHS tapes, and cassette tapes. What should you do with those media items?

Film, audio, and visual tape all have a relatively short shelf life. In some cases, the materials start to degrade after only a few years. After twenty years or so, the recorded signal might no longer be accessible. Such degradation doesn't result from improper storage or handling but occurs from within because of the nature of film and magnetic tape. As an archival storage medium, film and tape are simply not up to the job.

So the best first step when you encounter film or tape is to convert them to a digital form. Media conversion is not a complicated process, but it does require dedicated technology that you probably don't possess. So unlike picture scanning, conversion is something you probably will want to outsource. If you live near a university, check with their technology or information technology (IT) department to see if they offer inexpensive conversion services. If not, you can always find a service online to do the job.

Don't delay taking this step. Conversion will preserve your VHS home movies, recordings of kids' performances, and old soundless films on Super8.

In addition to digital files resulting from those conversions, your family history digital record will (if you followed the steps outlined in chapter 2) include recordings of your interviews with family members. Label these files with a consistent method that puts as much information into the file name as possible. As with image files from scanning, audio and video digital files can be edited to make them more accessible, attractive, and useful. You can learn to make "mash-up" videos to post on YouTube, or edit audio interviews to remove awkward pauses, interruptions, or inappropriate language.

No single program allows you to edit both audio and digital files. The best free program for audio editing is called Audacity (sourceforge.net/ projects/audacity). This audio recording and editing tool is a gold mine for family historians seeking to manage their growing collection of digital audio files. With Audacity, you can delete sections of a recorded interview, move them around, or combine them. For example, if the phone rang in the middle of an interview and you were forced to resume it later, you will end up with two separate audio files. With Audacity, you can combine the two files into one seamless interview session and even add comments later explaining about the phone call. You can also make improvements to the audio quality.

Don't forget to make transcriptions of your audio interviews; it's wonderful to have a recorded interview, but the information it contains is not searchable until you transcribe it word for word into a Microsoft Word file. As with many steps discussed in this chapter, the process takes time, but later on you'll be glad you did it.

Editing converted video is a little trickier but can be learned quickly. One good free video editor is OpenShot (www.openshot.org). There are others, both free and pay; do some online research to determine which is best for your needs and skill level. If you've got stacks of family home video and manage to get them converted, you will still have to do something to make them accessible. Most of your family members will prefer not to sit through hours and hours of unedited home movies but will happily view a ten-minute "greatest hits" that you post on YouTube or share via Facebook.

SUMMING IT UP

Managing genealogy records is a necessary part of family history re-search projects, but admittedly it isn't as much fun as discovering new information. If you don't stay organized, you will be unable to retrieve records quickly later on and might end up repeating earlier efforts. The best way to preserve your family's document records and photographs is to scan them and then share them (see chapter 8 for ideas). Remember:

- Scan all family papers and pictures, then put them away. Do your research using the digital copies only. Scan documents at 300 dpi and photos at 600 dpi; scan both in color.
- Purge, sort, and label your family photos before you scan them.
- Convert all audio and visual materials to digital; they are degrad-ing fast, and that process cannot be stopped.
- Make regular backups of your family history research files. Many people use an automatic backup service like Carbonite with great results; in addition to backing up newly created files in minutes, it allows you to access your files remotely.

Next: genealogy record types.

4

GENEALOGY RECORD TYPES

This chapter addresses:

- Census, immigration, military, and other federal records
- Birth, marriage, death, and other city/county records
- Court, church, and private records
- Problems with records

A genealogist's life is all about records: searching for them, analyzing them, and extracting information from them. This chapter outlines the many different record types used to build an evidence-based family history.

Remember that you are looking not only for the information records contain but also for the original records that contain information. All historians seek out and use original records wherever possible—records that can be studied and must be interpreted in order to establish historical connections and facts. Records are the foundation of a genealogy project; without them, you cannot provide the evidence needed to verify details from family stories and recollections.

Overall, records come in two varieties: *public* and *private*. Both types are vital to genealogy research.

Most records created by any government body are *public*. Federal records, unless they are otherwise restricted, fall into this category; state- and county-controlled records might or might not be considered public, depending on local laws. If a record falls under the "public" heading, it is theoretically available to be requested through the Freedom of Information Act, though the requestor usually pays for the copies. Almost all court proceedings are considered public records; that includes divorces (if the proceedings were court based) and traffic violations in addition to criminal cases. Depending on the jurisdiction, you can find a surprising amount of information about living people by searching court records. Records of births, marriages, and deaths (also called *vital records*) are generally public if the event occurred before certain established cutoff dates. Counties and cities, rather than states, are the entities that have customarily collected vital records, probably because of the sheer number of records to create, store, and retrieve upon request. In some counties, birth certificates can be ordered for people still alive if they were born before 1935 or so. In others, the birth record must be at least one hundred years old before it moves from private to public.

Private records, on the other hand, are those created by individuals and nongovernmental institutions, such as hospitals, churches, businesses, and social organizations. You have no right to see these records, but many organizations do make them available.

FEDERAL RECORDS

Fortunately for you, federal, state, county, and local government personnel have for hundreds of years created a paper record every time they interacted with citizens, and those records, because they were official, were usually preserved. Government record types sometimes overlap, but not usually. That means that a record available at the county level will not be available via the state, and vice versa. Finding where records are kept and what level of government controls them is part of the research process. The easiest records to find and use are federal. Following is an overview of federal records to use in your family history project.

Census

Without question, the U.S. federal census is the essential record set. Fortunately, both the information and, with a few exceptions, the microfilms of original records up through 1940 are fairly easy to access.

History of Census Taking

The idea of a census goes back to ancient times; the first government-mandated counting of people and assessment of households was done by an Egyptian pharaoh in 3340 BC for taxation and military purposes.[1] The practice has been part of human history ever since; documented references from ancient Israel, India, China, Greece, and Rome demonstrate how pervasive this record-keeping mode has been in written history.

Modern census taking began with the Romans, who initiated the practice of taking count every five years.[2] The word *census* comes from the Latin *censere* ("to estimate"). The Romans established an official government *censor* to carry out a regular census, which involved not only counting people and household goods but making a notation (*nota censoria*) when individuals committed some infraction or were living in a way contrary to custom or law. For example, a man living in an unmarried state when he had no reason not to marry was breaking custom; his duty as a citizen was to marry and provide the Roman state with more citizens. Other infractions worthy of a censorial notation were improper conduct toward wife and children (overly harsh or overly indulgent), extravagant spending and evidence of luxurious living, cruelty toward slaves, improper cultivation of fields, and theater acting.[3] This extra duty of noting which citizens were behaving badly gave us the modern concept of *censorship*.

The most famous medieval census has an imposing name: the Domesday Book (pronounced "doomsday"). It was completed in 1086 by order of the victorious William of Normandy ("the Conqueror"), who had taken the English crown in 1066 and thereafter ruled over the native Anglo-Saxon people. The census helped William assess his newly won territory: its households, farms, and industries. Because the decisions of the Norman census takers about the value of land and appropriate tax rates were not open to appeal, this census became known to the conquered natives as the Book of Judgment—that is, the Domesday Book (Anglo-Saxon *dōm* = "judgment, law").

Hundreds of years later, after the successful Revolutionary War, the new American government followed William's example. In 1790, under Secretary of State Thomas Jefferson, the first systematic, nationwide census was conducted in what had been England's thirteen colonies (earlier colonial ones had been compiled, some of which still exist). In fact, the new government of the "United States" wrote the need for a census into its constitution: Article 1, section 2, calls for a counting (more formally called an *enumeration*) of the population every ten years (hence, it is a *decennial* census), to be used primarily for apportioning each state's seats in the newly formed House of Representatives. That 1790 census was undertaken by U.S. marshals who went house to house on horseback. They counted 3.9 million inhabitants. As you can see in figure 4.1, the "forms" used to create the final copy of the 1790 census were just blank pages with the columns drawn in.

The most recent U.S. census, taken in 2010, counted 308,745,538 residents of the United States (details are available at factfinder .census.gov/faces/nav/jsf/pages/index.xhtml). Enumerating is both harder and easier today—harder because between then and now, the population has grown by over three hundred million, but easier because

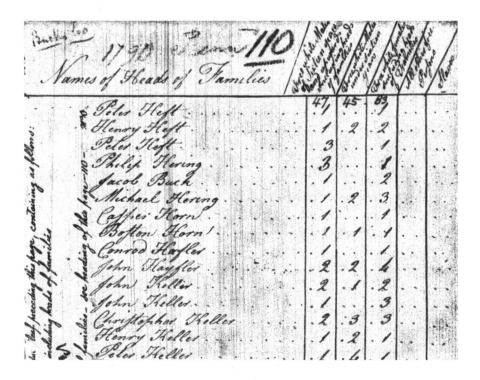

Figure 4.1. A page from the 1790 census in Bucks County, Pennsylvania. *Courtesy of the National Archives.*

face-to-face visits are no longer required for everyone (only for the people who do not complete and return a mailed questionnaire).

Prior to the 20th Century

In 1810, 1820, and systematically between 1850 and 1930, the federal government collected census information on different lists, called *schedules*, which resulted in genealogists today speaking of *agricultural schedules*, *slave schedules*, and *mortality schedules*. The main list of residents' names is called a *population schedule*; all the others are collectively called "special" schedules.

Most of the special schedules for 1810, 1890, and post-1900 were destroyed; the National Archive's filmed collection covers only 1850 to 1880. At the start you'll probably be most interested in the population schedules, with their satisfying lists of names, ages, relationships, and occupations. But the 1850–1880 special schedules can be enlightening. The agricultural schedules, for example, include data on farms, plantations, and community gardens, as well as the names of farm owners and managers. You can also find total acreage owned, land and animal value, and an inventory of machinery. Descriptions of other special schedules are available in several places online.

The individual census record sheets that survived into the 1940s were preserved on microfilm by the National Archives and Records Administration (NARA) in Washington, D.C. The microfilms are not perfect, but many record sets cannot be refilmed because the Commerce Department (keeper of the census records) destroyed the original pages after microfilming was completed. NARA does hold many original returns in bound volumes, and you can use them if a particular film is unreadable. Some census records created before microfilm preservation were damaged or lost over the years so are unavailable even on film; a complete list of what has survived can be found in a catalog called 1790–1890 Federal Population Censuses, available at the NARA site (www.archives.gov). The census pages that survive are fully indexed. Access to both indexes and record images is through subscription databases such as Ancestry and HeritageQuest Online, to which most libraries subscribe, or for free at FamilySearch. For privacy reasons, the federal schedules are released to the public seventy-two years after the census is taken; thus, 1940 was released in 2012, 1950 is marked for release in 2022, and so on.

Over the years, the amount of information requested by federal census enumerators has varied, and no set of questions is identical to any other. For a quick look at what questions were asked on each decennial census, check out the facsimile copies of the enumeration forms available online at usa.ipums.org/usa/voliii/tEnumForm.shtml. Generally, the further back you go, the fewer questions were asked and less information on each person is available. For the 1790–1840 population schedules, only the household heads are named, though other residents, including slaves, were represented by number. Not until 1830 did the government provide standard printed forms to the census takers, allowing a uniformity that makes searching easier (before that, the enumerators used blank paper that they lined by hand). The 1840 population schedule indicated, for the first time, a person's status as a Revolutionary War pensioner or pensioner's widow—vital information for those trying to link a family's history to that event.

In 1850, the census hit a milestone: it is the first population schedule to name every nonslave resident in every household (slaves were counted but not systematically named). Individuals uncounted in the census were those not residing in established households or institutions (primarily vagrants and homeless people) and people who were out of the country for an extended period. This census introduced slave schedules, which itemized the number of slaves owned by each head of household. Age, gender, and "color" (e.g., *black* or *mulatto*) are indicated; names were included only at the enumerator's discretion.

By 1870, the census enumerators were asking whether each resident's parents were foreign- or native-born—helpful data for identifying the immigrant generation within a family line. As the first census to occur after slave emancipation, 1870 is the first to list former slaves by name and, thus, the first to attempt listing *everyone* in the population schedule. The next one, 1880, became the first to list street names and house numbers, marital status, and how residents of a household were connected. With that one, you can identify in-laws, cousins, boarders, and stepchildren and know, with the marital status designation, whether you need to look for death or divorce records. At this time, the enumerators also asked in which state or country each person's parents were born, not just whether they were foreign-born. They also asked whether any of the household residents had any chronic disease or were "defective" in mind, body, sight, hearing, or speech.

The 1890 census, the first to have its data compiled on the tabulating machine invented by Herman Hollerith, revealed a U.S. population of between sixty-two and sixty-three million people—a figure arrived at within just six weeks of data completion. To see a picture of Hollerith's machine that made this quick figuring possible, go to Columbia University's page about computing history at www.columbia.edu/cu/compu tinghistory/census-tabulator.html. Hollerith's invention replaced an earlier, clumsier counting machine that was used to tabulate results from the 1870 census.

Enumerators in 1890 asked detailed questions about Civil War service (including which side a soldier or sailor fought on) and for precise racial self-identification (the options were *white, black, mulatto, quadroon, octoroon, Chinese, Japanese,* or *Indian*)—the first time this information had been collected. Residents were also questioned in detail about medical issues. The information was duly recorded by enumerators on preprinted sheets and shipped to Washington for copying to clean pages, which were used to tabulate results. After copying and tabulation, the field sheets and other notes were destroyed and the newly created "clean copy" pages were boxed up and stored. The boxes were then put into the Commerce Department basement, on open shelves. And there they sat for three decades.

In the late afternoon of January 10, 1921, a fire broke out in that basement, resulting in fire and water damage that destroyed almost all the unprotected 1890 census pages, for which no other copy existed. Unfortunately, no significant disaster recovery steps were taken when the blaze was finally extinguished several hours later; damaged records were left to soak in ankle-deep, sooty water until the following morning.

Recovery efforts were delayed further by insurance company examination of the fire scene. By the time the record sheets were dried out, the sad truth had become clear: although the tabulated data was available elsewhere, the original forms were unsalvageable, apart from a handful of sheets involving 6,160 individuals (from more than sixty-three million). No cause was ever determined for the fire, but the disaster inspired plans for a national archive, which was finally established in 1934.[4] If you are looking for people living in the United States during 1890, you have some other options, but nothing can replace the precious data that was lost. Fortunately for family historians, the 1900, 1910, and the recently completed 1920 census records were *not* in the

Commerce Department's basement that day. Other records were, but they received only minimal damage because they were not on open shelves.

The 20th Century

In 1900, census officials at the Commerce Department decided to ask not only for the age of each person but for the month and year of birth. You should view self-reported birth years with caution and take steps to verify them, but you can usually rely on the birth *month* being correct. People who misremember or misstate their age are fudging the year; they are unlikely to state the month incorrectly. Sadly, although the revised question in 1900 provided unique and interesting data, the experiment was dropped, and the next three population schedules reverted to "age since last birthday." This schedule also asked a new question about how many children each woman had borne and how many of those were still living. Between 1890 and 1900, the United States had absorbed millions of new residents, mostly from Europe. The population schedule for 1900 reflects the federal government's interest in the demographics of these immigrants. Not only was country of birth requested, but so was the year of arrival and whether an immigrant was naturalized. The answers provide a vital clue for tracking down passenger and citizenship paperwork.

In 1903, the nation finally got an official census bureau, which then (as now) operated out of the Commerce Department and had sole charge of the decennial census. Apart from minor modifications, the new bureau did not tinker with the 1900 question set when it created the 1910 form. New questions included a useful distinction regarding immigrants' status: they could have naturalization papers, a naturalization application pending ("papers"), or neither ("alien"). The 1910 census also noted whether an individual was a survivor of Civil War military service. Ten years later, the 1920 schedule dropped questions about Civil War service and number of children but added a question eliciting details about immigrant status: year of naturalization. Figure 4.2 shows a portion of a page from the 1920 census.

In the 1930 census, you will find much of interest. For one thing, you might know, or once knew, people listed on it. One new question asked "age at first marriage"; the answer can reveal a prior marriage to the one listed. Another new question, never again asked, is whether the

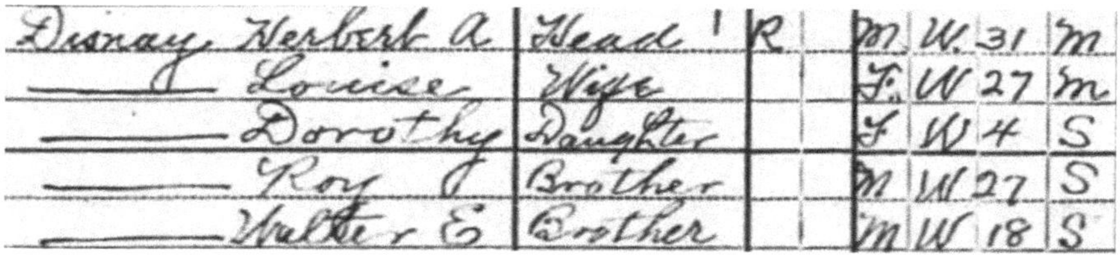

Disney, Herbert A.	Head	R	M	W	31	M
—— Louise	Wife		F	W	27	M
—— Dorothy	Daughter		F	W	4	S
—— Roy O.	Brother		M	W	27	S
—— Walter E.	Brother		M	W	18	S

Figure 4.2. Census showing Walt Disney in 1920, living with his brothers Herbert and Roy in Kansas City. *Courtesy of the National Archives.*

household possessed a radio. Radio ownership indicated at least some money in the family available for nonessentials and showed a willingness to embrace a new technology. It also gave the federal government solid data on who in the nation would be able to listen in when the president decided to speak to the nation, as Franklin D. Roosevelt did between 1933 and 1944 when he delivered a series of "fireside chats." Finally, the 1940 census had more questions than any previous ones, including where people had lived five years prior, their highest completed grade level, and the previous year's income.

The enumerators typically interviewed one member of a household, who would give the information for all the others. Thus, the recorded data was sometimes a best guess on the part of the person answering the questions. Only in 1940 did someone think to instruct enumerators to indicate (with an *X*) which household resident had answered the questions, which allowed for targeted follow-up. Children under eighteen could not legally provide information for a household. If all the adults were away from home, the enumerator would have to return later.

A note of caution: the census should never be taken as the final word for the spelling of someone's name. Back when the census was taken by going door-to-door, the overworked and underpaid enumerators knocked on every door, asking people to state their names. If the person could not, or did not, spell the names out, the enumerators recorded them as well as they could, often resorting to phonetic rendering. So the names written in the population schedules are often not accurate and usually do not reflect an individual's own choice of spelling.

Bottom line: the census is a wonderful and vital tool, but names, ages, race, and year of arrival (for immigrants) should always be verified with other sources.

Immigration, Naturalization, and Travel

The United States and Canada are nations of immigrants. Everyone in North America, apart from people descended wholly from indigenous tribes, has ancestors who made a long journey from another continent. After the census, the passenger lists and naturalization papers for those immigrants are the most useful federal documents, although records get sparser the further back you go. Detailed citizenship paperwork is not available for the Africans who were forced to make the transatlantic journey; information about those individuals must be sought from other sources.

Starting in 1819, lists of people who bought tickets for North America were created by shipping companies and submitted to U.S. officials upon arrival. These passenger arrival records (*manifests*) are stored at the National Archives and are available on microfilm, except those that were damaged or lost before filming took place. Only some naturalization records are at NARA; the rest are held by the U.S. Citizenship and Immigration Services, and others are held at local county courthouse archives. Indexes to the federal holdings are available through Ancestry and FamilySearch, among other places; indexing at the county level is intermittent. The actual records are not all on film yet, but requesting them is not difficult. Chapter 5 covers how to access these records.

Immigration Records

As noted in chapter 1, the popular but misguided idea that anyone's surname was changed at Ellis Island has long been discredited by genealogists and historians, and the passenger lists are proof that it did not happen. Those documents are full of names—millions of them—that were written down at the port of embarkation when the passenger purchased a ticket, not at Ellis Island or any other arrival port when they landed. If you are tracking immigrant ancestors who arrived in 1891 or later, you are lucky because the records contain more information and have been preserved better.

Colonial-period passage information for the British colonies is sparse, apart from the famous *Mayflower* voyage and a few others. For the French colony of Louisiana, much of the immigrant population can be accounted for with surviving ship rolls. For the most part, the men, women, and children who arrived before the conclusion of the Revolutionary War were subjects of European monarchs or slaves owned by those subjects; record keeping was better for Spanish and French people coming to colonies owned by their governments than for British subjects. Starting in 1727, non-British subjects coming to British America had to swear an oath of allegiance to the English king, which provided records for future genealogists to comb through. A useful resource for information on slaves that made the passage during this time, the Trans-Atlantic Slave Trade Database, is discussed in chapter 6.

In 1819, Congress passed a law[5] requiring shipping companies to record information about their passengers. Upon arrival at a U.S. port, each ship's captain was required to deliver the manifests showing passenger data, ship name, ports of departure and arrival, and date of arrival, to a U.S. customs officer; hence, they are also called *customs lists*; these lists became the property of the federal government. Those early lists contain only the basics about the passengers (name, age, gender, occupation, and nationality), much less than what later lists have. But the manifests are fully indexed and give you a solid record set for tracking immigrants to North America. Images of the original records are available through Ancestry, FamilySearch, and the Statue of Liberty–Ellis Island Foundation site at www.libertyellisfoundation.org (for New York arrivals).

Before Ellis Island opened in 1892, ships coming into port at New York unloaded their new arrivals at Castle Garden station, on the bottom edge of Manhattan where Battery Park is today. The circular, open-air structure, previously named Castle Clinton, had served as a U.S. Army fort until 1821, after which it was leased to the city of New York and became the site of many public entertainments. Starting in 1855, Castle Garden became the nation's first official immigrant-processing depot, the first stop on the journey into America or Canada taken by more than eight million people. It remained in operation by New York state officials until 1892. Among those who passed through this entry point: Hungarian native Harry Houdini (real name: Erik Weisz) and Irish cook Mary Mallon, better known to history as Typhoid

Mary. Castle Garden's biggest years were before the waves of southern and central European people arrived, so it saw mostly citizens of the United Kingdom, Germany, and the Scandinavian countries.

Castle Garden (under its former name of Castle Clinton) has been managed by the National Park Service as a national historic monument since 1946. A group called the Battery Conservancy runs a site (castle garden.org) with a free index to arrival records for this station (the lists are indexed with all other New York arrivals at Ancestry and other places).

In 1891, the federal government took over handling of immigration processing from New York state officials with new legislation[6] that established a Bureau of Immigration within the Treasury Department. This organization has seen its charter evolve over the years. It eventually became Immigration and Naturalization Services and then in 2003 changed its name to U.S. Citizenship and Immigration Services. In 1891, federal funds poured into a construction project on a small island close to the New Jersey shore named for its last private owner: Samuel Ellis, a colonial resident of New York. The island, which became federal property in 1808, made an ideal first stop for new immigrants because they could be processed before reaching the mainland; anyone deemed unacceptable could be detained and deported easily.

Originally about three acres, Ellis Island was doubled in size through landfill, and a complex of buildings was erected to cope with expected arrivals. The facility opened on January 1, 1892 and processed about 450,000 immigrants in its first year of operation.[7] Five years later, a fire broke out that destroyed the all-wooden buildings through which 1.5 million immigrants had passed. No one died or was seriously injured in the 1897 fire, but many records dating back to 1855 were destroyed, including hospital and office paperwork. Fortunately, the facility's passenger lists had mostly been shipped off-site already, so the fire destroyed only a small number of those.

Still, any loss of records affects someone's genealogy project; someone out there is searching for crossing records that no longer exist. After the fire, plans began immediately for a replacement structure, this time of fireproof brick; that new building still stands today. It was designed to process five thousand immigrants per day, which turned out to be barely sufficient to handle the numbers arriving between 1900 and 1914, when World War I stopped the influx. The new structure opened on December 17, 1900, and processed 2,251 arrivals on its first day. Before the facility closed in 1954, around 12 million people had been processed at the New York arrival stations, most of them at Ellis Island. The biggest year, 1907, saw 1,004,756 immigrants pass through. The all-time highest day of processing fell that year on April 17, when 11,747 people passed through the main building's Great Hall and many examination rooms. That is 11,747 people in a *single day*.

Many well-known individuals came through Ellis Island; an informal list can be found online.[8] Of course, not all arrivals on North American shores remained in the country. Apart from those brought to North America and the Caribbean by force or sent as prisoners, most immigrants had to choose whether or not to stay; Ellis Island and the other ports worked both ways, with ships departing daily for points in Europe, Asia, South America, and (albeit rarely) Africa. Many who came intended to remain only a few years and return to their homeland wealthier than before; others wanted to stay for good but were sent back. Most who came to investigate employment and living options decided to stay, but some of those people traveled back home briefly to retrieve other family members.

Others came intending to stay but found conditions unacceptable and headed back home. All these people left one or more arrival records. Unfortunately, even though most European ports maintained outbound passenger records, the United States and Canada did not regularly do so before Ellis Island closed. So you must infer outbound journeys when you find a later arrival. Some immigrants left as many as four or five as they ping-ponged between the old and new worlds. An enlightening and highly recommended source on this subject is Mark Wyman's 1996 book, *Round-Trip to America: The Immigrants Return to Europe, 1880–1930*.

At Ellis Island, would-be immigrants deemed "unfit" were detained in the shadow of the towering Statue of Liberty; after their detention period, they were returned to their home port at shipping company expense and expected to make their way back to where they had originated. Reasons for deportation were usually noted on the arrival lists, usually in cryptic codes that require examination and interpretation. Sometimes families arriving together were separated by this cruel winnowing; everyone but an elderly grandmother, for example, or a deaf adult sister was allowed entry. Arrivals "defective" in any identifiable way were personae non gratae to the federal government, even if they were part of a family who could care for them, at which point the whole group had to decide whether to stay without that person and let him or her travel back alone to face an unknown fate. Some families today still pass down stories of loved ones "lost" in this way.

New York harbor has always been the biggest, but over the years, America has offered numerous ports of arrival, including Boston, Phila-delphia, Baltimore, San Francisco, Miami, New Orleans, and even Galveston. West coast arrivals primarily went through Angel Island in San Francisco Bay. Travelers who disembarked in Canada crossed into the United States at one of several border-crossing stations, from Buffa-lo to Seattle. Records for federally controlled port arrivals are held at the National Archives; free indexes are available from a variety of sources, and the microfilmed images can be obtained at both free and subscription sites. A discussion of searching online for arrival records at the various ports and through Canada and Mexico is available in chapter 5.

If you are eager to learn more about immigration records and pro-cessing, check out John Philip Colletta's book *They Came in Ships: A Guide to Finding Your Immigrant Ancestor's Arrival Record* (3rd edi-tion, 2002). Colletta includes information on passenger records not held at NARA, which the serious researcher would want to consider. Also helpful on this subject is Michael H. Tepper's book *American Passenger Arrival Records* (1993).

Naturalization Records

One piece of information you will need to find immigrants in their homeland is the town or village they came from. Identifying this place is crucial for "crossing the pond" to continue researching, but the federal sources discussed so far are not much help. Later arrival lists often give the correct place, but remember that the question asked was "place of last residence," not "hometown," although for most people they were the same. On the decennial census, the question "Where were you born?" referred to country rather than to village, so that isn't much help either. To further complicate the matter, for people born in any town overseen by the Austro-Hungarian Empire, place of birth was usually stated as either "Austria" or "Hungary," regardless of the person's eth-nicity, which could be one of dozens not Austrian or Hungarian. Of course, many families have preserved that origin place-name in oral or written form, but spoken place-names are easy to misunderstand by people unfamiliar with the area and language. So, you need a more reliable record source—and you have one, for many of the millions who came here: the documents connected to an immigrant's naturalization into American society, which required each would-be citizen to state his (and later her) specific place of birth.

In addition to mandating a regular census, the post–Revolutionary War federal government established a set of rules for (white male) immigrants hoping to become American citizens. George J. Svejda, in a 1968 National Park Service document,[9] gives a detailed history of how naturalization laws evolved. The entire process involved the creation of many records, which means a paper trail to follow. Naturalization was then, and always has been, available through local courts so that people need not travel far to complete the process. But from 1790 to 1906, the paperwork was controlled by county courthouses, not the federal government. Some courts required more information than others, so you never know what you'll find. With the Naturalization Act of 1906,[10] the federal government issued standardized forms while still allowing the papers to be processed at local courthouses.

These forms required a great deal of information, including current residence, date and place of birth, port and date of arrival on U.S. shores, and the names of spouses and children. No other government-mandated document required this much information of the immigrant.

During the great waves of immigration (early 19th century to early 20th century), naturalization was a three-step process that took at least five years. First, the "alien" had to prove that he had resided in the country for at least two years. Until 1922, only males were required to file paperwork because women and children were naturalized by default with the male head of household. The Married Women's Independent Nationality Act of 1922 (sometimes called the Cable Act or the Married Women's Citizenship Act)[11] gave women the right to claim legal citizenship separate from a husband's and made it necessary that females henceforth apply for naturalization in their own names.

After proving a two-year residence, the alien filed a *declaration of intent* to renounce former allegiances and become an American citizen. After two to five more years and a further residency requirement, the alien could file a *petition for naturalization*. If that was granted, an official certificate was issued by a judge at a ceremony, often involving dozens of others seeking citizenship. Although many families preserved these stamped and sealed certificates acknowledging citizenship, those documents contain far less useful information than the declaration of intent that the individual submitted.

Thus, the declaration of intent is an excellent source for the specific place of birth. For arrival dates and ship names, however, exercise caution: immigrants being questioned by an official understood that they had to answer, but what if they could not remember the exact date or the name of the ship? Afraid of doing something to hinder their naturalization process, some of them made up that detail rather than admitting that they did not know.

Online indexes to naturalization records are available, but the original documents usually must be ordered from the county court where they are held or from the federal government (records after 1906 were customarily held at both places).

The U.S. Citizenship and Immigration Services Genealogy Program (www.uscis.gov) will, for a moderate fee, search indexes and make copies of naturalization records. Its processing time is slow, so if you know which county court was used by an immigrant, you can try requesting copies from there as well. The U.S. Citizenship and Immigration Services also holds "alien registration" forms from World War II, which non-naturalized residents had to complete. The Family History Library makes some naturalization records available via microfilm. One helpful source for further information is *They Became Americans: Finding Naturalization Records and Ethnic Origins*, by Loretto D. Szucs (1998). Figure 4.3 shows an unusual item: a naturalization process summary card signed by the individual concerned.

Passports

Letters requesting safe passage for travelers have been issued by rulers and governments since ancient times. The English word *passport* is borrowed directly from Middle French *passeport* ("authorization to pass through a port"), with *port* derived from Latin (*portus* = entrance). Today, governments all around the world issue a variety of passports (e.g., tourist, diplomatic, refugee); these little books remain the property of the issuing body and are subject to revocation.

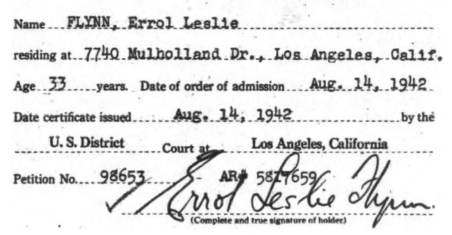

No. 5 5 0 3 0 1 6

Name ___ FLYNN, Errol Leslie _____

residing at__7740 Mulholland Dr., Los Angeles, Calif.

Age __33____years. Date of order of admission____Aug. 14, 1942

Date certificate issued_____Aug. 14, 1942_____by the

____U. S. District____Court at____Los Angeles, California____

Petition No.____98653____ AR# 5817659

(Complete and true signature of holder)

Figure 4.3. Naturalization summary card for Errol Flynn, signed by the film star. *Courtesy of the National Archives.*

A federally issued passport is not all that you need to enter a foreign country, however. To enter another country legally, travelers need a visa letter or passport stamp giving permission granted by that country. In other words, one governmental body cannot give permission for its citizens to enter another country. Many countries have reciprocal agreements that bypass the visa requirement. You do need the passport to return home.

According to Craig Robertson in *The Passport in America: The History of a Document*,[12] the first U.S. passport was issued in the late 18th century. Immigrants desiring a temporary return to their homeland or native-born citizens wanting to travel could apply for a passport, but it was not, except during wartime, required for return from travel abroad until 1952. After World War I, travel without a passport was not recommended, and the government saw a surge in applications. By 1930, the U.S. government had issued almost three million passports, each the product of a document file that could be of great interest. To get a passport, travelers filled out an application and submitted proof of citizenship. Application forms evolved over the years but usually asked for full name, date and place of birth, and intended destination. Other details likely to be found on these applications included name of spouse, residence, and date of naturalization, if foreign-born.

Passport records through 1925 are held at the National Archives; the Department of State maintains the rest. NARA has released thousands of microfilms containing passport records, registers, and indexes; those are now available at Ancestry. Figure 4.4 shows an early passport application, that of newspaper publisher Joseph Pulitzer. The document has been overwritten and scrawled upon by clerks indifferent to the eventual value of the document to genealogists and to the descendants of Mr. Pulitzer.

Military Records

Every war or military action, even if it is a simple moving of troops from one place to another, generates paperwork, and for family historians, this paperwork has always been crucial to tracing the movements of relatives in, and affected by, military actions. Some researchers will make more use of military records than others. For people with immigrant ancestors who arrived in the early 20th century, military records before the World War I draft will not be relevant. For people with ancestors whose arrival dates further back, Civil War records might come into the picture, and for those whose family lines go way back, Revolutionary War records are available. Military records are great sources for evidence of military service, of course, but also for residence history and (sometimes) physical descriptions. Many militia records (citizen groups providing military-type service, in contrast to the official national military) survive at the state and local level, and NARA does have some state militia rolls.

As a rule, military records get more interesting when trouble is involved. More paperwork was generated if a soldier was caught deserting than if he stayed in line, and pensions granted without question by federal officials generated fewer documents than pensions denied and then appealed. For the genealogist, all military records have inherent interest because they place a person within a known historical context that can be studied. An ancestor wounded at Antietam participated in a battle that has been extensively researched, written about, and even reenacted.

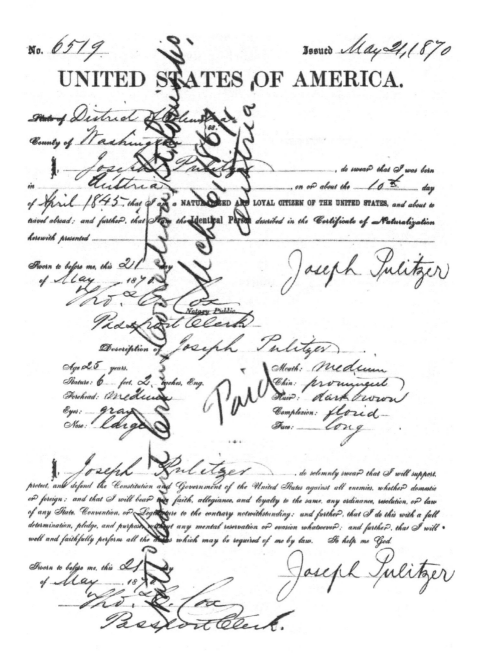

Figure 4.4. Passport application for Joseph Pulitzer (1870). *Courtesy of the National Archives.*

Although they are primarily federal, military records tend to reflect less centralization than the census and arrival lists, but most can be ordered from NARA or the National Personnel Records Center in St. Louis. The National Archives maintains a site called Access to Archival Databases (aad.archives.gov/aad), which is a good place to start; it provides record information (though not images) for about 475 data sets, including many of military relevance.

Ancestry offers subscribers more than a thousand military record sets (some quite small), which include downloadable images, as does Fold3 (www.fold3.com); see chapter 5 for details. The record sets that generate the most interest are from both World Wars, the Civil War, and the American Revolutionary War. However, records exist for the other wars that the United States has been involved in (though a statute of limitations might apply) and for peacetime as well. If you are not sure about the military status of someone in the past, the census is worth checking because some of the population schedules indicate veteran status: 1840 (Revolutionary War pensioners), 1890 (Civil War vets, for the six thousand or so names that were not destroyed by fire), 1910 (survivors of the Union and Confederate army or navy), and 1930 (general veteran status).

Following are the most common types of federal military records.

Draft Registration

Like the census, the idea of a military draft (more formally called *conscription*) has existed since ancient times. Compulsory military service made Rome great, and it has played a part in most global conflicts until recently. The U.S. government discontinued its draft in 1973 in favor of an all-volunteer service but still requires males between the ages of eighteen and twenty-five to register for the Selective Service contingency plan. These registrations will play a part in family histories of the future; for now, the only draft registrations you can access are those conducted during both World Wars. These registrations do not indicate enlistment in the military but rather a voluntary registration, making the registrant part of an available pool to be called on should the federal government deem it necessary. Only a small percentage of those who registered in either war were ultimately "called up."

The National Archives has microfilmed millions of completed draft registration forms. There were three draft calls in World War I and six in World War II, but so far only a small percentage from World War II are available online or through a records request. Sadly, original World War II cards for several Southern states were destroyed before they could be microfilmed. So, failure to find a person's draft registration does not indicate failure on his part to register.

The information requested on the registration forms is of interest to family historians because not many other record sources require the registrant to name his current employer and give the address of that employer. The template forms used during both World Wars ask for the name of someone close to the registrant, either "nearest relative" (World War I) or "someone who will always know" the registrant's address (World War II). Those are vital clues, along with the other information requested: current address, birth date and place, marital status, and physical description. The registrant signed his form or made an X; signatures were not required then as often as they are today, so finding one is special.

The World War I cards provide an excellent supplement to naturalization documents for identifying immigrants' hometowns, because the form asked for the registrant's birthplace.

Registration took place at federal offices (often referred to as draft boards), but the registration forms went to Washington. However, the local offices also gave each registrant a wallet card to carry indicating compliance with the federal law. Sometimes these small cards are preserved among family papers. Even famous men had to register for the draft, as you can see in figure 4.5.

Enlistment Records

There were, of course, many men who enlisted, rather than registering for the draft and waiting for possible call-up, and many who did both. Females were not subject to the draft, so their military participation was through enlistment only. Online sources for enlistment records parallel those given in chapter 5 for draft registration, but the two biggest can be found at the National Archives site and at Ancestry: World War II Army Enlistment Records, 1938–1946 and U.S. Army Register of Enlistments, 1798–1914. The records usually contain, among other things, place of residence, place and date of enlistment, year and state of birth, and education status. The pre–World War I list is especially helpful in

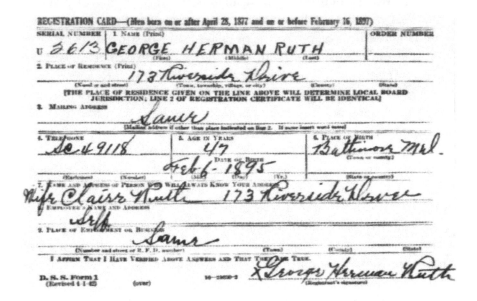

Figure 4.5.   George Herman "Babe" Ruth's World War II draft registration card.
Courtesy of the National Archives.

establishing the birthplace of people who came to the country between the late 18th and early 19th centuries.

Muster Rolls

Where there are soldiers, sailors, marines, and airmen (the term, with peculiar military logic, applies to females as well), there will be lists: lists of equipment and supplies, lists of duty assignments, and on and on. Military muster rolls are lists of people—a human inventory—that have been produced throughout the long history of American military maneuvers, during both war and peacetime. Many muster rolls are available online, but they represent only what has survived fire and other depredations of time. With luck, you can trace a particular soldier's movements almost year by year as he (or she) appears first on one muster roll and then another.

Personnel Records

The federal government divides the records it holds into two categories: archival and nonarchival, with split responsibilities for storage and access control. Military personnel records belong first to the Department of Defense (and all its predecessors), which created them. But according to an agreement between the Defense Department and the National Archives, the files are transferred to the latter sixty-two years after a service member has separated from the military, whether through discharge, death, or retirement. At that point, the records are considered "archival" and are available to the public through a simple ordering process. Archival military records no longer belong to the Department of Defense; they are transferred legally as well as physically to NARA.

Records for individuals who separated from military service less than sixty-two years ago are maintained in the Federal Records Center in St. Louis and are subject to access restrictions. Unfortunately, a 1973 fire at the St. Louis facility destroyed about sixteen to eighteen million personnel files that had no duplicates or microfilm backup. Chiefly affected were the records for army personnel discharged between 1912 and 1960 and air force personnel discharged between 1947 and 1964. This fire struck an especially hard blow because no indexes had yet been created for these records. So unlike the 1890 census destroyed in 1921, it is impossible to know exactly what was lost. However, some of the data has been reconstructed through unaffected medical and pay records for the individuals whose primary records were burned, so try your request(s) even if the individual records you seek were likely among those affected.

Personnel records are usually not online and must be requested through official channels. NARA's website (www.archives.gov) is the best source for information about what is available and how to request files.

Pension Records

Military personnel who survived various conflicts in U.S. history have been eligible to apply for pensions; if they died, their surviving spouse or minor orphans were eligible to apply for the pension money. Such pensions have been part of U.S. government spending since colonial days, when the new federal government promised financial support, sometimes in the form of land grants, to veterans of the Revolutionary War. Before these military offers of support, there were no public pensions. The first pension was granted by Congress in 1776: half-pay for a lifetime given to soldiers injured and disabled by military service and thus unable to earn their own living. Sometimes bounty land warrants were issued instead of cash payments; these records are sometimes combined with pension records.

If you are researching people who possibly served in the Revolutionary War, the War of 1812, the "Indian" War, the Mexican War, the Civil War, or the Spanish-American War, you will want to investigate pension and bounty land warrant record sets. Pension applications make excellent evidence for military service and contain information such as branch and dates of service, date and place of birth, names of heirs, and locations of service during conflicts. Sometimes (especially if there was an appeal) the files contain supplementary material, such as affidavits, marriage and death certificates, discharge papers, and other testimonials offered by the claimant in support of his or her application. The usual losses due to fire have affected the pension and land grant records of the federal government, including the earliest Revolutionary War applications, but most of the later ones still exist.

The National Archives holds pension applications and records of pension payments to veterans, their widows, and other heirs for service between 1775 and 1916, and these files can be requested; for more information, visit www.archives.gov/research/military. Indexes to military pensions can be found at Fold3 and Ancestry or through www.militaryindexes.com. Records of nonfederal pensions (some Confederate states granted these) can sometimes be found in state libraries. Bounty land grant applications and pension files are generally offered by the same providers.

Compiled Service Records

One useful military record set sprang out of a War Department initiative in the mid-1890s to reconstruct Union army and navy personnel information lost through fire, primarily to verify military service for veterans seeking pensions. The purpose was to create a single card, called a compiled service record (CSR), to hold in summary form all the militarily relevant information about an individual soldier—information that was extracted from original records. After the Union soldier card project was finished, War Department clerks began working on CSRs for Confederate soldiers and for participants in other conflicts, including the Revolutionary War, Spanish-American War, and War of 1812. The cards, which are held at the National Archives and at various state archives, range from 1798 to 1902; they usually provide, in addition to name, rank, and unit, the soldier's home state, enlistment date, and length of service. Also possible: age, physical description, wounds sustained, and date of discharge or death.

Remember that CSRs were not created at the time of service, like enlistment records and muster rolls, but represent a data summary created years after active service. Thus, they are derivative sources, not original—abstracts of information taken from original sources such as muster rolls, pay and casualty lists, regiment and hospital records, correspondence, and so on. They should be used as stepping-stones to primary resources such as those discussed previously. If data appears on the CSR, then data appeared in a primary source, a copy of which might still be available. CSRs are available for online order through NARA and can also be seen by subscription at Ancestry and Fold3; see chapter 5 for details.

The federal clerks creating the CSRs were doing exactly what genealogists do—researching an individual's history by gathering information from original records and creating a data sheet summarizing what they found. Decades before genealogy became America's favorite hobby, those War Department clerks were blazing a (paper) trail.

War Records

Conflict-specific documents have been carefully preserved by the federal government. For example, see the collection called "The War of the Rebellion: A Compilation of the Official Records of the Union and Confederate Armies," available at Cornell University's Making of America site (collections.library.cornell.edu/moa_new/waro.html).

Other Military Records

Of course, there are many other record collections relevant for military research, and the sharp researcher covers them all: casualty lists, lists of medal recipients, discharge papers, medical and hospital records, desertion and court-martial records, and regimental histories among them. Some are federal, some are state-controlled, and others might be held by private organizations. The availability of records, especially online access to them, is always evolving. Sometimes, if you are lucky, a library or archive holds locally relevant military records.

Social Security

If a person you are researching never served in the military, was not a naturalized citizen, and never mentioned a specific birthplace to family members, you have one more option for learning the birthplace: the application for a Social Security card. Since 1935, when Congress passed the Social Security Act, Americans have been required to submit an application (form SS-5) to receive a unique nine-digit number that connects them to future benefits. The goal of the act was to put a financial safety net under Americans who could no longer work because they were either elderly or disabled and to relieve the economic burden on widows whose working husbands had died. Applications began processing in November 1936, and by the following year, some thirty million Americans had received their number on a little printed card, which they signed.

That familiar blue-and-white card is sometimes found among personal papers, but the card has only a name and number, so it is not helpful unless it is used to connect you with the real gem: information supplied by the applicant on form SS-5, which asked for full name at birth, age at last birthday, date and place of birth, mailing address, father's and mother's full names, and current employer (this question was dropped after 1947). It also required a signature. Almost everyone who was employed by 1936 or later completed this application (subsequent amendments to the act allowed parents to request a number for newborns). No other governmental form asked for so much information. The SS-5 forms apply to an entire generation of people and are genealogical gold mines, because in each case, the information supplied is attested to by the applicant him- or herself. Figure 4.6 shows an SS-5 form that was completed in 1937.

Images of these applications are not available online, nor are they indexed online. Though federal documents, they are not held at the National Archives, as you might expect; copies must be requested directly from the Social Security Administration. The SSA, which microfilmed the records in the 1970s and then destroyed the originals, will release printed copies only for demonstrably deceased people, so you will first need to find a person's listing in the Social Security Death Index (SSDI) or else supply other documentation (obituary, death certificate). The SSDI is not made available online by the federal govern-

Figure 4.6. A Social Security Administration SS-5 form (1937). *Courtesy of the Social Security Administration.*

ment, but you can get it from multiple other sources, including Ancestry and FamilySearch. It does not include the names of every person who has died, even if those people had Social Security numbers, nor does it list everyone who received Social Security benefits. Only deceased individuals whose deaths were reported to the Social Security Administration are listed.

The SSDI—also known by the less mellifluous title of Social Security Death Master File—was created and is maintained by the Social Security Administration. In addition to the Social Security number of a deceased person, records usually contain the full name, dates of birth and death, zip code of last residence, and state where the deceased lived when the number was issued. This last piece of information can be helpful in distinguishing among people with similar or identical names. Remember, though, that the SSDI is not an original source for the spelling of names and the birth date and that "zip code of last residence" does not equal "place where person died."

Note: in compliance with section 203 of the Budget Act of 2013 ("Restriction on Access to the Death Master File"), data providers are no longer able to display SSDI records for individuals who have died within the previous three years. A copy of the new law is available at www.congress.gov/113/plaws/publ67/PLAW-113publ67.pdf.

NONFEDERAL RECORDS

Federal records are a must for a documented family history, but so too are those created at the state, county, and municipal levels. Into the category of nonfederal records fall those created at lower echelons of government, religious records, and anything created within the context of private ownership, such as business and medical records, newspapers, and family records.

Vital Records

Fortunately for you, local government offices tend to create a paper record each time they interact with citizens. The most useful are birth, marriage, and death records, collectively called "vital" records (and humorously designated as "hatch, match, and dispatch"). Many families store certified copies of them alongside other important documents.

Vital records are the best source for proving links between people. A birth certificate connects a person to his or her parents, regardless of who eventually raised that child; marriage certificates connect wedded couples regardless of whether the marriage lasted; and death certificates are good testimonials to immediate family, especially spouses. But unlike federal records, the availability of these records can vary from place to place. Some counties have digitized their archives and made the scanned documents available for purchase online, while others intend to do so but have not yet begun the process; still others have not yet digitized their records.

Access to vital records held at the state, county, or township level depends largely on each jurisdiction's particular laws. Restrictions vary as to who can access them and how many years must pass before they become available to anyone who asks. Costs also vary widely. See textbox 4.1 for a list of the best states for vital records before 1900.

Genealogists searching for family records in these states are luckier than those working within states not on the list. Remember that the kind of detailed paperwork now produced for each person born did not exist in the past. Before the 20th century, many states and counties did not even keep vital records systematically. Some towns in New England have extensive birth records going back to the 17th century, but several

Southern states have nothing before the second decade of the 20th century.

The term *vital records*, it should be noted, does not include records maintained by churches. A marriage that takes place at a church usually creates at least two records: one for the local government office and one for the church (see discussion of church and religious records later in this chapter). Ideally, you will get both.

TEXTBOX 4.1
BEST STATES FOR VITAL RECORDS BEFORE 1900

According to Megan Smolenyak's 2009 publication *Who Do You Think You Are? The Essential Guide to Tracing Your Family History* (Penguin), these are the best states for vital records before 1900:

Connecticut	Massachusetts
Delaware	Michigan
Florida	New Jersey
Hawaii (even pre-statehood)	New York
Iowa	Rhode Island
Maine	Vermont
Maryland	Washington, D.C.

If you are working with European records created centuries ago, you'll sometimes find that the record of baptism provides the only evidence of a birth and that these church-kept records are the de facto vital records for a town or city. (Chapter 6 gives details on accessing records outside the United States and Canada.)

The holdings at most vital records archives have been indexed, although these indexes might be available on-site only. If no index exists, you can still locate vital records if they are recorded chronologically in ledger-sized books. Costs and procedures for obtaining vital records depend on the municipality; the best approach is to find the appropriate website for the place that holds the documents and to follow the instructions. You can order many of these documents via the online service VitalChek, but this company charges a handling fee and has restrictions on who can receive documents.

Birth Records

Birth records make a solid link between two generations and sometimes contain information about how many other children a mother has had. At the very least, almost all modern-day, government-created birth records in the United States contain the date and place of birth (as attested to by the delivering physician/midwife); the gender, race, and given name of the child; and the full names of both parents, if available. Quite often, births were recorded in large books rather than on separate pieces of paper. For most of history, no birth "certificate" per se was created and given to the family.

Most states treat birth records as confidential if they were created within the past hundred years, but some use a seventy-five-year cutoff. If you can prove that the person is deceased, the county or state office will usually release the record. A few places make records available online once they are no longer covered by privacy restrictions.

Anyone old enough to have followed the news several years ago will remember the "controversy" surrounding President Barack Obama's Hawaii birth certificate. The document that he had originally made available to prove his status as a U.S.-born citizen (a requirement for the presidency) was not the "long form" of his birth record—that is, a full copy of the original—but rather a printed "short form" containing some information that appeared on the original (contrary to what many people believed, the short form, actually an official *extract*, is legal and acceptable for all occasions when a birth certificate is required).

In addition to the short and long forms of birth records, you will sometimes encounter *amended* and *delayed* birth records. If someone makes an official correction to a birth record, the result is a new, amended one. A delayed record substitutes for an original birth record that was never created or was lost. Imagine someone born in 1899 in a state that had not yet begun systematic tracking of local births. To apply for a passport as an adult, that person would first need to submit an application for a delayed birth record. The application required the individual to supply evidence of his or her birth (family Bible entries are sometimes acceptable, but school, military, and employment records are preferred). If the proof of birth is sufficient, a delayed birth record is created and is considered of equal validity to one created at birth. But for research purposes, a delayed birth record is *not* equal, because a record created closest to an event is usually a better guide than one created later. Record seekers should be aware that indexes to birth records sometimes list these delayed certificates separately.

If a delayed certificate is the only birth record available, the family historian can seek out and examine records that were created near the time of birth, especially baptismal records and "baby books" in which the parents record key events in an infant's life. Many baby books contain preprinted lines that encourage the parents to record such information as the exact time of birth, date and place of christening (if relevant), and the names of godparents and siblings. Often, the new parents received letters and cards from family members, which can provide attestation of birth details as well. But the practice of keeping such baby books was not common prior to the mid-20th century.

Marriage Records

The earliest marriage records were kept by religious institutions, but for the past few centuries, the event has created civil registration records as well. The typical sequence after the colonial period was marriage *bond*, marriage *license*, and marriage *return*. Thus, a "marriage record" at a courthouse might consist of all three or any one of these. Be careful not to assume that because a bond or license was obtained, the marriage took place. In previous centuries, European and American couples in the Christian tradition informed a church official of their intent to marry. The recording and publication of this intent was called the *banns* of marriage, after a Middle English word meaning "proclamation."

As with the marriage license, publication of banns does not indicate an actual marriage; that is a separate record. Standardized forms did not come into common use until the 19th century. Before that, church and civic officials handwrote everything in the document, sometimes first drawing lines on the blank pages of a ledger book.

Access laws for marriage records vary from county to county. In some places, the documents are contained in chronologically ordered books that cannot be examined; you must rely on clerks to make extracts of the records. Sometimes the license was a separate piece of paper issued to the couple intending to marry, who took it to the religious official or justice of the peace who performed the ceremony; then, the completed paper was returned to the issuing office; that record is known as a marriage *return*. In some places, the written *application for a license* can be obtained or is made available in digitized form along with the license itself. It is always worth asking for when seeking marriage records.

Marriage records contain a piece of information that sometimes proves elusive in North America: a woman's original (or maiden) name. Some even contain the names of the bride and groom's parents—with luck, even the maiden name of each mother. Marriage records usually contain at least the full names of both parties, the date and place of the marriage, and the name of the official who performed the ceremony. Some municipalities record the ages of the bride and groom, their addresses and occupations, and whether either has been married before. Sometimes the signatures of witnesses are included, but these are not necessarily relatives or even friends.

Marriage laws have changed over the past several centuries, especially the legal age for marriage. The careful researcher eyes with caution those brides' ages that are just at the minimum required by law. Many times, an underage bride simply lied about her age or had a parent falsely attest that she met the minimum age requirement. Sometimes these attestations are made available as part of the paper trail that a marriage generates. In any case, be sure to read the words of each question on the license application carefully. If it asks for a woman's name "before marriage," she might give her first married name rather than her "maiden" name.

If you do not know the date and place of a marriage, you'll have to find those details before the records can be obtained. Newspaper and church bulletin announcements are quite helpful in this regard. Some families preserve the formal wedding and shower invitations sent or received, and many record big events such as marriages in the family Bible or other religious book. Also, announcements of major anniversaries (e.g., 50th anniversary party invitations) can provide the key. Weddings are usually big events for families, so when interviewing people, the family historian can ask what weddings the person has attended.

Sometimes people do not remember the exact date, but they usually remember what age they themselves were (or possibly where they lived or were working at the time). So rather than ask, "When did Aunt Rose and Uncle Fred get married?" it is better to ask, "Do you remember Aunt Rose's wedding? How old were you at the time, and where were you living?" Chapter 2 has details on interviewing family members in a way that elicits the most useful information.

For marriages that ended in divorce, the records documenting legal dissolution will usually be held in county court archives. They might be available for copying but will take effort to acquire. They are almost never available for digital download. Even finding which courthouse holds the records can be a challenge. Often, the best approach is to hire a professional researcher with experience in the locality that contains the divorce records.

Once located, divorce records are always illuminating; they often include testimonials by the plaintiff (and rebuttals by the defendant) that reveal problems not usually made public before.

Death Records

Death records are fairly easy to find because they are the most recent documents created in a person's life and because state and county government offices place fewer restrictions on these records than they do for birth and marriage records. Death certificates usually contain the full name of the deceased; the date, time, and location of death; the deceased's last address and (sometimes) occupation; and (almost always) a physician's assessment of the cause of death, whether an autopsy was performed, and the disposition of the body (i.e., cremated or buried). On this document, the information surrounding the death is the most reliable because the doctor authorized to declare a person deceased can attest to it. Any piece of information not immediately observable must come from an informant (usually a family member)—date and place of birth, names of parents, occupation—and so should be viewed cautiously. A death certificate provides primary (firsthand) information for the date and place of death but only secondary (secondhand) information for earlier events.

Death certificates are the most familiar, but they are not the only record pertaining to an individual's demise. Other possible records include coroner's reports, inquest reports, and autopsy findings. If the death was originally recorded in a ledger book that has not been microfilmed, you will usually not be able to obtain a photocopy of the page but will instead be issued an extract or a certified copy of an entry. Sometimes death certificates are later amended, just like birth certificates, if corrections are necessary. Newspaper obituaries, burial and medical records, tombstones and cemetery records, and will/probate records are some other death-related sources of information. Most of these are discussed later in this chapter or in chapter 5, and don't forget the mortality schedules (1850–1885) and SSDI described earlier.

As with birth and marriage records, localities differed in their practices regarding death records, but most are open to a request for noncertified copies (a certified copy can usually be obtained only by family members or the executor of the will and is required for insurance and Social Security claims). In general, as time passed, death certificates became more detailed. The earliest ones in the United States gave only the deceased's name plus the date and place of death.

Sometimes a family's oral history differs from the facts recorded in vital records. As noted in chapter 1, you might want to prepare yourself for the inevitable revelation of a premarital birth, a divorce caused by infidelity or spousal abuse, or a suicide.

City Directories

Today almost every adult is familiar with the thick directories issued by phone companies and local publishers. These directories provide residential and business numbers and usually contain yellow pages that group businesses by type under specific headings. But what did people use before the invention of the telephone and the publication of phone books?

They used something similar called a *city directory*. These publications, like our modern phone books, helped individuals find where someone lived and see what businesses were listed under certain headings. Most of these city directories listed only the male adults in the household who were employed; a listing for a female usually meant that she was the primary wage earner in the household. The entries listed name and address and sometimes occupation, in highly abbreviated form. The directories were often sponsored by business owners, who used the results to target their advertising. The directory publishers hired people to go door-to-door collecting information, but unlike the federal census, no attempt was made to be comprehensive in these listings, so many residents were not listed.

Also like modern phone books, city directories usually contained listings of government offices, churches, schools, and other such organizations. Knowing these places might help you follow up on possibilities; the name of a church or club mentioned in family papers might be listed with an address. Even reading the advertisements can enlighten you about the products and services available at the time. As cities grew and directories became larger, cost considerations forced some directory publishers to cease creating them or produce them only occasionally. Eventually, of course, the telephone was invented, and phone numbers began appearing as well.

Small towns and rural areas generally did not produce directories before the invention of the telephone. However, sometimes larger towns and cities would list landowners in outlying areas, and some counties did produce farm directories, which often included a surprising amount of detail. Some libraries and historical societies hold copies of original printed city directories, but most directories were printed on cheap paper and so are fragile and not able to withstand much handling. You are better off using a microfilmed or digitized copy. Fold3 and Ancestry both have large collections of city directories, but don't forget to consult local libraries and archives as well; they might have the original books themselves. When using indexes and guides to city directories, remember that they often have a title that refers first to the publisher, as in *Polk's City Directories: Chicago*, rather than just the city name.

City directories can help you pin down a person's residences over time. In addition, if a woman is listed as a widow just a year after her husband was named in the directory, you gain a clue as to when he died. Taken together, these publications provide a unique snapshot of a locality at the time when someone walked the streets of a place.

Remember that, until the 1920s, these directories generally listed only the employed head of each household and not (like the census) every person in that household. Starting in the 1920s for some places and the 1930s for others, other adults in the household were listed, including spouses. But these city directories are not available for every location, as the census is. Also important to remember: although these documents have been indexed, it was done with optical character recognition software, which does not always represent text accurately. Fortunately, relying on the indexing for the city directories is unnecessary because the listings are alphabetical and the entries are easily found by browsing the record set.

One bit of record-keeping advice: if you locate a city that has directories available for a long stretch of years, make a graph chart to keep track of your searching progress. Along the x-axis, list every surname that you want to search in the directory, and on the y-axis, list every year available, as shown in the table. Then you can check off each year and surname searched as you go. Your future self will thank you, as this is not a searching job that you will be eager to repeat down the line.

State Census Records

Even researchers familiar with the federal census might not know that several states have, over the decades, conducted their own censuses and that these records are available from multiple sources. The state censuses were usually done in years other than the ones claimed by the federal census—most often, in the years ending in 2 or 5 (e.g., 1892 or 1905). These records can be obtained from state archives, historical societies, and libraries, as well as through Ancestry and FamilySearch.

Not every state conducted its own census. The popular genealogy reference guide *The Source* by Loretto D. Szucs and Sandra Hargreaves Luebking contains a listing of every state's census schedules, or a note that none were conducted, under the heading "State Census Schedules, 1623 to 1950" (available at Ancestry's wiki, now hosted at wiki.rootsweb.com/wiki/index.php/Main_Page).

Court Records

Students today learn about Johannes Gutenberg and William Shakespeare in their classes; rarely do they question how the teachers and textbook authors came to know all about these two men who lived hundreds of years ago. Neither of them kept a detailed diary, so how do we know, for example, that Gutenberg went bankrupt in 1456? Or that William Shakespeare married a woman eight years older than himself when he was eighteen?

Both facts have been discerned through *court records*, which have had better staying power as the years have passed than other record types. Court records include much more than proceedings of criminal cases. See textbox 4.2 for other records you can usually find in courthouse archives.

TEXTBOX 4.2
RECORDS IN COURTHOUSE ARCHIVES

Marriage and divorce	Guardianship and adoption
Land and property	Jury lists
Voter registration	Taxation
Wills and probate	Asylum and institution
Property maps	

Local courts more so than federal have generally been closely involved with the daily life of a community. Any profession that required a license intersected with an issuing court: lawyers, doctors, saloon owners, and transport operators had to appear, sign papers, and pay fees. Court-ordered building inspections, child support, fines, and tax collecting all generated paperwork, and that paperwork has endured surprisingly well overall because court records have tended to be protected and housed safely. Remember that each time a city, county, or federal court interacted with a citizen, a record was created; the Internet age has not changed that pattern. Today, some localities make public court records available through an online search; traffic violations and other minor criminal offenses pertaining to living people, for example, are often not considered private. Each jurisdiction has its own restrictions and access limitations.

Genealogists sometimes discover that a family member spent time in an institution such as a mental hospital or jail. But records from these institutions are difficult to obtain, as they are often discarded after a specified period. If they were kept, they are generally not made available because, with few exceptions, these institutions are private, and so their records are not subject to laws governing public records. However, if an individual was committed (sent involuntarily) to an institution for criminal or mental issues, that commitment resulted from a court order, which means that a court record once existed, probably still exists, and might be available.

Court records are public and subject to laws governing their availability. Start with available online indexes before traveling to where records are held. Restrictions apply for accessing court records, but with patience and time, they can be uncovered. When working with courthouse records, keep in mind that two index entries were created when the record involved two people. For example, a marriage record would normally be indexed twice: under the bride's original surname and the groom's. Property exchanges were typically indexed twice as well, once under the name of the seller (the *grantor*) and once under the name of the buyer (the *grantee*). Most indexes created before the 20th century were handwritten.

Some court records have been compiled—copied out by hand or retyped into a single manuscript. As discussed earlier in this chapter, military records have undergone this compilation process, and in some cases, the original records were destroyed, so the compilation is all that remains. Compiled records are useful if the originals are difficult to access, but you should never forget that whenever it was possible to introduce errors (as in copying or transcribing), errors could have been (and probably were) introduced.

Pursue the strategy called "follow the money." A family's whereabouts and well-being can best be established and assessed by searching out employment, tax, property, and inheritance records, all of which are the province of local courts. Often, these proceedings were required to be mentioned in the classified section of the local newspaper.

Church, Business, and Other Institutional Records

Births, marriages, and deaths often generate a companion church record to go with the civil record. A birth is often followed by one or more religious rituals, for which individual churches, synagogues, and mosques keep records. Where no government-issued record of a birth exists, church records can fill in the gap and provide unique information as well.

However, finding religious records is unlike finding civil ones. To identify the denomination and appropriate institution, you can find clues in family papers, especially holy books, funeral cards, and obituaries. Cemetery location might be another clue. Religious records tend to be held by the creating body, which is under no legal obligation to provide copies or even extracts from its records to those who inquire. Sometimes, smaller churches have joined forces and combined their record archives. City directories can help you identify which religious institutions existed at a specific time. Both FamilySearch and Ancestry provide access to millions of religious records from all over the world.

Business, law, professional, and medical directories often form part of the collections of local libraries and archives and should always be sought out. They are almost always private publications and so unconnected with laws governing the creation of records.

Obituaries and Cemetery Records

Obituaries range from terse to verbose and now appear both in print and online, sometimes in the form of extensive memorials.[13] Obituaries are usually written after someone has died; however, most news magazines and major newspapers have already researched and prepared extensive entries for famous people still living so that when the final event occurs, the obit is ready to go. For family historians, obituaries are an important record source because, unlike death certificates, they often link a person to surviving family members by name, which helps determine relationships. Obituaries are customary now, but the further back you go, the less frequently they appear. Finding obituaries published before the 20th century is a challenge because many early newspapers are still not fully digitized and indexed.

Obituaries are crucial for family history research, but no single source exists to make the task of finding them easy. They are the province of neither civil nor religious authorities but rather commercial publications (newspapers). Unlike birth, death, and marriage records, no laws mandate the preservation of obituaries or govern the public's access to them. The best approach is to make extensive use of any free access available and to use the obituary resources provided by or linked to existing subscriptions. Fortunately, many of the obits that once appeared only in print have now been digitized and are accessible online. Legacy.com offers free extracts of published obituaries, but users will quickly realize that the coverage is not extensive. Ancestry offers access to several obituary collections; the largest is the *United States Obituary Collection* (a compilation from various online sources), currently with just over twenty-seven million records. Caution: this collection consists only of those obits that appeared originally online, which means that anything before the last fifteen years or so is not here.

Your best bet for accessing obituaries and obtaining a full contemporary page image of the notice (the gold standard) is to subscribe to Newspapers.com, NewspaperArchive, or GenealogyBank (they do not overlap much). One of them should cover the newspapers you are most interested in. Linking genealogists to historical documents is a highly competitive online business, so access to obituaries is likely to remain complicated for some time.

One frequently overlooked source for informal obituaries not published in newspapers is the site Find A Grave (see chapter 5 for details). Like Wikipedia, Find A Grave relies on the contributions of users, many of whom have submitted several thousand entries on individual burials. People can post informal obits or even copy the text of published obituaries into the notes section of a person's memorial. You might find the obituary of someone you are researching before you even start looking for it, if you first locate a Find A Grave memorial for the person.

Remember that obituaries, while informative and helpful most of the time, contain secondary (i.e., secondhand) information, although a newspaper itself is an original source. Names, dates, addresses, and family relationships will need to be confirmed with original records. Even if the information supplied to the publisher of the obit is correct, errors can occur in the transfer to print or online. One final caution: the occurrence of an obituary in a place does not mean that death occurred there. A retired person might pass away in Florida after having spent decades in Philadelphia; in such a case, the family often chooses to memorialize the deceased in the newspaper of the hometown, sometimes not even mentioning that death occurred in another state.

Obituaries often mention religious affiliation and burial place; that information can be followed up. Cemeteries are not always the most user-friendly places, but you should always ask about burial permits and records. If you are lucky, the cemetery might be willing to share its grave-opening records, which sometimes reflect multiple burials, espe cially for large plots.

Home Records

The beginning genealogist lives in the best place to start researching: home. Every home has something useful, like papers left by a deceased relative, a collection of funeral cards, a box of photos, or an inscribed keepsake. Families often keep copies of birth and death certificates, burial deeds, obituaries, funeral sign-in books, baby books, and formal pictures. Someone in every family has a box or folder with such materials. Keep asking family members until you find these important papers. Once you do, follow the steps recommended in chapter 2 for preserving them and making them available to future generations by scanning them.

FINDING RECORDS

You can find records anywhere, and they do not necessarily have to be paper and certainly are not all online. A tombstone carving is a record and a valuable one. But most of the items that genealogists refer to as "records" will turn out to be pieces of paper with handwriting or typing on them. Almost always, you will encounter these records not in their original state but in digitized form. Many beginners have no idea what record sources exist and sometimes think that if it's not on Ancestry, it isn't anywhere. Online research is unavoidable for family history research today, but keep in mind that genealogically relevant information is also available in private (family) collections, in special libraries and archives, and in public libraries.

SUMMING IT UP

Learning to work with records is, for most novice researchers, a new enterprise; from the start, use a careful, methodical approach. Old records have their own reality that is worth learning about. Remember:

- Records are everywhere: in government offices, in libraries and archives, in churches, in home storage boxes, and in cemeteries. Many useful records are online, but most are not.
- In general, record keeping improved as time passed and more information was gathered about each individual. Older records often contain minimal information, especially by today's standards.
- When dealing with records in any form, be sure to examine them closely, and always prefer the original form to a copy, extract, or summary. Sometimes record keepers wrote marginal comments that were not indexed or transferred to an extract. Records can have all sorts of problems, as described in this chapter, but they are the building blocks of any genealogy project.

Next: the basics of online searching for genealogy records.

5

ONLINE RESEARCH—THE BASICS

This chapter addresses:

- Public versus private records
- Online records available
- Essential, useful, and worth exploring sites
- Search tips that get results

Genealogists today operate within a wired world. A novelist or journalist might opt to use an old manual typewriter, but no genealogist can pursue family history without online resources and digital files. In the prewired era, researchers consulted large, printed indexes in libraries and archives. Today, indexes are accessed almost completely online, so to research your family history, you must become comfortable with that process. To get a solid grasp on what's available, it's important to understand the differences between types of records and types of information.

PUBLIC VERSUS PRIVATE

The difference between public and private records was touched on in chapter 4. The distinction is so important, especially for beginners, that it's worth revisiting briefly.

The distinction between the two types is as close as your front yard. Your front yard is private property; no one has the right to stand within it unless they have your permission. The street that runs in front of the yard, however, is public; you as the owner of the adjacent yard cannot dictate who gets to use that street.

The same distinction is made with records. Public records are those that have few, if any, restrictions on who can access them. A real estate sale is an example of a public record; that's why you see them published in the newspaper classifieds. Most records created through the massive enterprise called the U.S. government are also public; you'll often hear the phrase "a matter of public record" to describe testimony given before Congress. Federal documents such as the decennial census and many others are also public records; access to them is unrestricted and free (though not necessarily by means of the most convenient path). You have a right under federal law to request and get access to public records through the Freedom of Information Act.

Examples of public records (with some exceptions, of course) that are essential for genealogy include the following:

- Court records
- Birth records (civil, not religious)
- Death records (civil, not religious)
- Marriage and divorce records

Private records, on the other hand, are those that you do not have a built-in right to see. Almost all medical records fall into this category, as do those pertaining to adoptions. If the record was created by a non-government entity such as a business, institution, or organization, the creating entity controls access. Most cemeteries are private enterprises; their records are often made available by the organization that controls them, but those records are still considered private. Churches keep records of births, marriages, and deaths along with the civil authorities; the civil records are public, but the church records are private (many do make their historic records available).

So the word *private* in genealogical terms has more to do with who controls access and how and when those records are made available rather than meaning "off-limits." See below for details on a site dedicated to helping you get access to public records (Public Records Online Directory).

Public versus Subscription Information Access

The issue of which records are private and which are public extends to the online world. In a sense, the invisible phenomenon we call "the Internet" or "the Web" is divided between public and subscription access information, which have distinct differences.

Public access information is what you get with a Google search. It is available to anyone who has a wired or wireless connection and a device—no passwords or fees required. For example, a Google search of *Barack Obama* retrieves millions of webpages. Those pages could be anything—government or organizational sites, news pages such as CNN or Fox News, individual blogs, online stores, and so forth. In short, you get a mixed bag of information types. Some of these sites might lead you to pages that require a password and payment; those pages are the doorway to *subscription access* information, which is behind a wall of sorts and virtually invisible to someone who does not seek it out. Behind that wall and millions of others like it is the "invisible Web"—the area of the Internet not uncovered in a Google search.

Public access information is free; subscription access information requires registration and (usually) payment. You can search Google and get results for no charge, but if you search Ancestry's portal as an unregistered user, you'll get only partial information until you pay for subscriber privileges. By the way, pornography sites operate in the same way: they give away some content in the public access area of their site and then offer the user much, much more—at a price. It is a business model that dominates the online world: the "good stuff" is behind a paywall, much as the good stuff in a pharmacy is behind the counter.

It is almost as easy to create public access information as it is to find it. Anybody with a minimum of know-how can create webpages, and there are few rules governing content. The Internet operates according to the rules of anarchy; no one polices it. The creators of public access content must not infringe copyright, misuse a trademark, or commit libel; other than that, content can be anything its creator desires. This information, because it is both created and accessed with no restrictions, has no filter; it can go from the mind of the creator to your eyes with no one to say, "Wait a minute, let's check that before it goes out."

Because of the technology that enables its creation, public access online information is almost 100 percent *Web original*: created online to appear online and thus completely bypassing the print stage. Unlike public access webpages, however, subscription access sources such as newspaper and magazine articles have been, until recent years, almost 100 percent *print original*: they appeared first in print and only subsequently (or simultaneously) appeared online. Today, some online journals have no print counterpart, but they go through the same review process that a publication intended for print does and are thus part of the *print original* category. Printed material is certainly susceptible to bias and error, but it has usually involved more eyes on the text than does content that has been created specifically for online consumption. Textbox 5.1 summarizes the general differences between the two types of information sources.

DIGITIZATION PROGRESS

For the past few decades, much available print original information has been digitized and made searchable. Google—as part of an ambitious project to digitize every known book—has scanned over thirty million titles, most of them in the public domain and thus not subject to copyright restrictions.

Genealogy records have also undergone a massive digitization effort. You now have online access to every federal census, to passenger arrival records for the major ports, to naturalization documents, and to state and county records where state law does not specifically prohibit access (e.g., Wisconsin). The progress has been truly astounding.

But a *New York Times* article makes clear that the job is nowhere near finished.[1] In 2007, the National Archives and Records Administration estimated that it had digitized only a fraction of its holdings. The text record holdings alone at the National Archives consisted of 9 billion pieces. Each piece had to be scanned and then the scanned image cleaned up and labeled. By 2007, the National Archives digital lab had achieved an annual rate of 500,000 completed scans. Pretty impressive, but at that rate, they will need *1,800 years* to complete the project. Since 2007, digitization efforts have ramped up, but the unscanned pieces of paper held in archives, libraries, and special collections in the United States still far outnumber the scanned. Fortunately for family historians, genealogically relevant documents—especially those of national importance—have been given priority.

TEXTBOX 5.1
GENERAL DIFFERENCES BETWEEN PUBLIC AND SUBSCRIPTION SOURCES

Public Access

- Free or no registration
- Mixed information types
- Usually does not go through traditional editing process
- Web original

Subscription Access

- Usually costs or requires registration
- Single information types
- Usually goes through traditional editing process
- Print original

The good news for genealogists is that many not-for-profit organizations are teaming up to digitize things faster. Indiana's Allen County Public Library is the second-largest genealogy library in the world, after the Family History Library in Salt Lake City; it has partnered with the Internet Archive to digitize public-domain materials. Groups and even individuals can submit files containing digitized texts to the collection.

Indexes and Databases Online

The Internet contains many genealogy-related sites, but relatively few offer the indexes and databases you will absolutely need, and even fewer offer original record images. Those few, the real power players in family history research, can supply the majority of information for your history. There are some excellent and useful public access sites requiring no registration or payment, but there is no escaping the fact that you will need at least two, and probably a few more, subscription-access sites. There is no master online index of every record available and no single conglomeration of records; you must deal with separate indexes made from discrete data sets and managed by different entities. The challenge of online genealogy research involves figuring out what sites give you access to the indexes and records you need. The most widely used indexes, such as the Social Security Death Index (SSDI), are available at multiple sites, but some of particular relevance to your research might be available through only one supplier (e.g., state birth and death indexes).

Casting a wide net when you begin searching online is fine, but once the initial flurry of downloading is over, the next step is to identify which indexes potentially contain the information you need and to search those thoroughly. Not all localities have the same coverage in their available indexes; for example, Florida offers an index of its divorce records between 1927 and 2001, a generous range. California's divorce index, however, covers only 1966–1984, not even twenty years. Most other states do not even make their divorce indexes available (and none make divorce records themselves available online). What you have access to online thus depends a great deal on where the records were created. You might need the same information for the California branch as for the Arizona branch of your family, but you will not get the same access. Nailing down the relevant indexes and keeping track of how they are updated or expanded is important.

You can track online news about how the resources relevant to your research are evolving. For example, people with family history in Pennsylvania have long been frustrated by the state's restrictive laws governing access to archival birth and death records. A not-for-profit group called the Pennsylvania Freedom of Information Coalition pushed hard for a change in the laws restricting access to archival records, and in 2009, a new "open records" state law was passed. Similar efforts are underway in other states, so access is always changing.

As discussed in chapter 4, genealogists deal with a variety of records, which are primarily created at the national, state, county, and city levels. But before you can use a record set, you need to find the index for it. Without an index, a record set is like a library without a catalog. There are many record sets available for which indexes have not yet been created, but the biggest ones have been done—namely, the federal and state censuses, the passenger arrival lists going back to the early 1800s, and the most popular military records.

Vital Records Online

There is no national index for births and marriages; those records are the province of states and counties, not the federal government. But for the last several decades, the federal government has tracked almost every death that has occurred in the United States by way of its Social Security Death Index, a database that contains extracted files from the Social Security Administration's Death Master File. Widely used and for years available free from multiple sources, the SSDI contains information for people who had a Social Security number. Those with no number or whose death was not reported to the SSA will not appear in the index. Most of the information is from 1962 and after, although the database includes information on deaths going back to 1937.

The SSDI's value for genealogists is obvious, as it contains around ninety million names, each with multiple data points in the record and all of it searchable. It also includes around four hundred thousand railroad retirement records; after 1935, railroad employees had a separate Social Security–like retirement plan. The SSDI records usually contain the deceased person's first name and surname, birth and death dates, Social Security number, the state where that SSN was issued, and the last known residence (not the same as the location where death occurred). With the extracted information in the SSDI, you can take the next step and request a copy of the application for a number (called the SS-5 form) filled out by the person, which you have legal access to through the Freedom of Information Act. Instructions for ordering can be found at the Social Security Administration website (www.ssa.gov/foia/request.html).

It's pricey, but a copy of someone's original SSN application can give you, in the applicant's own handwriting, the full name at birth, parents' names, date and place of birth, and signature. If already employed, the applicant included the employer's name on the application. You can request a copy even if you do not have the Social Security number, but the charge is a little more and the search might take longer. The SSA will not release copies of the application form for anyone under 120 years old unless you submit proof that the person is deceased. It will also black out parents' names on the SS-5 application unless you provide proof that they too are deceased (or unless they were born more than 120 years ago). Despite these restrictions, the SS-5 is a useful record to obtain. Chapter 4 has details and an example of this record type.

Remember that the online SSDI records you see are extracts and so are not original sources for any of the information. The SSDI contains errors, as any database does, because it resulted from data entry. In late 2011, following reports that identity thieves were targeting recently deceased people's Social Security numbers, genealogy sites were pressured by Congress to remove the SSDI from their offerings; several did so. Ancestry kept the SSDI but put it behind its paywall and removed the numbers from records less than ten years old. Ironically, the SSDI has been used since its inception to *prevent* identity theft; it allows institutions such as government offices and businesses to avoid paying benefits, issuing policies, and approving credit cards in the name of, and with the Social Security number of, a deceased person because they can search the SSDI for that number.

The federal government has not usually been involved in vital records, apart from the SSDI; those records have long been the province of states, counties, and small municipalities. Some places began requiring registration of key life events in the mid-17th century, but others did not begin systematically collecting that data until well into the 20th century. Even when registration of births and deaths was mandated, compliance took some years to achieve, so the record you are searching for might not exist, even though it should have been created. Before telephone and e-mail, it was not easy to report births and deaths; doing so often meant taking time off work and traveling to a government office. As time passed, the compliance rate for registrations gradually climbed until it reached today's 99.9 percent, so the closer your target documents are to the present, the more likely it is they were created.

State and county indexes are an excellent way to track down original documents; you can find many of them at Ancestry and FamilySearch, or you can search each state's official website for instructions on access-ing available indexes and ordering certificates. Remember that, like all indexes, the ones created from vital records are subject to processing errors, and the indexes themselves are an extracted form of the records, not the records themselves. Textbox 5.2 contains tips for searching the Social Security Death Index.

TEXTBOX 5.2
TIPS FOR SEARCHING THE SOCIAL SECURITY DEATH INDEX

- Remember that numbers are easy to transpose during data en-try. If you are searching dates, try reversing numbers (*1997* instead of *1979*). Errors in copying numbers occur more often when the date is given in numeral form (9/10/1960) rather than written out (September 10, 1960), so search *October 9* (i.e., *10/9*) if you have no luck with the correct date (September 10 or 9/10).
- Don't get stuck on the spelling of a name as you know it; try any other spellings or variations you can think of. If you're looking for *Childs*, try *Child* or *Childe*, and use wildcard symbols (? to replaces one letter and * to replace multiple letters). See later in this chapter for more details on using wildcard symbols to search.
- Reverse the name fields; put the last name in the first name box and vice versa.
- If you know the middle name of your search target, try that instead of the first name.
- Search using different combinations of known data—for exam-ple, every person named *Loretta* who died in Ohio between 2000 and 2010 or everyone whose name began with the letters *Penn* who died in a specific year.

Census Records Online

Each U.S. federal and state census has its own index, but you can search them all at once at several sites. Although the images themselves are not always included in free access, census records are easy to find; Family-Search and the Internet Archive both offer them, and public library card holders can use HeritageQuest Online (details on all three are given later in this chapter).

Finding someone in the census is easy if the enumerator spelled the family's name correctly. If not, you might still find your target family if you have the address or other information. Chapter 6 gives details on using census ward maps and address locator tools. Fortunately for gene-alogists, the census record sets were indexed more than once. That means a mistake made by one indexer might not have been made by another, which gives you another shot at finding an elusive record. For example, *Mary Christiano* is indexed correctly at FamilySearch in the 1940 census but incorrectly at Ancestry as *Mary Christians*. In short, Ancestry's census index is different from the one in FamilySearch, and both are different from HeritageQuest Online. So try all three if you can't find someone; don't give up on finding a census record until you have done some creative searching with wildcard symbols and checked all available census sources.

Also, because of Ancestry's option for users to submit corrections, you are more likely to find a record that was indexed incorrectly (i.e., someone might have caught the error and made a change). In 1920, Walter Elias Disney, the creator of Mickey Mouse, was living in Kansas City with his brother's family (see figure 4.2 in the previous chapter). The enumeration sheet lists the family name as *Disnay*—a mistake that might prevent someone from finding this record. But in 2006, an An-cestry user submitted a correction, ensuring that henceforth, this record would be retrieved in a search for *Disney*. At FamilySearch, however, the record was also indexed as *Disnay*, and that error (which originated with the enumerator) has remained in the index. In other words, a search there on *Disney* will not pull up the 1920 census record for Uncle Walt.

Enumerator and indexer errors are not the only reason why you might have difficulty finding a census record. Sometimes the infor-mants lied or unknowingly gave false information. Sometimes people did not know how to spell their family names or exactly how old they were. And sometimes, a family's reality was too complicated for the questions. The head of a household might be raising his unmarried daughter's child but claiming it as his own, or a wife might want to disguise the fact that her husband had abandoned the family.

Immigration Records Online

At 6:00 p.m. on April 17, 2001, a new site called Ellis Island Records went live; it offered, with registration, free access to passenger arrival records that previously had been accessible only on microfilm. The Ellis Island arrival records, a subset of the immigration records held at the National Archives, cover more than twenty million immigrants and take up 3,700 rolls of microfilm. The project to digitize those microfilmed records and create a searchable database took several years, millions of dollars, and many volunteers (most of them LDS church members), but by 2001 the site was ready to go. Its creators anticipated high demand; hundreds of millions of Americans trace their ancestry back to people who set foot on that scrap of land known as Ellis Island, and the site organizers knew quite a few of them would give the new database a try.

Within hours of going live, the site recorded fifty million visitors, and within days it was clocking about twenty-seven thousand users *per second*. From the start, however, many searchers got this message instead of their hoped-for results: "Thank you for your interest. . . . Due to an extraordinary number of visitors, we must limit access to the site. Please keep trying or check back later." The organization behind the new site, the American Family History Immigration Center, scrambled to put a dozen or so more servers into use to handle ever-increasing demand. While the site never crashed, access remained difficult for months; eventually, the traffic slowed, and access became more stable. A few years later, other subscription sites began adding passenger records. Today, genealogists have multiple online sources for immigration data.

Most passengers traveling from Europe and entering the United States between the mid-19th and mid-20th centuries disembarked at one of five major ports: New York, Philadelphia, Boston, Baltimore, and New Orleans. If you do not know where your ancestor landed, most likely it is one of the first three. But people entered America at many other places; small cities up and down the coasts had ports, and people crossed at several Mexican and Canadian border points. The free site called U.S. Ports of Arrival and Their Available Passenger Lists, 1820–1957 (www.genesearch.com/ports.html) lists every sea or border station that has published immigration records; links are organized by state.

Citizenship and naturalization documents are part of immigration records; Ancestry has an excellent index that includes images of application summary cards, and sometimes the documents themselves are included. Some of the summary cards are even signed by applicants. Though small, these cards contain the information you need to order the naturalization document set from either the federal government or the court where the event occurred. Before September 17, 1906, when the U.S. Naturalization Service was created, naturalization records were held locally; as explained in chapter 4, any court could grant U.S. citizenship. Citizenship applications usually generated four distinct documents over the long process, the first three of which are often available to order or are available online already:

- Declaration of intent
- Petition for naturalization
- Oath of allegiance
- Certificate of naturalization

The summary card will point you in the right direction, if you can track it down. See chapter 4 for definitions and details about the four document types. In recent years, passport applications have been offered for online access.

Although not online, many immigration-related documents held by the U.S. Citizenship and Immigration Services—formerly the Immigration and Naturalization Service—are available under the Freedom of Information Act, which is a 1966 statute that allows the release of information and documents held by the federal government. Requests can be made only through form G-639 (available at www.uscis.gov). Usually there is no charge for the copies, which are sent in the mail. With a little digging, you can establish whether the U.S. Citizenship and Immigration Services holds relevant records for your research; among its holdings are naturalization certificate files after September 26, 1906 (prior records are held in local court jurisdictions); immigrant visa files from

July 1, 1924, to 1944; alien registration forms from August 1940 to April 1, 1944; and alien files after April 1, 1944. If you are willing to pay for assistance with U.S. Citizenship and Immigration Services records, you can hire research help through its Genealogy Program (www.uscis.gov/genealogy).

Military Records Online

Military records rank high with genealogists in usefulness and interest, but they are not as easy to access online as those discussed earlier. For one thing, they do not exist as a single record set but cover multiple branches of the service for well over two hundred years. Each of the major conflicts during that time involved personnel from the various service branches, all keeping their own records.

Military records can be dazzlingly precise and fascinating, as shown in figure 5.1. According to this document—held at the New York State Archives and available in Ancestry's U.S., Union Soldiers Compiled Service Records, 1861–1865—a soldier named August Woellert enlisted in the Union Army in Rochester, New York, on July 18, 1862, and was discharged July 24, 1863, "on account of wounds" incurred at Antietam and Chancellorsville, both major Civil War battles. A native of Germany, this 5'10" soldier was twenty-six years old and worked as a "ship carpenter" before his soldiering activity. Before his discharge, he was "reduced to the ranks," with no explanation given for that action.

That's a lot of information for one small card, which is only one among millions in a series of record sets called *compiled service records* (chapter 4 has details). A few decades ago, these records could be ordered only through the mail, but they can now be ordered or even accessed online. Fold3 (now a subsidiary of Ancestry), offers subscription-based online access to these compiled service records from the Revolutionary War and Civil War, among other military records.

Genealogists researching people who fought in the Civil War will find extensive documentation for every aspect of that conflict. One of the best free resources is a database maintained by the National Park Service. Called the Civil War Soldiers and Sailors Database, this free index has extracted records of six million Confederate and Union military personnel. Much of the information came from the compiled service records, but because this database includes information from other

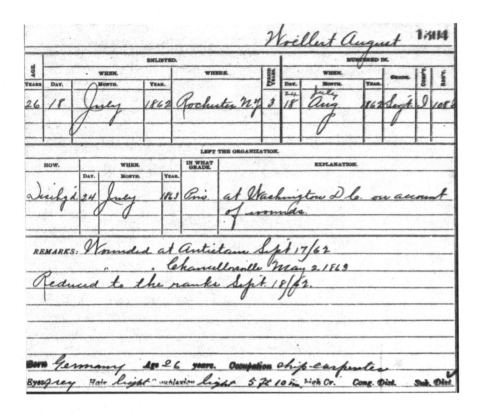

Figure 5.1. **A compiled service record for a Civil War soldier who was wounded in two battles.** *Courtesy of the New York State Archives.*

sources, it should be searched in addition to the compiled service record indexes. The system has unique information as well: regimental histories, which can give you a fascinating picture of a soldier's movements; detailed descriptions of significant battles; lists of prisoners; and burial records. You can access the Civil War Soldiers and Sailors Database at www.nps.gov/civilwar/soldiers-and-sailors-database.htm.

Many military pension records and veterans' claims are available online through Fold3 and can be ordered through the National Archives (www.archives.gov). Bounty land records, which indicate grants of land from the federal and state governments as reward for military service, are usually not available online but can be ordered from the National Archives. The Bureau of Land Management maintains a searchable database of land records (discussed in the next chapter) at glorecords.blm.gov/default.aspx, and Ancestry has an index called U.S. War Bounty Land Warrants, 1789–1858.

The military record images that you can find easiest online are some of the draft registration cards collected by the federal government during the two World Wars. During World War I, the president issued a call for three draft registrations; more than twenty-four million men complied. The cards of a limited group of registrants in World War II are also available. Unfortunately, many military records were lost in a disastrous 1973 fire at the National Personnel Records Center near St. Louis (chapter 4 has details). Because no microfilming or duplication had been done before the fire, the loss was quite serious for genealogists.

For a regularly updated summary of what military-related indexes are available online and where, check out Online Military Indexes & Records: A Genealogy Guide (www.militaryindexes.com). The links are organized by conflict name.

Newspapers Online

Digitized newspapers have increasingly played a role in our understanding of past political and social contexts and are quite valuable to genealogy research. For example, if your mother was born in Brooklyn in 1947, you can search the archives of the *New York Times* to see what headlines appeared the day she was born, what issues were on the minds of city residents that day, and what advertisements the paper's subscribers were viewing.

Of primary interest are obituaries, engagement and marriage announcements, birth announcements, news about military activity, hospital admissions and releases, activities in police reports, car accidents, and so on. Real estate transactions and legal proceedings that were required to be published in newspapers give a glimpse into who sold what property to whom, who had not paid their taxes, and who was notified in the case of probate. Every time you find someone mentioned in a local newspaper, you gain insight into that person's movements and context. In general, the smaller the place, the more newsworthy each person's actions were. Items reported in a small-town paper (visits abroad, anniversary parties) did not have a place in big-city publica-

tions, but most cities had neighborhood papers that contain such material.

As explained in chapter 4, newspaper items (including obituaries)
are sometimes difficult to come by because they are not public records
and citizens have no special right to see them. Instead, newspaper
archives are made available at the publisher's discretion. This elusive
record type has become a big business online, and today's researchers
have unprecedented access, usually through subscription sites. The collections don't overlap all that much, so you might need multiple subscriptions to get the newspaper records you need.

Of course, some local publications make their archives available for
free, but generally the entries do not go back more than a few decades.
One major free source for older newspapers is the Library of Congress's
Chronicling America: Historic American Newspapers (chronicling
america.loc.gov), with about seven million historic newspapers available
at no cost to you.

It's always worth checking to see if the town or city you are researching has digitized papers. Some localities are following the Library of
Congress model and digitizing issues of their papers going back to the
beginning—in many cases, access is free. For example, one volunteer
has dedicated himself to making digitized images from New York state
and other area newspapers currently only available on microfilm (ful
tonhistory.com). He has more than twenty-five million pages available
online so far, indexed through optical character recognition, searchable,
and free to download. If your relatives lived anywhere in New York
during the period covered by this guy's efforts, you cannot afford to
miss this site.

Several subscription sites—especially Newspapers.com, Newspaper-
Archive, and GenealogyBank—offer access to newspapers and are
worth exploring. Do a quick browse on the localities you're researching
in each of the three to see if the local papers are represented. Chances
are, one of those three will have what you need. Ancestry, in addition to
its myriad other offerings, provides access to more than a thousand
historic newspaper publications.

One newspaper resource that many beginning genealogists often
overlook is the ProQuest Historical Newspapers database, accessible
through library subscription (usually academic libraries). This major
resource offers the full text of many city papers; if you have ancestors

from large urban areas, you might benefit from tracking down a sub-scriber library and arranging access through the Friends of the Library or guest program. This underutilized resource is perfect for genealo-gists seeking not only a firsthand picture of the political and social context for their ancestors but also name-dropping records such as obit-uaries. ProQuest has a sophisticated and flexible search interface; you can limit the article type, specify an exact date range, and select the publication to search in.

Obituaries are the most sought-after newspaper items but can be the most difficult searches to execute satisfactorily. You can find obituary extracts at several sites, but original publication images are harder to come by. There are free sites, but usually records do not go back more than a few decades. For recent obituary notices, Ancestry has its U.S. Obituary Collection, 1930–2018; the Obituary Daily Times Index, 1995–2012 is another useful source; it contains extracts of published obituaries from around the world. It is distributed by e-mail list and is also available on Ancestry. This is an index, not a collection of record images, but it can give you the details you need to track down the original. About 2,500 entries are added each day.

Another terrific free source for recent obits is Legacy.com's Obit-Finder, a trademarked searching tool that covers more than a thousand newspapers in the United States and Canada. Searching is free, but access to some documents requires payment.

SEARCH STRATEGIES AND RECORD PROBLEMS

Each type of record brings with it a unique set of conventions and potential problems. In general, your strategy should be to cast a wide net at first and then close in on the records you need. Learning effective online searching takes time, so be patient during the process. Stay alert to the possibility of errors, and always seek to corroborate the informa-tion you find in one record with what appears in others. Following are four general categories of record errors and problems.

Category 1. Errors That Result from Incorrect Information Given by the Supplier

Though rare, such errors did creep into the official records. Sometimes during the federal census-takings, for example, the individual supplying information for an entire household did not know exactly how old each person was, so merely took a guess. A family member might give a nickname instead of a proper name when asked by the census-taker to list the individuals in a household (*Jack* instead of *John*, *Lizzie* instead of *Elizabeth*). In other instances, people deliberately misrepresented their ages and relationships.

Category 2. Errors Introduced by the Person Who Created the Record

The U.S. federal census is a perfect example of a record set replete with errors introduced by the individuals who created the records. In fact, a better setup for introducing errors could hardly be imagined: underpaid men and women—exhausted after trudging through urban streets and down country roads asking the same set of questions over and over—recorded this vitally important information by hand while standing in doorways.

Also, in many areas, especially during the late 19th and early 20th centuries, the enumerators dealt with people who did not speak English as their native language; as a result, names were often recorded phonetically. Sometimes the record creator was given a full first name but recorded an abbreviation for it, writing *Chas.* instead of *Charles* or *Wm.* instead of *William*. Later indexers or abstractors would faithfully copy these abbreviations, leaving *Chas.* and *Wm.* on the forms that someone would have to search to retrieve the record by name. In addition to recording information incorrectly, the record creators sometimes had terrible handwriting, so when a later clerk was making the fair copy, the names were misinterpreted.

Category 3. Errors Created by the Person Who Indexed the Record

Almost all records you can obtain online are accessed via index. An index allows you to find that one record among millions. But what happens when the index listing—the link between you and the record you are seeking—is faulty? Usually, it means that the record stays lost unless you apply other strategies. Given the importance of extracting the data into an accurate index, you might assume that this all-important task was completed by professionals with care and accuracy, at least for federal documents such as the census and the arrival lists held at the National Archives. In reality, most indexing was done rapidly and by people who were instructed to record exactly what they saw regardless of whether it made any sense.

Sometimes a problem was created by a combination of creator error and indexer failure. The shipping company agents who completed the passenger manifests were instructed to write the surname, then the first name of each individual. But the clerks were human, and sometimes their fatigue or another distraction led them to reverse this customary recording order and put the first name before the surname. That is the first error, but it becomes a problem only if the indexer does not realize that the reversal has occurred and indexes the name incorrectly (i.e., with the first and surnames reversed).

For example, if a record creator wrote *John Wood* instead of *Wood John* on one line of a passenger manifest, and a later indexer compounded the problem by entering *Wood* into the first-name field and *John* into the surname field, someone trying to find John Wood would not retrieve this record with a name search. This problem occurred many times in the census and on the passenger manifests but could have been avoided if the indexer had recognized what was obviously a surname, even though it was in the first-name field, and vice versa.

Congress required a great deal regarding the information on passenger manifests but missed the chance to mandate that the information be *printed* rather than given in cursive script. Reading other people's cursive handwriting can be difficult even when the writing is done by a contemporary. On the manifests, the English and Irish names were easiest for native English speakers to index, but if the names were unfamiliar and also written in a style difficult to read, names got misrepresented easily.

Figure 5.2 shows a segment of a manifest record showing an individual's name that was misunderstood by indexers. His name was *Sebastiano Famiglietti*, and he sailed from Italy and landed at Ellis Island, as millions of his compatriots had already done. His was a typical southern Italian name, not difficult or unusual to the Italian clerk who sold him his ticket. But when an American indexer pulled up the record decades later and entered the name as part of the indexing project, he or she simply could not read the handwriting and entered the name as *Fannoslietti Sebattiano*. That clearly nonsensical entry stands as the indexed name of Sebastiano Famiglietti in Ancestry.

The indexer's problem reading the handwriting was compounded by the original record-creator's mistake in the order of the name. Customarily, an individual's surname was written first, then the first name (today we would separate names written that way with a comma). But the clerk failed to follow custom and recorded Sebastiano's name the way someone might say it: first name, then surname. The indexer in this case did not realize the clerk's error so has indexed the name not only with completely incorrect spelling but also with the first and surnames reversed.

It is unlikely that the family of Sebastiano Famiglietti would find him unless someone makes a correction—in other words, does the work of indexing again. Ancestry allows such corrections, even invites them, but unfortunately, FamilySearch has no mechanism in place for inputting corrections directly on the record. The Ellis Island database does invite corrections, but they have to be submitted via e-mail.

The indexers of the manifests also misread relationship words for surnames, which means even more errors. Federal law since the mid-1800s has required passengers arriving at U.S. ports to be listed in family groups, for ease of processing. The shipping clerks in other countries who were selling tickets and writing out the passenger lists wanted,

Figure 5.2.   An Italian name on a 1900 passenger list. *Courtesy of the National Archives.*

of course, to follow American laws pertaining to the shipping industry. So some of them indicated, with words or abbreviations, the relationship between passengers in a group. Figure 5.3 shows a section of a manifest with the words *fratello, moglie,* and *figlie* (the Italian words for *brother, wife,* and *child*) written next to the names. At the top of this partial page image is a man's name: *Biagio Giordano* (given in reverse order on the form, according to custom). Below his name we see *Fratello Giovanni.* The original recording clerk was indicating that Giovanni is Biagio's brother—*fratello* is not Giovanni's surname (which was, of course, *Giordano*). And yet, this record for Giovanni Giordano is indexed as *Giovanni Fratello.*

Other added words just below those names created the same problem. You can see the name *Stefano Geraci;* below is the name of Stefano's wife, *Giuseppa Granata,* with the word *moglie* written next to it. The recording clerk is saying, "Here is Stefano Geraci and his wife, Giuseppa Granata" (Italian women did not change their surnames upon marriage). You probably will not be surprised to learn that this woman's name is indexed in Ancestry as if *Moglie* were her surname.

There are thousands of such errors on the manifests and in the census, in both Ancestry and FamilySearch. As you work with these records, keep in mind that where the possibility of error exists, errors will certainly exist.

The process of indexing records has improved a great deal in recent years; now, indexers working with FamilySearch use a double-blind

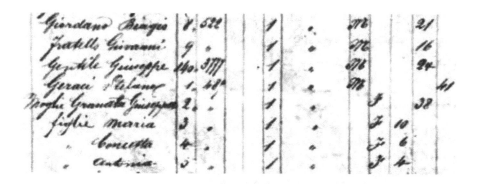

Figure 5.3.   Words added to a passenger manifest by an Italian shipping clerk to indicate relationships between members of a traveling group. *Courtesy of the National Archives.*

process designed to decrease errors. Two people independently extract or transcribe the records, and if they disagree, a third person analyzes the original and determines the correct version. That is great news for records being processed today, but for the pages indexed when the process was in its earlier days, we are stuck with error-filled indexes.

Category 4. Lost Information Caused by Damage to the Record

A picture, they say, is worth a thousand words. Figures 5.4, 5.5, and 5.6 supply about three thousand. As these images show, precious, nationally significant records have not always been treated with care. Over and over, vulnerable paper records have been lost because they were not given basic protection from fire and water. On a smaller scale, repairs were made with cellophane tape with little thought to how that tape would hold up decades down the line.

Cellophane tape (usually called Scotch tape in America), like almost all adhesives, leaves residue behind after the top layer of plastic has

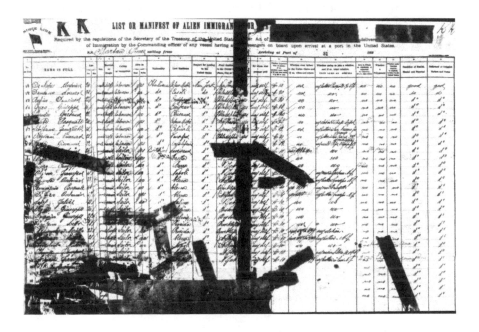

Figure 5.4. Damage to a record caused by cellophane tape. *Courtesy of the National Archives.*

Figure 5.5.   Records destroyed in the Washington, D.C., Post Office Building fire on December 13, 1935. *Courtesy of the National Archives.*

fallen off. Over time, that sticky residue attracts dirt and darkens, eventually creating the effect seen in figure 5.4. A professional restorer could, perhaps, remove the residue that obscures the names at the bottom of this record, but these paper records are not works of art; they contain information important to only a few people, so advanced restoration is unlikely to occur. If your ancestor's name was covered by the liberal application of cellophane tape, you'll most likely need some clever search strategies to uncover it.

Paper records are fragile things. They succumb immediately when exposed to fire and are easily damaged by moisture and insects. The loss of important records creates an effect that cannot be measured and that makes the work of all historians more difficult. Each loss is significant, but the 1890 federal census and the millions of unique military records in the 1973 fire in St. Louis at National Personnel Records Center are surely the two most significant for family history research (see chapter 4 for details on both disasters).

Figure 5.6. War Department records housed in the White House garage prior to the establishment of the National Archives. *Courtesy of the National Archives.*

A few more points need to be made about searching for online records. The nature of each record type correlates with errors and problems that can make successful searching a challenge. The federal census and many vital records indexes contain their own special error types.

Federal Census

The census indexers worked with documents that themselves were the product of transcription. As explained in chapter 4, the enumerators who went door-to-door created field notes. Later, someone else made a clean copy from those notes, which were then destroyed. If the copyist made a transfer error, that error remained in the official version of the census page. By copying what they saw, modern indexers replicated those errors.

Transcribers and indexers of the census were also copying many numbers in addition to names and other words, and numbers are notoriously difficult to keep in short-term memory, even for a few microseconds. Furthermore, numbers are easy to transpose and sometimes difficult to read in handwritten script because, unlike letters—which are parts of words that make sense in themselves, even if each letter is not clear—an illegible single digit could be anything from zero to nine.

Vital Records

The legibility and even comprehensibility of birth, death, and marriage records depended on whether the original record creator could understand the person giving the information. Genealogists who work with vital records for non-English-speaking immigrants in large cities will be familiar with this problem. For example, in 1905, a recently arrived Italian immigrant gave birth in a Chicago tenement apartment. The birth attendant was a Polish midwife who lived nearby; no other medical assistance was at hand. Although she had been in the United States longer than her clients, the midwife spoke very little English and not more than a few words of Italian, so communicating with the parents was difficult.

The birth record she created reflects that linguistic barrier. The parents told the midwife that the baby's name was *Ida Agata*. The midwife wrote *Adioargreta*. That unrecognizable "name" became part of the official birth record for this child, and that's how it is indexed in FamilySearch. The surname, which the parents could not spell out themselves, was *Pennavaria*. The midwife, capturing most of the sounds that she heard, wrote that down as *Pinvaria*.

The midwife was on firmer ground when she heard the mother's name: *Francesca*. She understood the name, but without knowing how to spell it in Italian, she used something like the Polish spelling: *Fransiska*. The mother's surname, *Nasca*, was apparently a puzzle to the midwife; she wrote a tentative capital *N*, then added *AS* before inscribing a confusing letter that could be a *C* or an *E*. Then, for reasons of her own, she ended the written name with an *H*, creating *Naseh*. The father's first name (*Nunzio*) also gave her trouble because it has no counterpart in Polish; she swung wildly and wrote *Naunisi*.

Decades later, the indexer working with this birth record dutifully copied out what was written and thus created an entry in the database for an *Adioargreta* born to *Fransiska Naseh* and her husband *Naunisi Pinvari*. If you were searching for *Ida Agata*, with parents *Nunzio Pennavaria* and *Francesca Nasca*, the original errors make finding this record quite difficult. The mistakes are not the fault of the indexer but the original record creator, and such mistakes abound in county archives that contain records created in neighborhoods with high concentrations of recently arrived immigrants. The writing is clear in the record, but the information is incorrect, so the resulting index entry is also incorrect. This is only one of millions of examples.

Bottom line: if you are working with vital records created within non-English-speaking populations, you should assume that names were not taken down accurately every time. *You* might know how to spell a family's surname, but it's possible that earlier members could not, so the people creating birth and death certificates (midwives and doctors) made their best guess. Ironically, the accusation often leveled at the port officials at Ellis Island (that they couldn't understand some surnames and thus wrote them down wrong) was certainly true of officials in cities where the immigrants took up residence, although those mangled versions did not become their actual names. See chapter 1 for details on why the idea of names being changed at Ellis Island is a movie-generated myth completely unsupported by evidence. The situation for English, Irish, and Scottish names was not much better, given the tendency of record creators to use abbreviations for first names (see search tip #5 below).

SEARCH TIPS THAT GET RESULTS

During an initial search of a database, you will usually find relevant items right away; those are the records that do not have errors in the extracted information. But when this low-hanging fruit has been picked, it's time to get clever.

1. Use Wildcard Symbols

If you're searching a name with possible spelling variants (*Green/ Greene*) or easily mistaken letters (*N*'s and *M*'s, *A*'s and *O*'s), use wildcard symbols to replace letters. Just as a wild card in poker can stand for any card, a wildcard symbol (? or *) can stand for letters. The question mark stands in for a single letter; the asterisk for multiple. For example, if you are looking for *Galbraith*, try *G?lbr*th* as your search term. You will get results that have any single letter between *G* and *L* and any combination of letters that appear between *R* and *TH* (up to a certain number of characters, depending on the database): *Gilbraith, Galbreath, Gelbrith*, and so on. That means more results to look at, but if one of those is the person you're looking for, it's well-spent effort. Check each database's help section for specifics on what wildcard searching it allows. Usually, you must include at least three letters in the word or name, and you cannot use wildcards for both the first and last letters.

2. Enter Search Terms Sparingly

If you know that John McKay was born in 1902 in Philadelphia, was married in 1927, and died in 1974, you might think entering all that information is the best way to find his records. It's not. If you're looking for his birth record, adding the birth year is a good idea because the record itself is concerned with the birth and will have the year right. If, however, you are looking for his marriage record, adding the birth year might prevent you from finding it if the original record didn't contain that information.

Older marriage and death records usually gave the ages of the participants, not the birth dates. If the database has automatically computed a birth year based on the age given, that date will appear in the index entry for the record. Imagine that John McKay, when he was married in 1927, gave his age as twenty-six on the application for a marriage license; the computer comes up with 1901 as his birth year. If you entered *1902* (the correct birth year) as part of your search, you will not retrieve this record. The same is true if you enter *Philadelphia* as the birthplace. If the record itself does not list a birthplace, you won't retrieve it because the search algorithm is looking only for records that list Philadelphia as birthplace.

Stick with search terms and dates that connect to relevant data points in the record that you seek. Names are always appropriate, but other information should be entered only if you are sure that it is given in the record itself.

3. Use Data Combinations Other Than Names

Most beginning genealogists use only the names of the people that they are researching to retrieve records. But what if the name is incorrect in the database? Instead, try combinations like these:

> Birth record: year and/or place + father's first name and/or mother's name + gender
>
> Census record: place living + state/country born in + birth year (within two years)
>
> Passenger record: year of arrival (within five years) + nationality + city of departure

In other words, leave the name field blank and pull up other lists. For example, aim at getting a list of all males born in Philadelphia around 1902 to a mother named Mary or a list of all German females who departed from the port of Bremen and arrived in Boston around 1900.

4. Search for Relatives

Sometimes one person's name might be incorrect in the database, but someone else's in the family is right. For example, if you have looked for the census record of *Thomas Hope* without success, switch your search to his wife and children. You will find this sidestep searching especially valuable when your target has a common name, such as John, James, or Mary. If you are looking for *John Smith*, you stand a better chance of finding his census record if you instead search for his daughter named *Winifred* or son *Merton*. Before you give up on locating any particular census record, do your search using the names of the other family members who lived at that address.

5. Use Abbreviations Instead of First Names

Common male first names, such as William, Thomas, James, and George, were occasionally recorded in abbreviated form. To see the extent of this problem, do a search in Ancestry using *Wm.* (not *William*, just *Wm.*) as a first name (you need at least three characters, so include the period). The many records giving *Wm.* as a man's actual name will give you an idea of how bad the problem is. The same results occur if you search under *Thos.* (Thomas), *Jas.* (James), and *Geo.* (George). In each case, the original record creator used an abbreviation that of course stood in for a longer name, but the indexer entered the abbreviation itself in place of the name. These records do not overlap; the ones retrieved under "Jas. Smith" will not be shown in results for "James Smith" and vice versa. Only if someone has input a correction, turning *Jas.* into *James*, will the searcher find the record.

This problem with abbreviations indexed as first names occurs less frequently with female names, but anyone looking for an *Elizabeth* should never give up before trying *Liz, Lizzie, Eliz, Eliza, Liza*, and so forth. The good news is that the newest search algorithms available in the larger databases have begun to address this problem and eventually might retrieve all variations on a first name, no matter which version you enter.

6. Ignore Vowels

Experienced searchers know not to get stuck on one spelling of a name, especially the vowels. If your target name is *Woellert*, you should anticipate some records or databases that give the name as *Wellert* or *Wollart*. Bypass the vowels by replacing them with wildcards (e.g., *W*l*rt*)

7. Replace Capital Letters

Capital letters written in cursive script are sometimes difficult to read. They are less common than lowercase letters and are often written with a flourish. Handwriting conventions vary across space and time and even within localities and generations. Replace easily misunderstood capital letters with the single-letter wildcard symbol (?). So instead of searching Marshall, use *?arshall*. You'll pull up records where the indexer mistook the M for an N.

8. Reverse the Fields

As explained earlier, it occasionally happened that names were entered into the databases backward, with the first name in the surname field and vice versa. Remember that the database algorithm cannot think. It cannot recognize that a name like *Katherine* is obviously a first name. If an indexer put *Katherine* in the surname field, the database treats it as a surname. Ancestry and FamilySearch both require you to choose the first- or last-name field when entering a name. But if the name has been indexed backward, you won't retrieve the record unless a correction has been made. Work around the problem and find elusive records by reversing the fields. If you are looking for *Daniel Dougherty* or *Patrick Kelly*, try *Dougherty* (in first-name field) *Daniel* (in last-name field) or *Kelly Patrick*.

9. Check Multiple Sources

For the census and some other record sets, multiple entities offer access online, which means that a different set of extractions might have been done. If you do not find your target person in Ancestry, try FamilySearch; chances are, a second indexer saw the name correctly when the first one did not. The Ellis Island database contains passenger list indexing and transcriptions that were done independently of the other two, so you have a third set to search.

WEBSITES FOR GENEALOGY RESEARCH

If you are serious about genealogy, you will need the big aggregator sites that offer indexes and records; with one major exception, those all cost money. There is no way to do genealogy extensively using only free access sites. However, just because someone must pay does not mean that every individual has to. Public libraries across the nation subscribe to Ancestry and HeritageQuest Online, so library card holders have free access to the major record sets for genealogy research. But public libraries are busy places, and most of them limit computer time for patrons, so if you have an ambitious agenda you will need to consider one or more individual subscriptions. Before you commit, use the free trial option to determine whether the data in the package is useful and contains the records you need.

User comments on genealogy-related sites are full of gripes about paying for access to records and about the way the largest site, Ancestry, has "gobbled up" smaller competitors. Reality check: selling information is a business—a highly competitive one. Like other business sectors in the United States, the big fish swallow the little ones, profits are maximized, and consumers inevitably complain. The subscription sites charge for access because they invest money in organizing and storing records and in providing reliable access and high-quality images. With the exception of FamilySearch, all the big players charge their users; 21st-century researchers benefit from this model because the subscription money not only covers overhead but also allows the companies to process new data sets.

Even before the Internet, genealogy was not an activity you could pursue without financial outlay. The prices for individual subscriptions might seem exorbitant when compared with free access, but that's the wrong comparison. Compare, instead, the cost of accessing the records offline: traveling to the National Archives, printing records from microfilm, staying in a hotel. For the price of a subscription, you get access from your living room, with no flight reservations and no time in hotel rooms. Looked at this way, the subscription costs seem quite reasonable. Excellent free sites are available, but they do take someone's time and money to manage. If the site grows, it might become too big for the founder to handle; sale to a large, profit-based site makes sense at that point.

The following section describes sites that are *essential, useful,* or *worth exploring*. Each category contains both free and pay sites. Breaking a list down into *free* and *pay* makes little sense to the experienced genealogist; if you want to research your family effectively and thoroughly, you will use both. What matters is the usefulness of a site, whether it has unique information, and whether you go back to it time after time. The site information given will inevitably become outdated at some point. As the Internet evolves, content gets added and withdrawn, site name and domain designations change, and pages become unavailable or hidden. The focus of this list is on Web resources that facilitate research rather than on other aspects of genealogy, such as tree building, data sharing, artifact preservation, or community connections (all covered elsewhere in this book).

ESSENTIAL GENEALOGY SITES

Ancestry

www.ancestry.com. Ancestry is the number one player in the game—the Facebook of genealogy. Its founders have seen it grow phenomenally since their early days selling print publications. As it has grown, the company has absorbed competitors and bought smaller sites that offered unique tools. For a fee, Ancestry provides not only access to original records but also the technology to create a graphically displayed family history and the means to connect with other subscribers. You can also upload a GEDCOM file (i.e., a genealogy-database file ending in .*ged*) created with another program. Others can view your data, send you inquiries, and share documents. Most of the records offered are from the United States, but image files from other countries are being added rapidly. A few of its indexes and databases are free to access, but most of what this site has can be seen only with a paid subscription.

Ancestry does not have it all, but it certainly has a great deal of what genealogists need: original records images and a chance to share data with other people researching the same lines. Users have access to about thirty thousand searchable indexes (which you can search together or separately) containing around 10 billion records. Content is added regularly, so the failed search of today can be successful tomorrow. Additionally, this site has an exceptionally good learning center, where you can find video tutorials, webinars, discussion boards on subjects and surnames, and an authoritative wiki. User contributions (family trees, stories, and photographs) round out the value of this go-to site for genealogists. It offers a free trial membership and different pricing options.

Based in Provo, Utah, Ancestry is the largest genealogy business in the world. It runs not only the Ancestry site but also several other genealogy sites in the United States and abroad, including Fold3, Newspapers.com, Genealogy.com, RootsWeb, Find A Grave, and Archives (not to be confused with Archives.gov, the National Archives site). Ancestry's current behemoth presence belies its humble beginnings. Though Ancestry's founder, John Sittner, was a member of the LDS church, it is not a part of that church and has no official connection with it.

One strength of the Ancestry search engines is flexibility. You can use any combination of data points and limit dates precisely. It has some glitches, of course, but savvy users can work around these. The invitation to users to submit corrections is unique among sites offering indexes; this correction tool ensures that users will return, because a record buried under an incorrect transcription or indexing might be corrected one day by someone and be retrieved in a later search.

Ancestry's holdings are truly staggering; the complete list of indexes and databases, plus its learning center offerings and family history software details, would fill a book. It has the documents every genealogist needs: the completely indexed federal census, along with record images for each one except that of 1890 (destroyed in a fire); arrival records from Ellis Island and several other ports; military draft registrations and pension records; city directories from all across the nation; birth, death, and marriage indexes from every state; school yearbooks—the list is seemingly endless. It is the best site for advanced researchers and beginners both.

FamilySearch

www.familysearch.org. No genealogist can afford to pass up the treasures offered here. And it's all free! FamilySearch stands alone in the online world because of both its provenance (the Family History Library in Salt Lake City) and its depth (millions of records compiled over many decades). The library and vault in Salt Lake City house a collection of records that you will find nowhere else, and most of it is available online.

As noted in chapter 1, the LDS church has long been a promoter of family history research and virtually created many modern American genealogy practices. For decades, the LDS organization has been photographing and microfilming records from all over the world. For much of the time since it began collecting records, access was only through those microfilms, either on-site in Salt Lake City or at one of the many Family History Centers across the nation. Recent innovations in digitization, however, have brought those record images to your computer: millions of records, once available only on microfilm, are now viewable and downloadable online. What's more, LDS teams are still out there with their cameras, digitizing old records all over the world, records that would otherwise be unavailable to you. As the Family History Library's collection grows, the organization maintains its dedication to providing access to these vitally important record sets at no cost. In short, the LDS church is giving away what it could easily sell access to.

Viewing/downloading the site's many indexes and images is free, but you must create a sign-in account to see the record images. Registration will not lead to uninvited e-mails or spam from the LDS church; it is simply its way of monitoring access to its records and resolving problems that get reported. Navigating is a little more complicated than Ancestry because the original purpose of the site was to assist church members in tracing and compiling their family histories, not to cater to the general public's needs. The current site thus serves two constituencies. Furthermore, unlike Ancestry, it also serves to connect users with an actual library containing printed materials not available online. The multiple purposes of FamilySearch can sometimes make navigating difficult for the user seeking only the online resources.

At the opening screen at FamilySearch, you have two options for searching. You can use search boxes on the left to search all the available indexes and databases within this system, or you can do a search of specific record sets by finding the right one under "Browse all published collections" on the right.

The list of collections allows you to select and search them individually, but it's also possible to do combined index searches. The advantages of a targeted search are obvious if you are working with fairly common names or if you know the relevant locality. For example, to find Thomas Smith from Alabama who served in the Civil War, you could do a broad search from the opening screen, but that will retrieve every *Thomas Smith* in all the indexes. Instead, you could select the database called Alabama, Civil War Service Records of Confederate Soldiers, 1861–1865 and search for Thomas Smith in that index alone. The little image of a camera next to the index name means that record images are available; the far-right columns show how many records are covered by that index and when it was last updated.

Downloadable images are available for many indexes, but for the rest, FamilySearch either says "image not available" or links to a partner site that has them (Ancestry and the Statue of Liberty–Ellis Island Foundation site are two). You can get full access to these images at one of the main local branches of the Family History Library. Find the nearest one at www.familysearch.org/locations.

One interesting offering at FamilySearch is the International Genealogical Index. This index, unlike the others discussed in this chapter, is an LDS-specific one and available nowhere else. That is, it originated with the Genealogical Society of Utah and is still used to carry out church doctrine regarding baptisms for the deceased. It contains data from birth, death, and marriage records from all over the world extracted by or contributed by LDS researchers using a variety of sources. As with all databases, use this one with caution: The information is presented in extracted form—that is, somebody copied information from other records and later contributed it to the database—and should be verified with original records where possible.

A link within each index to the FamilySearch wiki offers excellent explanations of the record sets and terminology that the user will find in the records. Like Wikipedia, these wiki entries are created and updated by users, many of them with highly specialized knowledge about certain aspects of genealogy. This is the place to go when the going gets tough with records or to get a good idea of where to begin with a particular search. For instance, if you have "jumped the pond" and are using the Family History Library records from another country, you might find that someone has already compiled a guide to interpreting records of that country. Other research help is available—chiefly, articles and video tutorials. The FamilySearch site administrators provide excellent customer service and technical support. If a user cannot access an online database or has a question, the site offers several options for getting help, including live chat—specifically, getting online with a staff member at the library in Salt Lake City (Ancestry does not offer this option).

Like Ancestry, FamilySearch has some negatives. One serious problem: users cannot easily submit corrections the way they can in Ancestry. FamilySearch accepts suggestions for corrections, but it does not allow users to make them on the record index summaries themselves. As a result, the indexes at FamilySearch are mostly static; a failed search here is not likely to transform into success by next year because of a correction.

Find A Grave

www.findagrave.com. Find A Grave began in 1995 as founder Jim Tipton's way of sharing his hobby of locating celebrity gravesites, and it has morphed into the biggest online registry of burials. Tipton's quirky site grew quickly as people began using it to record and search for non-celebrity graves. Cemeteries contain genealogical records literally by the acre, and Find A Grave offers you a way to access them. Here's how it works: all across the country—and increasingly across the globe as well—volunteers visit cemeteries in their area and photograph or record tombstone information, then upload that data. Interment records are also added by genealogical societies or from the records of institutions such as the U.S. Veterans Department. Thousands of memorials are added weekly, so the person whose burial you could not find today might just be listed tomorrow.

This site's relevance to genealogy research is undeniable. Information available nowhere else can be obtained here for nothing, not even a mandatory registration (necessary only to create records and participate in the discussions). Each memorial indicates, at minimum, the location of a burial, but it usually contains dates as well, and many who volunteer data supply photographs of burial sites. Any memorial can potentially contain more; photographs of the individual and a transcription of the obituary are occasionally added. Each memorial is managed by its creator unless management is transferred to someone else.

The search function is flexible; you can search across the entire database, within a state or county, or within a particular cemetery. The best feature of Find A Grave is the tombstone photographs, which provide verifiable evidence of death and burial, and if you find a memorial with no tombstone photo, you can submit a request for one, which might be fulfilled by a volunteer who lives near the cemetery. There are other free burial site databases available that are worth checking if Find A Grave does not yield the data that you need: BillionGraves and Interment.net are two big ones.

In 2013, Ancestry bought Find A Grave and made its records available to subscribers. But you do not need Ancestry to view it; the site is still free to the public. Bonus: because it requires no registration, its records are retrieved in a Google search. As of late 2017, Find A Grave contained around 165 million memorials and was showing no signs of slowing down. Don't miss this vital and immensely useful site!

Google

www.google.com. Perhaps Google does not immediately strike you as an essential genealogy tool, but it is. The Internet is the planet's global data bank, and Google has the passkey. It will return results using the smartest algorithm around, and all for free. Google began in 1998 as one among several search engines that helped people sort out the rapidly expanding Internet, and it quickly outpaced them all to become number one. Then it really started to grow.

Even middle schoolers know how to "Google" something, but Googling effectively to retrieve targeted results takes practice. For one thing, Google has search options that are not obvious from its home page, which has long been an ocean of white space broken up by a single search box and some regularly changing, quirky graphics. Nowhere on that deceptively simple page will the user find links to the most useful tools that Google offers the genealogist. Only once you enter a search term does the screen show you options other than webpages. You can see a range of other options in the toolbar.

Here is a breakdown of the most genealogically useful options under Google's sub-categories.

Web. Google will sort through billions of webpages in a few seconds. New content is added every day; digitization projects, especially for newspapers, are ongoing. Perhaps your ancestor's name has been recently indexed, either through data entry or optical character recognition. The Google algorithm is smart, but it is not capable of intuitive thinking, so learn to search smart. Use wildcard symbols to expand a search and other symbols to restrict it. If you put two search terms in, the default connecting operator is AND; for example, *North Carolina* retrieves everything with *North* and with *Carolina*, not necessarily together. If you want results with only that phrase, use quotation marks (*"North Carolina"*). Also, eliminate irrelevant search results by using the minus sign. If you have an ancestor with a common name, such as *Marie Jones*, your search will get several hundred thousand hits even if you use quotation marks. Scan the list and identify the *Marie Jones* items that are definitely not yours; then eliminate those by taking an unusual word from each false-positive entry and adding it to your search terms with a minus sign in front of it (e.g., *"Marie Jones" –Montreal*). Just be careful not to eliminate common words or place-names that might appear in the records that you really do want. For more strategies on searching Google Web effectively, check out genealogist Kimberley Powell's excellent article at www.thoughtco.com/google-genealogy-style-1422365.

News. The Google News option is next to Web in the toolbar or under the More tab. It will retrieve different results from the Web search and is always worth checking. The articles retrieved are recent, so this tool is more useful for preserving ongoing family history. At one time, Google offered an extensive News Archive search option, which gave searchers free access to archived newspaper articles. Google removed this option from their site in August 2011, although you can still browse current issues. You can set up a Google Alert to notify your e-mail inbox whenever a news story appears that features select keywords. Also, you can search back issues of many newspapers by title at news.google.com/newspapers.

Maps. Google Maps (www.google.com/maps) can't be beat. Other mapping sites exist, but only this one has the power of Google Earth behind it. You can choose the traditional map view or the satellite view (i.e., from above), or you can use the animated figure Google calls "Pegman" to navigate the street view. As you collect addresses from records, enter them into Google Maps to see whether the buildings are still there. Your family members will think that you are amazing when you show them current images of homes long since left behind. Keeping track of addresses can also help you answer the *why* questions that come up in family history research. For example, why did your grandfather's brother become an undertaker? Use Google Maps to study the locations of all known addresses for him. Is there a funeral home down the street from where the family lived? That might explain great-uncle's career choice. Wonder how your great-grandparents met? Map their known locations and see if neighborly proximity is the answer. As a rule, people in the past did not move around as much as their descendants have. Quite often, people were born, grew up, worked, and died all within a few square miles. Google's mapping feature can help you get to know that one crucial bit of geography and assist with navigation should you decide to visit the area.

Books. In the decades since the Google think tank came up with the idea to scan entire libraries, this search tool has gone through multiple names, but the concept remains the same. Introduced as Google Print in late 2004 and now called Google Books, this option allowed users to search the full text of books and magazines. It was a great idea, but when Google included copyrighted material in its stored database, it ran into legal trouble. In its current state, Google Books offers searchers millions of scanned books. Search results range from the downloadable full text of public domain material to snippets from publications still under copyright (if relevant, a "purchase e-book" option is given).

The Books option on the toolbar is usually hidden under the More tab. It is important to know that it is there, because full-text results will not appear in a regular Web search. Google Books can turn up unexpected findings, such as your Civil War ancestor's name in an 1892 book listing the soldiers of his regiment or an article about your great-aunt's performance in a local theater production. This feature is also useful if you are researching the context for an individual. For example, if your great-grandfather worked as a blacksmith, a search in Google Books for *blacksmith* will turn up back issues of *The American Blacksmith*, a monthly journal packed with news of the trade, advertisements, and even diagrams of tool innovations. It is possible that your ancestor read this very publication.

In addition to published books and journals, Google Books will pick up unpublished or self-published material, such as family histories and pamphlets. If one of your relatives did a genealogy project in the 1970s and donated a manuscript summarizing the family's history to a local library, it might end up digitized and available in Google Books. You just never know what will turn up.

The free access site called HathiTrust (www.hathitrust.org) plays a similar role. It has digitized thousands of public-domain books and is fully searchable.

USEFUL GENEALOGY SITES

The sites listed in this section all have something to offer, and they deserve a place in your online toolbox. They focus primarily on U.S. research; for online sources of information from countries other than the United States, see chapter 6. This list focuses on sites that facilitate genealogy research; for online resources focused on forums, news, and data sharing, see chapter 8. It is far from comprehensive, even for U.S. research, and no doubt leaves out sites many people value.

Cyndi's List of Genealogy Sites on the Internet

cyndislist.com. Founded and maintained by experienced genealogist and author Cyndi Ingle (formerly Cyndi Ingle Howells), Cyndi's List began in 1995 as a list of bookmarks shared among members of the Tacoma-Pierce County Genealogical Society and morphed into the biggest collection of genealogy links available today. It is the gateway to around 332,000 online resources in two hundred categories and has more than once been voted the best genealogy site on the Web. The site clocks about two million visits per month; use it to get your bearings when researching a particular place or topic.

Ellis Island and Castle Garden

www.libertyellisfoundation.org and castlegarden.org. The opening of the Ellis Island database in 2001 ignited many peoples' interest in their immigrant ancestors. Despite its initial problems handling demand, the site remains a popular destination and has allowed millions of people to see, free of charge, the arrival lists showing their ancestors' names. If yours were among the twenty-two million who came through Ellis Island, give this database a try. Searching is free, but registration is required to view the manifests. You can see them but not download or print them (although you can probably get a screen shot of part of the document). To obtain a full-size hard copy, you must order one, and the price is steep. If your ancestor is on a double-paged manifest, you must pay for both pages. It might be more cost-effective to subscribe to Ancestry for three months—then you can download and print as many pages as you want.

The Ellis Island site is run by the Statue of Liberty–Ellis Island Foundation. It provides indexed information for travelers who disembarked at Ellis Island, record images, and (unlike any other resource) historical photographs of the ships that brought so many people to America. That is, it provides these things if you can manage to find your

ancestor. The indexing problems discussed earlier in this chapter permeate the Ellis Island database, and because no simple error correction
method is available, the incorrectly indexed names have remained a
barrier. As if the indexing problem weren't bad enough, the site's
search interface is rather inflexible. But a helpful tool exists to correct
the inadequacies of the Ellis Island database index; see the "One-Step
Webpages" section in chapter 6.

Even though many people think *Ellis Island* is synonymous with
New York in terms of passenger arrival, it was only one of two major
processing stations; the other was Castle Garden (chapter 4 has more
on that place). Genealogists researching immigrant ancestors who arrived in New York City between 1855 and 1890 can search the free
Castle Garden database made available by the New York Battery Conservancy. It offers the index only; the digital images must be obtained at
Ancestry. Like the Ellis Island database, the Castle Garden database
has no mechanism for corrections.

If you are seeking an alternative to the passenger indexes provided
by Ancestry, it is inconvenient that these two New York dedicated port
indexes are split. Many people, even if they know someone came
through New York, do not know which station was used. The inconven-
ience might be ameliorated if the two sites linked to each other's
records, but they don't; in fact, neither even mentions the other's exis-
tence!

Fold3 (formerly Footnote)

www.fold3.com. This site, named for the military's flag-folding ceremony, is an important resource for records unavailable elsewhere, including some naturalization documents, newspapers, and city directories.
But its greatest contribution is military records, especially service and
pension records from the Civil War and Revolutionary War. In fact,
many genealogists consider it the best online source for military
records, period. The document viewer gets high marks, but users will
need the latest version of Flash, or the site may have loading problems.

The site began as Footnote.com in 2006, an access provider to five
million historical documents; it has grown much bigger and today has
nearly seventy million searchable documents. Footnote.com was acquired by Ancestry in 2010 and renamed Fold3. It operates as a separ-

ate company from Ancestry, with its own content and subscription payments. As of early 2019, it offered about 530 million records.

HeritageQuest Online

Available only through library patron accounts. ProQuest's Heritage-Quest Online (HQO) has a great name; it sounds like a fun 1990s computer game rather than a businesslike genealogy resource. Individuals cannot subscribe to HQO; only libraries can, and they make it available to their cardholders. Its offerings include digital images from every census, thousands of digitized local history publications, pension files for the Revolutionary War, part of the Freedman's Bank archives, and the Periodical Source Index, a subject index to genealogy-related and local history periodical articles. The notebook feature is useful for keeping track of searches, and the search interface is easy to use. HeritageQuest Online is a great alternative for census images because this set resulted from a digitization project separate from Ancestry's.

If you don't want to subscribe to Ancestry yet but would like to get started researching, you can access the full set of federal population schedules here (1790 to 1940, with all U.S. territories and military/naval forces). Images for the population schedules are included, as are images for the following schedules:

- Indian census rolls (1885–1940)
- Mortality schedules (1850–1880)
- 1880 schedules of defective, dependent, and delinquent classes
- Selected other nonpopulation schedules (1850–1880)

HQO is a great option for starting your census research at no cost. Library patrons who access HQO remotely can view vitally important record sets without leaving home. If you haven't used it in a few years, check it out. As a result of an expanded partnership agreement between Ancestry and ProQuest, HeritageQuest Online underwent major renovation in 2015 and got a brand-new interface with expanded content.

Joe Beine's Indexes

Online genealogy has its superstars, and in the minds of many family historians, Joe Beine is one. In addition to his index listings for military records (www.militaryindexes.com) and a site aimed at beginners (www.researchguides.net), Beine has created the most popular directory for death indexes across the nation (www.deathindexes.com). He does not have a Wikipedia entry (yet), but most genealogists know his name.

The death indexes site is especially clean and well organized and has only modest ads from Ancestry. The links are mostly to online resources, but you will see some offline info as well. Beine's motivation for creating the death indexes site was personal: his grandfather went missing in 1948, and in the late 1990s, Joe made finding out what happened to him a priority. He began collecting state and other death indexes as they went online (Kentucky was the first) and attached an HTML file to his already-established German Roots site. The death indexes page rapidly ran up hit counts as user after user found this convenient grouping, and in 2003, Beine decided to create a dedicated site. It is not limited to death indexes. You will find links to online obituary resources, burials, probate records, and death certificates (where available). Joe has not found his grandfather yet, but his efforts to do so have benefited everyone looking for their deceased ancestors.

National Archives and Records Administration

www.archives.gov. Every state and county government holds genealogy records, especially those relating to births, deaths, and marriages. Access to those records depends on the policies established by each municipality; some offer free online access to their records, while others make them available only to on-site visitors or through the mail. Some areas have allowed their archival records to be made available through FamilySearch; others allow the index only and require copies to be ordered from the record-holding office. Fortunately, access to federal records does not follow this haphazard fashion.

Once, the only place you could get copies of federal records was the National Archives and Records Administration. Until the Internet arrived and made access to federal records a breeze, researchers often had to make trips to Washington, D.C., just to find one or two census or immigration records. Although much of its information is now available elsewhere, you can access indexes and many record images for free at the National Archives site. When you get there, look under the Access to Archival Databases and the Archival Research Catalog links—that's where the genealogical goods are. You will find access to databases (e.g., Enemy Alien Registration Affidavits), World War II draft registration cards, casualty lists from several conflicts, bounty land applications, and criminal case files.

Note: the site address can be easily confused with the similar URLs *archives.com* or *archive.org*.

Public Records Online Directory

publicrecords.netronline.com. Every state and county has public records useful to a genealogist that are not accessible through subscription sites. For example, the Detroit tax assessor's office might have a crucial piece of documentation relating to the sale of your grandparents' home. Public records consist of such documents as law court proceedings; records of births, marriages, and deaths; demographic data; and taxes assessed. They are available for the asking, though not always for free. Finding the appropriate source for these records in each locale can be a challenge; this site solves that problem for you. It operates as a portal to official state and county offices, most of which have an online presence (a phone number is provided if not). It is supported by advertisements and costs nothing to use.

RootsWeb

rootsweb.com. RootsWeb has been around since 1993. It began as an attempt to collate surnames online and morphed into a robust genealogy community site. Long the go-to place to check the Social Security Death Index (SSDI), RootsWeb was folded into Ancestry in 2008 and removed its SSDI access in 2011. But it still has a family tree builder, user-submitted family trees (its World Connect project), a surname list (around one million names so far), database links, and many discussion forums, all of which are archived and searchable. Buried on the busy home page for RootsWeb is a useful mailing list feature. Sign up for a topic-, place-, or surname-specific mailing list, or just search the archives by keyword. For example, if your ancestor came from a town in western Romania—once part of Central Europe's Banat region—you can search all the message posts in the *Banat-L* mailing list for the specific town name. That way, you can see what questions others have posted and, better yet, see what answers more experienced researchers have provided. This resource, plus the three hundred thousand family trees uploaded by users, makes RootsWeb an excellent spot to begin research on a family.

USGenWeb Project

usgenweb.org. USGenWeb was once aligned with RootsWeb but is now a separate entity. The site's motto is "Land of the Free . . . Genealogy." Run by volunteers and dedicated to promoting free access to records, the USGenWeb Project consists of fifty-plus state projects. Volunteers "adopt" counties within each state and maintain a page with information, links, updates, and so on. For example, from the USGenWeb home page list of states, you can click on "New York," which will connect you to "NYGenWeb" (all the state pages follow that naming pattern). Within the state home page, you can find a list of counties; select one and get a series of pages devoted to the history, people, and resources of that county. From the county page, you can go to city or town pages. The pages all have a different look; each is designed by the volunteer who maintains it. USGenWeb is a great place to start if you do not know what resources a certain county or city has.

The USGenWeb Project inevitably spawned a global twin: World-GenWeb (www.worldgenweb.org). If you are researching immigrant ancestors, this site can link you to the appropriate GenWeb pages. For example, if you select "Europe" from the map, you will see a list of countries. Select "Bosnia" and be taken to MediterraneanGenWeb, which will lead you to BosniaGenWeb and on down to info pages about provinces and towns. Think of it as the ultimate geographical drill-down menu.

WikiTree

www.wikitree.com. WikiTree has been around since 2008 but has experienced a surge in popularity in recent years. It's a free social networking site designed to help genealogists share the information and data they've collected, with the goal of creating a worldwide "tree" of connections. It's similar to RootsWeb in that sense but has a fresher interface.

WORTH EXPLORING

You can get far in your family history research without the sites that follow, but they are always worth a quick look to see if something relevant pops up.

Allen County Public Library Genealogy Center

genealogycenter.org. The Allen County Public Library in Fort Wayne, Indiana, is one of the highest-profile public libraries in the nation. They have been in the genealogy business for a long time, and their website is a powerhouse of information. This site is worth a look, especially for the beginner. Genealogy trivia buffs might be interested to know that the HeritageQuest Online database PERSI (Periodical Source Index) was created by Allen County Library staff members.

Ancestral Findings

ancestralfindings.com. This free site offers one lookup per day in a wide range of records, so it makes a great place for a beginner. You can get the free search by filling out a short form. The home page is cluttered and a little difficult to sort through, but some digging reveals, among other resources, connections to free public records, a virtual cemetery, advice and fact sheets, and a surnames list.

Archives

www.archives.com. This is one of three sites that have confusingly similar names; *archives.gov* and *archive.org* are the others (this one is the only commercial venture). The site was founded in 2009 and in 2012 was acquired by Ancestry, which maintains it as separate entity. Used most often by beginning researchers, it can be good for someone on a budget. Archives offers access to billions of records at a modest annual fee (less than what Ancestry charges), but many of the records that it sells access to are available for free elsewhere (because they are public records) or with an Ancestry subscription. As with Ancestry and many other databases, the free trial requires registration of a credit card, which will be billed if the user does not cancel the trial.

Dead Fred

deadfred.com. In the past decade, a number of specialty sites have sprung up that focus on pictures rather than written records—not a database but a "photobase." They invite users to upload old family photographs, and they usually have a section with mystery photos that need to be identified. The photobase site with the best name and arguably the most traffic is Dead Fred, founded by Joe Bott and named after German king Frederick III, who was not his ancestor but who once ruled over some of his ancestors. You can search the site by name and location. Odds are, you will not find a picture of a long-ago relation, but there's always a chance and it's free. Joe/Fred is responsible for thousands of reunions through the site; you can read moving testimonials about them.

Internet Archive

archive.org. This free site is not genealogy specific but has many offerings relevant to that pursuit. Its home page billing says it's a "non-profit library of millions of free books, movies, software, music, websites, and more." The site includes digitized books, articles, and records, including census images. Most of the material is made available through partnership with several libraries and with Project Gutenberg, a volunteer project started in 1971 by Michael Hart to make e-books available for free.

Family historians will not regret checking out the American Libraries collection here, which has city directories and published family histories; everything can be downloaded or printed. Here too you can also find the Wayback Machine—a tool for finding stored copies of sites that have closed or changed URL. Searching this site is not easy, given the large number of texts and records, but patient efforts might be rewarded.

Olive Tree Genealogy

www.olivetreegenealogy.com/index.shtml. Olive Tree is one of those "you never know what you're going to find" sites, which makes it interesting to browse but less useful for targeted searching. Since 1996, its creator, Lorine McGinnis Schulze, has pulled together free genealogy records plus links to other databases, including some subscription sites.

VitalChek

www.vitalchek.com. VitalChek is a LexisNexis company headquartered in Brentwood, Tennessee. It is not in the genealogy business per se, but it does operate as a clearinghouse for birth, death, and marriage certificates. You will see a link to its service next to many Ancestry records. Be sure you read the fine print, however, before you order. VitalChek charges you not only for the certificate but also a "processing fee" to order the same certificates that you could order direct from the state or county office for no extra fee. Still, VitalChek is fast; you can get certificates in a few days that would otherwise take several weeks to receive directly. In short, it offers convenience for a price.

MyHeritage

www.myheritage.com. It requires courage to take on a giant, but for the last several years, MyHeritage has taken aim at Ancestry—or rather, at Ancestry's customers. Like Ancestry, it offers a powerful, flexible tree software program, searchable indexes, original record images, a messaging feature, and DNA kits. In short, it aims to be an alternative to Ancestry in every way. MyHeritage was founded in 2003 by an Israeli company and has grown rapidly since then. It acquired the award-winning records site WorldVitalRecords in 2011 and in 2012 absorbed its primary competitor, Geni.com. Since then, multiple other small sites and services have been folded into MyHeritage, most of them based in Europe, where the majority of its users reside. These acquisitions are, on the whole, a positive development because they result in multiple search options being streamlined and made easier to work with.

SUMMING IT UP

Many online sites with information to sell give something away as bait, such as free access for a specified period or access to a certain record set. Other sites ask you to pay for something you could otherwise access for free, because the records are public. Don't sign up to pay for anything before researching it and verifying that the information offered is unique and the price is acceptable. Remember:

- Most subscription sites are for-profit. They are interested in getting you to part with your money. Read the fine print before you commit. But don't think you can do significant genealogy research without paying something.
- Ancestry, FamilySearch, and HeritageQuest Online all have their own indexes for the census, and Ellis Island database and Ancestry have different indexes for the passenger lists. If you cannot find it one place, try one of the others before calling off the search.

Next: advanced research techniques and specialized resources.

6

ADVANCED RESEARCH TECHNIQUES AND SPECIALIZED RESOURCES

This chapter addresses:

- Public-domain and unpublished books
- Maps and land/property records
- Non-U.S. records, including translation help and hiring experts

Once you have mastered user-friendly sources such as Ancestry and FamilySearch and checked out the sites recommended in the previous chapter, you're ready for some advanced research options. Keep in mind that every project is different. Let your findings lead you to the best resources to get the information on the family you are researching. The topics listed here might not be relevant to your current family history efforts, but somewhere down the line, if you keep at it long enough, you'll probably find a use for most of them.

PUBLIC-DOMAIN BOOKS

As explained in chapter 5, Google has undertaken the monumental project of digitizing everything. That goal is impractical, given copyright laws, but there is a vast library of printed texts whose copyrights have expired, and Google is free to digitize those. Something no longer under copyright is considered to be in the *public domain*.

Anything created after January 1, 1978, is under copyright protection for the life of the author plus seventy years. For something published prior to that date, the terms vary, but in general all works published in the United States prior to 1923 are now free of copyright, as are works published between 1923 and 1963 without copyright renewal. That means quite a lot of family history–relevant texts are out there and available.

Google Books and Internet Archive (both discussed in chapter 5) are excellent ways to access public-domain texts; both allow you to search by keyword and to narrow results. But there is a third option you won't want to miss: HathiTrust Digital Library (www.hathitrust.org). Though it has some downloading restrictions, you can freely view everything.

Digitization of public-domain materials is most useful for genealogists when it makes available things that would otherwise not be easy to access. For example, someone with ancestors who passed through Ellis Island might not know about a 1925 book by Victor Safford called *Immigration Problems: Personal Experiences of an Official* (briefly described in chapter 1). This fascinating little volume, now in the public domain, describes in colorful, personal language the firsthand experiences of a doctor hired to help process arrivals at Ellis Island in the early 20th century. This man was on the spot where history was being made. Every day for years, he interacted with arrivals from all over the world and absorbed the loud, grimy reality of that busy port. Safford's book was scanned as part of the Google project and is available at HathiTrust.

Given that you simply don't know what is there to be found, it makes sense to search public-domain repositories regularly. It's happened for many researchers that they discover that someone long ago wrote and published a detailed history of one piece of the family they are researching.

Note: the guidelines for quoting material from public-domain texts are the same as for things under copyright. If you plan to write up your family history and distribute it, follow the citation practices you would normally use when quoting someone else—acknowledge the source and give the full bibliographic information.

UNPUBLISHED BOOKS AND OTHER DOCUMENTS

Searching for interesting and relevant published material on public-domain sites is a great idea; so is looking for stuff that has never been published in the first place, such as diaries, letters, and autobiographical manuscripts. It's not as easy as searching Google Books or HathiTrust, but careful efforts might be rewarded.

To understand how you can access unpublished material, you need to know about WorldCat—a gigantic online catalog featuring the combined holdings of thousands and thousands of participating libraries. In the old days, when libraries used to keep their records of holdings organized in card catalogs, such a comprehensive combined catalog was, of course, not possible. There were attempts to create combined listings for a group of catalogs; those results were called *union catalogs*, and they took up many linear feet of shelf space in library reference rooms.

WorldCat is a digitized union catalog. It itemizes the collections of around seventy-two thousand libraries in almost two hundred countries, including the Family History Library in Salt Lake City, and currently has just over three hundred million itemized records. Think of World-Cat as a catalog of catalogs—the largest bibliographic database anywhere, ever.

So how is WorldCat useful to genealogists? In addition to the published books held in those seventy-two thousand libraries, it contains catalog records for unpublished and ephemeral material. If someone in your family wrote, but did not publish, a family history and donated the result to a local library, and that library cataloged it, the manuscript listing most likely appears in WorldCat. If one of your ancestors was interviewed as part of an oral history project, you might find a transcript of that interview in WorldCat. In short, nowhere else will you have such easy access to listings of unpublished or privately published material.

An anecdote illustrating WorldCat's usefulness might help convey how you might use it. In 2003, the Disney Company was in production for a film called *Hidalgo*, which centered on an early 20th-century American named Frank T. Hopkins. Hopkins had made many claims about his past, including having won a long-distance horse race across Arabia—claims that he detailed in his unpublished autobiography. Newspapers picked up the story and, over time, Hopkins became known as the macho American cowboy whose mustang horse Hidalgo beat out Arabian horses across the sea.

Disney announced that they planned to bill the movie as "based on a true story"—a fact that interested the History Channel, which had decided to make its own documentary about Hopkins. The History Channel producers sought to verify the stories about Hopkins winning long-distance horse races, so they contacted the Long Riders Guild, an international association of equestrian explorers dedicated to researching and writing original books and articles relating to traveling on horseback and to publishing works on that topic that have fallen out of copyright.

The first thing the guild did was turn to WorldCat to obtain a copy of Hopkins's unpublished autobiography, the basis of his claims. They found a listing for the original manuscript at a library in Wyoming and ordered a full photocopy, which was provided to them.

After months of studying the manuscript and researching its statements, the Long Riders Guild determined that precisely *none* of the claims Hopkins had made in his autobiography could be verified—not even the ones about his early life, marriage, and employment. One of the guild members was then interviewed for the History Channel documentary and explained the findings. Hopkins's stories, he said, were simply tall tales told by a man with a vivid imagination but few actual accomplishments. The guild then sent a letter to the Disney Company outlining its research and explaining that the film should not be labeled as "based on a true story." Disney ignored them.

The guild members were dismayed by Disney's refusal to remove "based on a true story," so they decided to publish the Hopkins autobiography under their own imprint with annotations analyzing each claim and outlining their research findings. Since the manuscript had never been published, it had never been under copyright, and the guild was as free as anyone to publish it.[1] The truth about Hopkins's misrepresentations is now available in a published version of his own autobiography; the Long Riders Guild has to be satisfied with that.

Try a WorldCat search with the surnames you are working with and see what turns up. Getting a copy of something listed isn't guaranteed—WorldCat has only the catalog listing, not the original text—but it will tell you which participating libraries own a copy of the item you want, and you can use the Interlibrary Loan services of your local public library to request the item. In the event that the item is not loanable, you can contact the holding library to inquire about getting a photo-copy, as the Long Riders Guild did with the Hopkins manuscript.

You can access WorldCat through most library sites or directly at www.worldcat.org.

LAND AND PROPERTY RECORDS

For many Americans, a deep dive into property records will be necessary to reveal a fuller picture of their ancestors in this country. After all, everybody has to live someplace. Land management has always been a complex process involving a great deal of paperwork (excellent news for genealogists) and subject to local and federal laws. Records are available for a wide variety of property types but usually cover ownership, not rentals. You can get an excellent snapshot of who owned and who rented in the 1930 census, but that's the only easily accessed record type that contains rental information.

To begin working with property records, assemble a master list of locations and dates associated with the families you are working on. If your family owned nonresidential property, keep a list of those address-es as well. Farm ownership is represented in multiple record types, including the agricultural census schedules of 1850, 1860, and 1870. Not every farm was included, but those special schedules are an excellent resource for you if your family owned farm property in the mid-19th century. All the agricultural schedules are fully indexed and available from multiple sources online.

If you have a family history that includes someone given or sold land by the federal government (as happened with Revolutionary War veterans), check out the General Land Office Records (glorecords.blm.gov/default.aspx). This Bureau of Land Management site offers a free searchable database for federal land conveyance records plus millions of land title records issued between 1820 and 1908 in the thirty public land states.

If you are researching urban locations, you will probably find local county tax assessor information online. These public records reveal a surprising amount about property transfers and values. One of the ways land management records were kept in urban areas was the Torrens land title system, in which a municipality creates and maintains a central location for all title transfers, thus eliminating the need for individual paper deeds to change hands. Whichever city or town you are researching will have some well-established method for you to follow when pursuing property records.

And don't forget to make extensive use of the ever-growing online collection of city and town directories; with those scanned books, you can potentially track a family's location over many years. Most directory publications have been private enterprises, so their quality and quantity vary widely by location. Ancestry has a nice collection, as does Fold3.

MAPS

Maps are useful for your family history research in multiple ways. Online, you can find dozens of excellent map collections for most geographical areas of the United States, and Google Maps can both show you what a property address looks like now and let you do a virtual walk through the streets of a town.

Hard-copy maps are useful as well. One way to help you maintain a sense of the geographical relationships between people and locations is to pin a large-scale city, town, or county map on the wall. Then you can plot the addresses you collect in your documents.

In addition to these general map tools, there are the specialized maps that you might not have needed yet. The ones described below are online and mostly available free of charge.

Ward Maps

Census records form the backbone of all genealogy projects and can be accessed through multiple searchable indexes (Ancestry, FamilySearch, HeritageQuest Online). Sometimes, however, you cannot find a census record because the name you are searching for has been recorded incorrectly. Why were the names written incorrectly? The answer to that question has to do with how the census-takers obtained the data. The thing that many people think happened at Ellis Island but didn't (names were misunderstood and written down wrong) really *did* happen with the census. Enumerators, starting with the U.S. federal marshals on horseback in 1790, went door-to-door asking people for their names and other household information. Those people spoke their names out loud, and the enumerators wrote what they heard. You can imagine the potential for misunderstanding.

Compounding this problem was the influx of non-English speakers. By the end of the 19th century, millions had arrived and more were arriving every day. Enumerators faced a special challenge in asking those people for their personal details when census-taking time rolled around. The resulting name misspellings run throughout every page of the federal census record set, although of course those misspellings had no effect on the actual spelling of a family's name. Any official changes to spelling of names occurred at the request of the individual (or the head of a family, in many cases) and usually happened during the naturalization process.

This unfortunate situation with incorrectly recorded names in the census means that you will not find everyone you are looking for right away, even though each census is fully indexed and searchable in multiple databases. But don't be discouraged; there are several ways you can work around the problem. See chapter 5 for some creative search strategies that can help reveal the records you seek; those strategies are also useful for record types other than the census. But if you are stuck specifically on the census, consider using a resource called *ward maps*.

To create an accurate portrait of its citizenry, the U.S. federal government carves up the entire country on paper into *wards* and, within the wards, *enumeration districts*. Ward maps are redrawn for every decennial census, so they change over time.

Ward maps are most helpful when you know your target's address at the time of the census. Using the address, you can identify the precise enumeration district (ED) within a ward for that address, and then, using the "browse" option at Ancestry or HeritageQuest, flip through all the pages for that ED until you find the address. This workaround has uncovered many census documents that would otherwise be unfindable because a name had been recorded incorrectly.

Fortunately for all genealogists, libraries across the nation have made great progress in digitizing their local area map collections, which often include maps showing ward and enumeration boundaries for each census. Search online using [location name] and *ward maps*. If you are lucky, the municipality will have a freely accessible collection. Most likely, you will find multiple versions of these maps. Remember that a city or town's street layout and names are likely to have undergone changes. Using a modern-day map side by side with a ward map can help orient you to the geography of the past.

Ward maps are helpful only if you know a research target's address, so keep a list of addresses that you encounter in records, noting who lived where and during what time period. Input each address you see in a saved document into the file name for that document; that way you can quickly retrieve every record associated with an address.

To find a ward number and enumeration district, rely on a unique resource developed by a genealogist named Stephen P. Morse. Morse is one of genealogy's superstars, though you've probably never heard of him. He was the chief brain behind the development of the Intel 8086 chip in the late 1970s, which led to the development of personal computers. He went on to use his expertise in data processing to develop tools for searching census and immigration records that many genealogists have come to rely on. He calls his search tools "One-Step" programs, and they can be accessed for free at stevemorse.org. Note: the domain ending is important; stevemorse.*com* is the home page for a musician.

Morse was inspired to create the One-Step site after the problematic opening of the Ellis Island database in 2001. Long an enthusiastic researcher of his family history, Morse was one of the millions frustrated by the time it took to search the Ellis Island database and with the primitive search parameters at the site. Unlike the other grumblers, however, he did something about it: he created a program to make his searching easier and more effective. He shared his program with the research community, and genealogists have been thanking him ever since.

Morse decided early on that he needed the ability to search by *town* and by *Soundex*, both of which the Ellis Island site did not allow. Soundex, a phonetic algorithm for indexing names by sound, is designed to match names despite spelling differences. It has been around a while (patented in 1922) and has long been used by the National Archives to analyze census data. Details on the Soundex system can be found at the National Archives and Records Administration site under "The Soundex Indexing System" (www.archives.gov/research/census/soundex .html). Using Soundex, names such as *Robert* and *Rupert* score the same, as do *Taylor* and *Tyler*. The point is to ignore incidental variations in spelling and focus on the sound similarities. In addition to adding town and Soundex search options, Morse folded in the Castle Garden database records, erasing the irrelevant (for researchers) difference between the two data sets.

Although the passenger lists in the Ellis Island database all contain a place-name, the capacity to search by place-name is not available (yet) in Ancestry, and neither is the capacity to search by Soundex. That means that records can be uncovered through the One-Step tool that you would likely not find using the Ancestry or the Ellis Island search interfaces. If you are looking for people who passed through a New York City port, this site ranks under *essential*.

Morse did not stop at making arrival records easier to find; he soon turned his eye to the U.S. census indexes. He teamed up with researchers Joel Weintraub and David Kehs to create an enumeration district finder for the 1930 census, and they went on to create searching aids for other census record sets. Details of how the three began working on this project can be found in Megan Smolenyak's 2004 article "Steve Morse: A Genealogical Mensch."[2] An explanation of the One-Step offerings was published by the superstar himself in a specialized genealogical journal.[3]

At Morse's site, you can find the ward and enumeration district for a particular location by entering the known address, along with bordering streets. The site then links you directly to the batch of pages in the census for that ED. To find your target family, page through until you locate the correct street and house number.

Note that such information is not readily available for every census; the most complete information is for the 1940 census, and it gets less available the further back you go. Also, every location is not represented in Morse's algorithm. Despite these limitations, many have found the census-searching tools immensely helpful; you should definitely give this site a try. Morse even has the ward and ED search tools already available for the 2022 release of the 1950 census.

Sanborn Fire Insurance Maps

If you are researching a family that lived in an urban area in the late 19th through the mid-20th century, you might find that the Sanborn Map Company included that family's dwellings on one of its many specially created maps. These maps are scaled architectural drawings with details that will astound you—closer to blueprints than traditional maps. Figure 6.1 shows a typical Sanborn map.

Fire maps came about in the United States because of expanded building and city growth following the Civil War. Following a model established by London insurance underwriters, the property insurance industry hired the Sanborn Company to produce maps for them. Prior to the map creation scheme, underwriters had to visit each potentially insurable site to determine square footage and other structural details. With business booming, they needed a way to do that step remotely, from their offices. The competing companies shared the cost of what

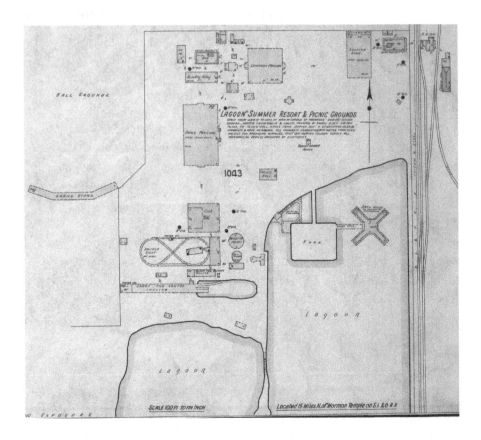

Figure 6.1.   Sanborn map showing Lagoon Amusement Park in Utah (1911). *Public-domain image.*

clearly benefited all of them, thus creating a shared library with limited users.

By the time Sanborn produced its last commissioned map in 1977, they had created detailed depictions for buildings in about twelve thousand U.S. cities and towns. Initially, of course, these maps were kept in the files of the insurance companies; they were working copies, commissioned for a business purpose. But after a time, the maps became obsolete and were usually donated to local public or university libraries. The resulting collection of historical maps has been treasured by historians ever since.

You can access many Sanborn maps online, either through local archives and library sites or through the Library of Congress (www .loc.gov/collections/sanborn-maps/about-this-collection).

NON-U.S. RECORDS

One popular misconception many people have about genealogy relates to finding information from outside the United States. Over and over, travelers make plans to visit a place in Europe or elsewhere so they can do some research on their family history. Once they get there, however, they usually wind up disappointed and return home without much progress made.

Here are several reasons why you aren't likely to get access to original paper records in other countries:

- Americans barging in with cameras and waving money around has long been a clichéd image abroad. It strikes non-Americans as rather presumptuous that we expect to be given what we want despite knowing little of the local culture. Even if you do get lucky and find yourself working with a cooperative civil or religious official, it's unlikely they will hand over old record books to you. More likely they will offer to search the books for information you require and provide you with extracts of that information.
- Historical records aren't always held in the place they originated. Quite often, especially in smaller countries, a centralized archive was created and all historical records from thousands of towns and villages were transferred there. In larger countries, regional de-

positories played a similar role. In short, the civil records you seek are unlikely to be in the place they started. The major exception to this is church records, which often do still reside in the church offices that created them.

- Working with local people in non-English-speaking countries is never an easy thing. Your phrase book might help you find the nearest restroom or train station easily enough, but it won't be much help when you want to ask nuanced questions like "How long has this church been here?" or "Where is the oldest cemetery in the town?" You could always hire a translator, of course, but that's costly and unnecessary, if the purpose of the translator is to help you find original records to research your family history.

In any case, you won't have enough time to search the record books carefully even if you got access to them. Enjoy your visit abroad and leave the research work for home (ideally *before* you travel). Most likely, if you've uncovered your family history back to the immigrant generation, you can research your family lines outside the United States right from your own living room.

Thanks to the Family History Library and its decades of efforts to photograph and preserve on microfilm vital records from all over the world, you will most likely find at least some of the non-U.S. information you're looking for. As explained earlier, the Family History Library's website (FamilySearch) offers free access to millions of original record images, many of them from outside the United States. Ancestry also offers non-U.S. records through its international subscription option.

Furthermore, countries abroad have experienced their own genealogy boom in recent years, and most have a site similar to Ancestry for census and vital records. See the following chapter for details on country-specific resources. To pursue the non-U.S. history of your family, follow these four steps:

1. Establish your American family history back to the immigrant generation. For some people, this will take them back to the 17th century. For others, the immigrant generation arrived in the 20th century. Several document types will tell you whether someone is native-born or not: the census, naturalization paperwork, draft

registration, Social Security application, and death certificates, among others. All these record types are described in chapter 4.

2. Find out the name of the "home place" for each immigrant—their town, village, or city of birth. People in other countries did not move around much before they left for America, so the place someone was born is likely the same place he or she grew up. Finding the home place for someone born outside the United States isn't always possible, but you should pursue that piece of information doggedly; it's your key to finding the relevant non-U.S. records. When non-natives were asked where they were from, they usually named not a country but a town or perhaps a province. So Irish immigrants would say they were from "County Leitrim" instead of "Ireland" and an Italian would say he was "Calabrese" rather than "Italian." People strongly identified with the specific locale they hailed from more so than we tend to do today. Once you have the place-name, figure out the county/province it's in, and then the state/region. For example, the Republic of Ireland town of Glenamaddy is in County Galway, and County Galway is in Connaght Province. It's important to know all those geographical names, because record sets might be held at any level. It also helps to know religious geographical designations in the area. For example, Catholic church records are often organized according to parish names.

3. Find and use the international records available in FamilySearch and Ancestry. Both sites are searchable by location.

4. Find and use country-specific resources outlined in chapter 7.

If you know the municipality name where your ancestors lived, look it up in the Family History Library catalog and see what resources are available. Remember that records might be held in different repositories—some local, some provincial, and some at the state level. Getting to know the record-keeping conventions of the place you are researching will pay off. To find the records for a specific location in FamilySearch, follow the "Search/Catalog" link from the home screen.

Almost all the microfilmed record images held by the Family History Library have been digitized and are available to view and download at FamilySearch, but keep in mind that the indexing of those records is a project that will be ongoing for many years to come. To work with unindexed records, you'll have to "browse." Click through the entire set, image by image. It is time-consuming, but if no searchable database with indexed records exists, that is your only means to retrieve the information.

Working with original records takes time and patience, even if those records are in your own language and the handwriting is easy to read. With effort and the use of translation tools, however, you can probably find many relevant non-U.S. records for your family history. Then you can start planning your trip.

Non-U.S. Record-Keeping Conventions

As you begin working with records from outside the United States, you will experience a fairly steep learning curve. Other places do things differently; they always have and always will. Record-keeping norms are different from place to place, so keep an open mind and stay eager to learn and understand. Here are some general points to remember as you deal with non-U.S. records:

- Records all over the world have been lost as time has passed. Fire has been the chief enemy, but mold and insects have played a role in record destruction as well. Furthermore, sometimes a location was the epicenter of local conflicts or war activity that resulted in destruction and damage to buildings and the records residing within those buildings. In the American South, many records were lost during the Civil War. In the same way, countless Irish records were lost during the multiple conflicts centered around Irish independence.
- Some records required the entering of information into fields on a form, the same way we do today. In other places, the information was written out in sentences and paragraphs.
- In many places, women kept their birth names for life. In other words, a married woman did not change her name. She had the surname of her father and was known by that name from birth through death.
- Handwriting conventions vary widely all over the world, for written numbers as well as letters. Go slowly and learn the local styles.

- Americans write dates differently from Europeans. If we write "9/2" we mean September 2. But a European would interpret that as February 9. When you encounter abbreviations for the months, keep in mind that in some places, the month *names* still govern the abbreviation, not the place in the calendar. For example, Italian records regularly abbreviate the month of September as "7bre" because when it was given its name, September was the *seventh* month in the calendar year (from Latin *septem*, seven). Similarly, December is the twelfth month of our calendar, but Italian records abbreviate it as "Xbre"—the X being the Roman numeral representation of ten, because December was named when it was the tenth month of the year. Potential for confusion lurks in every record.
- Sometimes with civil and church records, birth records are annotated with information about later events (marriage and death). That's because when the clerk wanted to create a marriage or death record, he was required to consult the original birth (or baptism) record to verify the person's age and place of birth. While he had the record book open, he would often indicate the later event. Sometimes, if the birth record was for an infant that died, the clerk made a small cross on the record (and sometimes those crosses look like swastikas, which they are not). As you work with birth records, watch for those annotations; they give you a fuller picture of an individual's life than you might be expecting from a birth record.
- In many places, including the United States, a marriage "record" consists of several documents—the publication of banns, supporting documents, the civil marriage record, and the church marriage record. If you're lucky, all these documents will be available.
- There are many ways of correcting mistakes in handwritten records, not all of them immediately obvious for what they are. Whereas in the United States we would most likely scratch out or put a line through the incorrect word and write the correct one over it, in other places the record clerks put a line above and below the incorrect word and wrote the correct one in the margin. One not-so-obvious Italian mistake-correcting method was to write the word *dico* after the mistaken word. *Dico* literally means "I say" but in terms of correcting mistakes it means "whoops," and

the correct word or name follows. So you might see *Angela Tolve dico Antonia Garramone* and (the clerk assumed) understand that the person's name was Antonia Garramone, not Angela Tolve.

- For as long as there's been wedlock, there have been children born outside of it. Every location has records for these babies, and they can give a fascinating glimpse into cultural and religious prejudices. Keeping track of a child's biological parents was especially important at a time when people didn't move around much; the possibility of consanguinity had to be guarded against. Foundling children were often given made-up names (à la Oliver Twist) to distinguish them from "legitimate" members of their society. That means for the rest of their lives, they carried the stigma of their illegitimacy, and males even passed it on (in the form of their surname) to their own children. Encountering a foundling in your family line means you have hit an impassable wall. You simply will not be able to link that child to a known mother or father and thus carry on researching the family line back in time. Life was extremely difficult for foundlings; if you discover you have a foundling ancestor, take a moment to recognize that individual's strength of mind and body. After all, that person managed to grow up and have his or her own children; that says something worth acknowledging.

Translating Records

If you need to work with records not in English, make the task easier by preparing translated lists of words that commonly occur in vital records, and keep that list nearby as you work. No matter what country's records you are looking at, they are likely to use roughly the same terminology to record births, deaths, and marriages. In other words, records have a rather limited vocabulary.

Textbox 6.1 shows a recommended list of words to know when you deal with non-English records. Master these in the language you are dealing with and you'll soon get the gist of the records. In addition to those words, make a translated list for all the names of the months; usually they were written out in the records rather than indicated with a number.

TEXTBOX 6.1
ESSENTIAL WORDS TO KNOW IN NON-ENGLISH RECORDS

baptism	female	named
birth	first name	peasant
born	godparents	profession
burial	grandfather	priest
child	grandmother	rabbi
church	husband	record
day	il/legitimate	residence
death	male	soldier
died	marriage	surname
farmer	month	widow/er
father	mother	year

Even if you go in armed with translated words, you can expect to find records that look bafflingly unlike American ones. The style of recording varied from place to place; many localities did not use pre-printed forms—just large blank books with lines drawn in. The resulting records look like dense blocks of handwritten text, with no line or paragraph breaks, and can be a challenge to interpret.

By the end of the 19th century, most localities began using pre-printed forms, which are easier to translate. These were not like our certificates given to the people involved but information recorded in large books by the civil authority; families were not usually issued a copy.

And best news of all: full translations of most non-English record forms you will encounter are available at the FamilySearch wiki.

HIRING RESEARCHERS AND TRANSLATORS

At some point you might find yourself in need of outside help with your genealogy. Ancestry offers research services for a fee, but you also might want to check out a smaller site called GenLighten (genlight en.com). After registration at GenLighten, you can search a locality for someone to do lookups in local records or find a specialist in pursuing some particular heritage research. Once you identify a potential researcher you'd like to hire, you submit a description of your project and get a quote back. If you accept the terms, the researcher will do the work and upload the results at the site. There are other specialized sites to suit many research needs.

If you have non-English documents that have been passed down in your family, you will probably want to hire a professional translator (relying on Google Translate will not work). Try Proz (www.proz.com) to find a translator to match your needs; you can search by language and document type. Proz has quite a few participating translators, so you have some negotiating power on the pricing.

SUMMING IT UP

Researching beyond the basic level means you've come a long way since you started. The more complicated the project gets, however, the easier it is to get discouraged. Advanced research is not just for genealogy professionals; anyone who plans to do a thorough, carefully researched family history will need many of the "beyond the basics" tools and techniques discussed in this chapter. Remember:

- There is a mountain of material not available online that can be identified in WorldCat and found in specialized libraries and archives.
- The tools necessary for advanced research, such as ward and enumeration district finders, are not available at Ancestry but at specialized sites.

- Visits to Europe in search of records usually end in disappointment. Do your research at home, before you leave, with the vast digitized record collection made available for free at FamilySearch and for a cost at Ancestry.

Next: heritage research and DNA for genealogy.

7

SPECIALIZED SUBJECTS, INCLUDING DNA FOR GENEALOGY

This chapter addresses:

- Ethnic and cultural heritage research
- DNA testing for genealogy

The databases discussed in the previous two chapters are potentially useful to all research projects, but eventually you might need information that does not apply to everyone. For example, if you are descended from immigrants who arrived around 1900, you can ignore Revolutionary War– and Civil War–era resources, but you'll want to explore non-U.S. records thoroughly. If you are descended from people who came to America from the United Kingdom in the 18th and early 19th centuries, you will not need the international resources from the 19th and 20th centuries. As you explore the more advanced and project-specific resources, remember that specialized lists, databases, and record sets relating to ethnic and cultural heritage are often the product of dedicated volunteers, so the quality and verifiability will vary.

COUNTRIES OF ORIGIN AND ETHNIC GROUPS

Whatever ethnic groups your family history contains, more than likely someone has compiled something useful, such as a research guide, an overview of customs, tombstone transcriptions, or a list of surnames from a particular town. You can often find a lineage or heritage society that makes available specialized publications by members. If you live in the area where your family history played out, you might find mentions in privately published genealogies. All these resources are specialized and generally not available through Ancestry, FamilySearch, and the other big sites.

The following list of resources for specialized research is not meant to be comprehensive for each research interest or to cover every group represented by descendants today but to provide a starting point for the major groups that took up residence in North America (or, in the case of Native Americans, were here already when the Europeans arrived).

Note: this list covers immigrant groups whose greatest numbers arrived in the United States prior to the mid-1900s. This arbitrary cutoff means that arrivals from many places (e.g., Vietnam, Cambodia, India, Pakistan, Somalia) are not covered here. Information on heritage research for those groups is available from other sources; the FamilySearch wiki covers the basics for most ethnic groups and can get you started.

If you aren't sure what ethnic heritage you have, you might want to do a DNA test for genealogy results. Among other things, it will tell you exactly what ethnicities went into making you. See later in this chapter for details.

United Kingdom: English, Welsh, Scottish, and Scots-Irish

The Europeans who settled the "New World" in the greatest numbers were from today's English-speaking United Kingdom and Republic of Ireland. But the inhabitants of the British Isles were not the first Europeans to take up residence in North America. Spanish and French trappers and explorers preceded the English arrivals, and Dutch colonists established a presence on the small but significant island known even then as Manhattan.

And even before Columbus made his famous voyage, the intrepid Vikings had already come and gone. Archaeological research at a site called L'Anse aux Meadows in Newfoundland, Canada, has proved conclusively that Norse mariners (i.e., Vikings) had a settlement on the coast around 1000 AD, about five hundred years before Columbus's arrival. Columbus himself was a citizen of Genoa in northern Italy but was working for the rulers of Spain, so the Spanish crown was the first to capitalize on his discovery of a land that, though inhabited by millions of natives, had previously been unknown to the European powers.

When Spanish colonizers came in Columbus's wake, they concentrated primarily on exploiting the resources of the Caribbean, Mexico, and the coast of South America. But they also had a significant presence in what is today the continental United States, establishing the city of St. Augustine in Florida in 1565; it is the oldest continuously inhabited European-founded city in the United States. We owe many place-names, including *Florida*, to these Spanish settlers. Along with the early Spanish arrivals (most of whom were looking for gold rather than planning to stay), Portuguese, French, and Dutch colonists, among others, settled the eastern coast of North America, the Gulf, and the Mississippi Valley.

Despite the well-documented presence of these Spanish, Dutch, and Portuguese arrivals before the English ever showed up, the emphasis in most American elementary school history textbooks is usually on the *Mayflower* Pilgrims, who arrived in 1620. That was fifty-five years after St. Augustine was founded, and later even than the Jamestown Colony (founded in 1607).

Eventually, English-speaking people did come to dominate the American colonies and establish the English language and cultural habits of the British Isles as the standard. Despite their head start, those with English heritage did not remain the majority. The U.S. Census Bureau's 2010 American Community Survey[1] indicates that Americans with self-reported English ancestry form only the third-largest European ancestry group, behind those with German and Irish/Scots-Irish ancestry. Only in the late 19th century did immigration from England taper off, to be replaced by arrivals from southern and central Europe, among other places.

If you want more information on researching all the biggest groups in today's United Kingdom, check out Kathy Chater's book *How to Trace Your Family Tree in England, Ireland, Scotland, and Wales* (2017). For area-specific resources, see the sites listed below.

England and Wales

If you have English or Welsh heritage, you can probably find relevant records through Ancestry and FamilySearch. English administrative records are generally thorough and reliably available back to the start of the 19th century; some record sets go back even further. You must know a specific location for your ancestors in England to find their records, because pre–19th century records are generally held at the county level. Be aware that several counties have changed names and boundaries over the years. The Gazetteer of British Place Names (www.gazetteer.org.uk) should help if the records you seek were thus affected.

Anyone researching non-U.S. records should learn the specific date when the creation of civil records for births, marriages, and deaths was mandated by a central government. For England and Wales, that date is July 1837; vital records created after that date are held by the General Register Office (www.gro.gov.uk/gro/content). Its site contains ordering instructions, or you can get digitized copies where available through some of the sites discussed in this chapter. Before July 1837, English and Welsh records were created and held by local parishes; some of those records were kept starting in the early 16th century. The International Genealogical Index, created by the Genealogical Society of Utah, contains data drawn from these and other countries' parish registers; images of the original records were not created for that project, just transcriptions or extracts. Parish register transcriptions in general are sometimes available from local historical societies. In addition to vital records, FamilySearch makes available decennial census records for England and Wales through 1911.

Another important date for English and Welsh genealogy searches is January 11, 1858. Beginning in the 14th century and going up to that date, the church in England decided all matters pertaining to wills and probate. Thus, records about the disposition of property before 1858 are in ecclesiastical offices, including the Prerogative Court of Canterbury, which covers southern England. Today those records are held at the U.K. National Archives (nationalarchives.gov.uk) and are available to be downloaded for a fee. Welsh wills up to 1858 are held at the Llyfrgell Genedlaethol Cymru—the National Library of Wales (www.llyfrgell.cymru). Beginning in 1858, all English and Welsh wills and probate matters were handled by civil courts.

Here are some good online sources for United Kingdom heritage research (the order is alphabetical):

England GenWeb. www.englandgenweb.org. Use this free gateway service to do county-specific research.

FindMyPast. www.findmypast.co.uk. The United Kingdom's version of Ancestry, with the heft and breadth to make it essential for researchers with U.K. roots. FindMyPast offers a choice of either a subscription or a "pay as you go" option. With the latter, you pay per download. This site offers millions of records, most pertaining to the United Kingdom but with some from Canada, Australia, and New Zealand. It has every census as well as civil registries, parish records, passenger lists for ships leaving the United Kingdom, military records, court records, and newspaper archives. If you have ancestors from the U.K., you will need this site to do thorough research. FindMyPast, like its American cousin, Ancestry, has been acquiring smaller sites; in recent years, it acquired Origins.net and the U.S.-based Mocavo. Also like Ancestry, it is rapidly expanding its DNA program. Note: it was formerly called 1837online.

FreeBMD. www.freebmd.org.uk. Standing for "Free Births, Marriages, and Deaths," this site is a volunteer effort to transcribe the civil registrations of England and Wales that date from 1837. Parallel sites exist for access to the census (www.freecen.org.uk) and parish registers (www.freereg.org.uk). The three sites are part of a larger project called Free UKGEN.

The Genealogist. www.thegenealogist.co.uk. A modestly priced pay-per-view site worth investigating if you are looking for the standard genealogy documents (vital records, census, directories).

GENUKI: U.K. and Ireland Genealogy. www.genuki.org.uk. A large site maintained by volunteers with thousands of links, records, and tutorials.

Society of Genealogists. www.sog.org.uk. Based in London, Britain's biggest family history society has a library and educational center; it also has many unpublished manuscripts. Consider this Britain's equivalent of America's Family History Library—a good place to begin.

Scotland

Scottish and Scots-Irish ancestry are closely related, but many of the records pertaining to immigrants who came directly from Scotland are

held in Scotland, whereas the Scots-Irish immigrants departed from
Northern Ireland, where their families had lived for generations after
emigrating from Scotland (these people are sometimes called Ulster
Scots).

So their records are not in Scotland but are either in England or
Northern Ireland, which is part of the United Kingdom but across a
body of water from the mainland. Scots-Irish ancestry research involves
working with records in both places, if you can get back that far. If you
are looking for Scottish ancestors, you will first have to determine which
group they belong to. Today, about 8 percent of Americans claim Scottish ancestry, and about 10 percent claim Scots-Irish. The Scots who
spoke Gaelic brought several words that were absorbed into English:
clan, *galore*, *pet*, *plaid*, *shindig*, *slogan*, and *trousers*.

Scottish records are covered by most of the sites listed, but here are
a few specialized ones:

Gazetteer for Scotland. www.scottish-places.info. Given the importance of learning the specific place-name where your ancestors
hailed from, this site provides an important assist. It's a geographical
encyclopedia, the first comprehensive one produced for Scotland since
1885. With more than twenty-two thousand detailed entries, this site
will certainly play a role as you dig for Scottish records.

National Records of Scotland. www.nrscotland.gov.uk. In April
2011, the National Archives of Scotland merged with Scotland's General Register Office to create a new entity, the National Records of Scotland; use this site to research business, estate, family, and church
records.

Scotland's People. www.scotlandspeople.gov.uk. This well-orga-
nized government site is vital for anyone researching Scottish ancestry;
here you can access indexes and, for a fee, a large collection of image
records.

Ireland

At almost 12 percent of the American population, those with Irish ancestry are the second-largest group, just behind Germans—and that
figure does not include people who claim descent from Scots-Irish immigrants. Irish people began heading to America when it was still just a
handful of colonies, and they kept arriving in large numbers until the
20th century. Many were Irish Gaelic speakers, and they left their im-

print on American English in the words *clock, hooligan, leprechaun,* and *shamrock*. Dozens of published guides and Internet pages are designed specifically for Irish ancestry research.

Irish records have not fared as well as those from the United Kingdom. Among other disasters, a 1922 fire in the Ireland Public Record Office destroyed countless civil and parish documents, including almost all the earliest census returns. Fortunately, some of these records were transcribed or extracted before being lost. Your Irish research will be most successful if you first create an accurate family history back to the immigrant generation and then nail down the place where they came from. Many American and Canadian records for incoming immigrants just say "Ireland" for place of birth, but you'll need something more specific. The IreAtlas Townland Database (thecore.com/seanruad) is a good resource for place-names.

National-level civil registration in the Republic of Ireland dates only from 1864, although parish records exist for centuries before that. FamilySearch and Ancestry both have indexes for Irish civil records, as do many of the sites discussed in this chapter. Irish census records are a sad story; many sets were lost in the 1922 fire or were shredded by the government. The earliest complete census returns are for 1901. Church records are therefore the most reliable resource; land and property records are important supplements. The following sites are potentially helpful for Irish research:

Emerald Ancestors. www.emeraldancestors.com. This paid membership site is dedicated to genealogy research for Northern Ireland and Ulster. Its offerings, mostly just indexes, cover civil registrations, parish registers, and historical information for the northern counties. If you have Scots-Irish heritage or English ancestors who settled in Northern Ireland, this site is worth checking out.

Irish Genealogy. www.irishgenealogy.ie. Set up by Ireland's official tourism department, this free site offers millions of parish records throughout the country, and it is still growing.

Irish Newspaper Archives. www.irishnewsarchive.com. This subscription site is the largest digital archive of Irish newspapers, with access to millions of articles over a three-hundred-year span. Searching the index is free, but you must pay to access the images.

The National Archives of Ireland. www.nationalarchives.ie. You will find free access here to the 1901 and 1911 censuses (nothing earlier survives in a complete state) and other searchable indexes and research guides.

RootsIreland. www.rootsireland.ie. Register for an account to search for free among the twenty million digitized records at this site created by the Irish Family History Foundation. The focus is on church records, especially baptisms, marriages, and burials. Downloading is on the pay-per-piece system.

U.S. National Archives and Records Administration. aad.archives.gov/aad/index.jsp. If you have successfully traced your family history back to the immigrant generation and determined that your ancestors were among the millions of Irish who arrived during the potato famine years (1846–1851), you might find a transcription of their passenger records in a special index called Records for Passengers Who Arrived at the Port of New York During the Irish Famine, available at the National Archives site. Go to the URL above and search *famine*. That will bring up the record set. From there you can search by surname.

In addition to those websites, check out these two excellent publications: *Researching Scots-Irish Ancestors* by William Roulston (2nd edition, 2018) and *How to Trace Your Irish Ancestors* by Ian Maxwell (3rd edition, 2019).

Scandinavia: Denmark, Sweden, Norway, Finland

Although they have much in common, the Scandinavian countries are not usually grouped in genealogy research guides. They each have well-managed national archives, and the civic and religious records from these four countries are widely available. Thus, this research is not as challenging as some other ethnic lines, but the language barrier can prevent easy access (chapter 6 has a suggested word list for reading non-English records). Swedish, Danish, and Norwegian are all Germanic languages and are similar to one another, but Finnish is a Uralic-Altaic language—not even in the Indo-European language family (it is related to Hungarian and Estonian). The FamilySearch wiki has good overviews on conducting genealogy research in all four countries (entitled "Sweden Genealogy," "Denmark Genealogy," etc.). Also look at these resources:

Sweden: The journal *Swedish American Genealogist* (www.augustana.edu/swenson/sag) and a site in Swedish maintained by the Federation of Swedish Genealogical Societies (www.rotter.se/swed ish-roots/about-us/the-federation)

Norway: The Norwegian American Genealogical Center (www.nagcnl.org) and the Digital Archives of Norway (www .digitalarkivet.no)

Denmark: The National Danish-American Genealogical Society (danishgenealogy.org) and the Danish Emigration Archives (aemi.eu/ the-danish-emigration-archives)

Finland: The Finland GenWeb pages (www.worldgenweb.net/fin land) and the Migration Institute of Finland (www.migrationinstitute.fi)

African American Ancestry

Few family historians have worked so diligently and traveled so far to put a story together as African American writer Alex Haley. Working long before the advent of Internet searching and digitized records and trying to piece together a family history for which records often did not exist, Haley published his results in 1976 as a novel called *Roots: The Saga of an American Family*. Every genealogist should read this book because Haley tells not only the story of his family but of the project itself—his years of research and travel and the many hours spent poring over slave ship records. Fortunately for people today trying to trace African lineage, much of the work can be done without extensive travel outside the United States.

Most African Americans in the United States and the Caribbean descend from the Africans brought over as slaves before the practice was outlawed. The best place to begin researching is with Tony Bur-roughs's *Black Roots: A Beginner's Guide to Tracing the African American Family Tree* (2001). Though dated, Burroughs's guide is nevertheless a terrific resource for this particular research challenge. Burroughs recommends a six-step strategy, which is paraphrased here. More recent information can be found online in the sites described below.

Step 1. Find Family Sources. As with any genealogy project, the best place to begin is at home. Search family homes for letters, Bibles, saved papers from employers or insurance companies, and the like, and put together a detailed history of names, places, and movements. Interview family members, making note of unusual names or naming patterns and any unusual occupations, such as blacksmith or tailor.

Step 2. Take Your Family Back to 1870. All your work with family records and interviews can help you establish your line backward in time, step by step. Ideally, the home sources plus the usual genealogy records—vital records, the census, wills, newspapers, obituaries, military records, cemeteries—will give you enough to trace your history back as far as 1870, the first year that the federal census listed all African Americans by name. Going back further involves a different strategy.

Step 3. Identify the Last Slave Owner. Roughly one out of every ten African Americans in the United States was already free by the Emancipation Proclamation in 1863. Those individuals would most likely be listed in the 1860 census, in the Free Population schedules. The rest would be counted only by number and listed with their slave owners, so identifying the owners is the key to going back further. Finding a slave owner's name is a challenge but has never been easier than it is now. Sources for finding slave owners' names include the records of the Freedmen's Bureau and the Southern Claims Commission, individual slave narratives, some military records, and county histories. The Freedmen's Bureau was established in 1865; it took charge of all activities relating to newly freed slaves and managed property confiscated from the Confederate states. Bureau records are available at the Freedmen's Bureau Online (freedmensbureau.com). The corresponding Freedman's Bank records from 1865 to 1874 are available through HeritageQuest Online and Ancestry. The most relevant military records are for the "U.S. Colored Troops" in the Civil War Soldiers and Sailors Database (described in chapter 5), available at www.nps.gov/civilwar/soldiers-and-sailors-database.htm.

Between 1871 and 1880, the Southern Claims Commission processed claims by people living in the South who lost property to the Union forces. Citizens had to prove their loyalty to the Union and provide evidence of ownership. Most claims were rejected, but the process created a paper trail regardless of outcome. Among the details provided with claim evidence were names and ages of former slaves, names and residences of slave owners, manumission records, and information about slave businesses and property ownership. The Southern

Claims Commission documents are held at the National Archives. The seminal work on this subject is Gary B. Mills's "Southern Loyalists in the Civil War: The Southern Claims Commission" (1994), which was digitized by Ancestry and made available as the "U.S. Southern Claims Commission Master Index, 1871–1880" (search the catalog for it); digitized images of the documents themselves are available through Fold3.

For an excellent overview of the relevance these records have to African American genealogy, see the 1999 article "The Southern Claims Commission: A Source for African American Roots" by Reginald Washington.[2]

Step 4. Research Potential Slave Owners. Because slaves were considered property, they were mentioned in documents pertaining to maintenance and disposal of land and personal goods, such as wills and probate records, plantation management and sale records, land and deed records, and newspaper notices about runaway slaves. Finding the records of slave owners often involves travel; do as much research in advance as you can. With luck, you will find the correct slave owners who affected your ancestors and, from there, work your way through the property records to determine slave lineage back to the individuals who were brought from Africa. Records of slave sales and advertisements are available in some states, though not usually online.

Step 5: Research African Places Where Ancestors Originated. For African American genealogists, this step might not be possible. But if your research has uncovered an African ancestor's origin place, you can research the slave trade practices for that area. The best online resource for information on the slave trade is the Trans-Atlantic Slave Trade Database (slavevoyages.org), which contains information on the roughly thirty-five thousand slave ship voyages that brought millions of Africans to the Americas between the 16th and 19th century. You will not find individual slaves named, but if your research has revealed the name of a ship or ship captain, this site is the place to go for further details.

Step 6. See Who Came from the Caribbean. After the Haitian Revolution, and again after World War II, the United States saw an influx of immigrants from Caribbean countries, most of them descendants of slaves held by British, Dutch, and French plantation owners. If your ancestors originated in Africa but came to the United States by way of the Caribbean, you have an extra piece of the slave trade puzzle to learn about.

In addition to Burroughs's book, check out the FamilySearch guide (www.familysearch.org/wiki/en/Quick_Guide_to_African_American_Records), which covers investigating African ancestors who arrived after the abolishment of slavery. Another useful source for this topic is AfriGeneas (afrigeneas.com), a loosely organized site that offers, among other things, a surname database, slave sale information, school lists, city directories, a beginner's guide to research, a newsletter, and a mailing list. The Afro-American Historical and Genealogical Society (www.aahgs.org) is a member organization that publishes a journal and sponsors an annual conference; it promotes scholarly research and offers members help in documenting African American family histories.

Finally, a state-by-state guide to resources is available from professional genealogist Joe Beine at www.genealogybranches.com/african american.html.

Hispanic Ancestry

To start researching Hispanic family origins, check out the resources given in the FamilySearch and Ancestry wikis (respectively, "Hispanic Genealogy Resources Online" and "Overview of Hispanic Research"). A couple things to keep in mind: First, many of the relevant records for Hispanic genealogy were kept by the Roman Catholic Church and usually concerned sacramental events (baptism, confirmation, marriage, last rites). So even if civil records are available, make sure you follow the religious record trail as well. Second, in many Hispanic or Latino countries, people usually have two surnames, one from each parent. The first surname, which often becomes a middle name, is customarily the father's surname, and the second one is the mother's surname. Occasionally, the two names are separated by the letter y ("and"); more recent records will have the names reversed, with the father's name last. Also, women usually retained their maiden names upon marriage. Both naming conventions mean that genealogists have an easier time connecting people and tracking families back through the generations.

George R. Ryskamp's book *Finding Your Hispanic Roots* (2009) is a good resource on this topic.

Jewish Ancestry

The earliest Jewish settlers in the United States came from the Mediterranean area and so were Sephardic. Later arrivals from Germany, Poland, and Russia were Ashkenazic; they have different histories and different historical records. Before the Immigration Act of 1924, which contained a "national origins quota," about two million Jews had come to America. More arrived later when the quotas were lifted. Researching Jewish genealogy is both easier and harder than other ethnic heritages—easier because there is a widespread active community of fellow researchers but harder because the ancestral lines often cover multiple places, sometimes on different continents.

Tracing Jewish family history begins, of course, with establishing an accurate family history back to the immigrant generation and then, if possible, learning the name of the city, town, village, or even province where its members came from. Online resources for accessing vital records in Europe and other places abound, but they are not much use if you don't have a place-name. Sometimes the surname can be a clue. As with other European groups, many Jewish surnames occur only within a small region; using historical surname research tools might help you identify the area. Multiple options are available, including the Consolidated Jewish Surname Index (avotaynu.com/csi/csi-home.htm), which connects you with records covering about seven hundred thousand surnames. This index is provided by Avotaynu, a publisher of books and a journal about Jewish genealogy.

Another good resource is the JewishGen Family Finder (www.jewishgen.org/jgff); registration is required. Place-names in Europe changed as the land came under governance by different entities; for example, the Russian city now called *Volgograd* was named *Stalingrad* between 1925 and 1961 and called *Tsaritsyn* before 1925. So you might not be able to locate your special places with Google Maps or a modern world atlas. Instead, look to historical atlases and maps. The JewishGen site, an affiliate of the Museum of Jewish History, provides the Jewish-Gen Gazetteer (formerly ShtetlSeeker), which contains the names of about a million localities in fifty-four countries in Europe, North Africa, the Middle East, and Central Asia. Map coordinates are given with the search results, which makes pinpointing that place on a modern map fairly easy. Find the gazetteer at www.jewishgen.org/com

munities/loctown.asp. The FamilySearch wiki entry to check for guidance is "Jewish Genealogy Research"; the Ancestry wiki entry is called "Overview of Jewish American Research."

Central and Eastern Europe

This large category covers people who lived primarily in Central and Eastern Europe; most Slavic immigrants to the United States came from Russia, Ukraine, Poland, the Czech Republic, Slovakia, Bulgaria, Croatia, Serbia, and Slovenia. Hungarians, Albanians, and Romanians are not Slavic peoples, but because they originated in areas dominated by Slavs, they are sometimes thrown in with this group for research guide purposes.

After establishing your history back to the immigrant generation, it is vital to establish locality names in their homeland. That piece of information can often be found on the declaration of intent created during the naturalization process (see chapter 4 for details). The spelling of a place-name might be different from what you see on a map because its original form is in the Cyrillic alphabet used by Russian and Serb immigrants, among others. Even the Slavic languages that use the Roman alphabet have unique accent marks, which change the pronunciation of certain consonants. For example, the Croatian names *Dundović* and *Yanković* were almost never written with the accent marks on American documents, even on the passenger lists (because they were intended for English speakers). That final accented letter, which makes a "ch" sound, was written either without the accent mark (*Yankovic*) or converted to the letters *ch* (e.g., *Dundovich*). Place-name spellings underwent similar transformations as accent marks were dropped.

The research guides available online generally break down by ethnic group (e.g., Czech, Slovak, Polish), but if you have Slavic ancestry, make the acquaintance of the Federation of East European Family History Societies (FEEFHS). This group provides country-specific links, articles, and community connections, making its site an important source for Central and Eastern European heritage research. The FEEFHS site also has a section on the Banat region of Europe, which overlaps the borders of several modern-day countries.

One useful book that covers several large Slavic groups is Lisa Alzo's *The Family Tree Polish, Czech, and Slovak Genealogy Guide* (2016).

Italy

In March 1891, after the arrest of eleven alleged murderers of a police chief, a vigilante mob stormed the New Orleans city jail and clubbed all eleven men to death. The men killed by the mob were all Italians. That's right—the largest mass lynching ever recorded in the United States involved not whites against African Americans but one group of European ancestry against another. This incident is described in an engaging book by Richard Gambino called *Vendetta: The True Story of the Largest Lynching in U.S. History*[3] (1977). The book was later made into a film starring Christopher Walken.

The New Orleans lynch mob was organized by John M. Parker, who later became the governor of Louisiana. In 1911, Parker was famously quoted as saying that the Italian immigrant was "just a little worse than the Negro, being if anything filthier in [his] habits, lawless, and treacherous."[4] His opinion, unfortunately for the millions of Italians newly arrived in North America, was shared by many; this group experienced widespread discrimination before becoming assimilated and passing the mantle of "hated other" on to later arrivals. By the time the waves of European immigrants slowed to a steady drip in the 1930s, about five million Italians had taken up residence in the United States, most of them from Sicily and the southern mainland.

An American with Italian heritage will have no trouble finding online research guides and access to exceptionally thorough record sets online through the Family History Library, which seem to cover every tiny village and hamlet throughout Italy, including Sicily and the other islands. We owe the availability of these records primarily to the government of Italy, which in the early 19th century implemented a uniform record-keeping method and also facilitated the efforts of LDS record photographers in the 1980s and 1990s. The Family History Library holds about twenty-eight thousand rolls of microfilm pertaining to Italy—a staggering number compared with its holdings for less represented countries, such as Russia and Romania, whose governments were not so cooperative.

Understanding the European part of your Italian family history begins with the place where the immigrants lived before they left—a piece of information that is usually not difficult to find for Italians. If you can locate the original passenger list or the declaration of intent, you will most likely find the village name; Catholic Church records in the United States frequently name the place of origin as well. Citizens of the Italian peninsula have a long history of staying put; many families remained in the same area generation after generation.

Italy has been inhabited for millennia and has many well-defined subcultures, each with its own dialect and traditions. The deep roots in a single place make researching one family easier, but that paradigm underscores the importance of having the right place-name. Once you know it, more than likely it will appear on a modern map of Italy; place-names there have not changed much over the centuries. Pinpointing the place on a map will give you the name of the province and region it falls into, and that information can help you find the original records.

Italy became a united country only in 1861. Civil record keeping had been officially mandated decades before, but only after the mid-1860s are you likely to find, for each locality, the standardized *atto di nascita* (birth records), *atto di matrimonio* (marriage records), and *atto di morto* (death records), along with census tallies. Roman Catholic parish records round out the thoroughly documented Italian citizen's life in the 19th and early 20th centuries; in many places, these church records go back to the 16th century, and a few go back to the 13th.

The Family History Library's catalog lists hundreds of place-names in Italy, each with numerous record sets available in microfilm or online. From there, check out some of these specialized tools:

Finding Italian Records. daddezio.com/genealogy/italian/records/index.html. Use this site when you want records beyond what the Family History Library can supply. You enter the province or region name and get an address in Italy to which you can send your inquiry, which should be in Italian (use Google Translate to convert your English).

Scopri la diffusione del tuo cognomen. www.gens.info/italia. The name means "discover the distribution of your surname." If you put in a surname (look for the box that says *cerca un cognomen*), you will get an interesting map of Italy showing, with colored dots of varying sizes, the distribution of that surname according to the latest demographic data. This tool can help if you are trying to narrow down where in Italy your ancestors came from or are wondering whether a surname is common or unusual there.

Also check out Suzanne Russo Adams's book *Finding Your Italian Ancestors: A Beginner's Guide* (2009) and Melanie D. Holtz's *The Family Tree Italian Genealogy Guide* (2017).

Germany

German immigrants began arriving in the American colonies in the 17th century and did not stop until the World Wars of the 20th century. Like many other relocated Europeans, the Germans sought landownership and relief from political and religious oppression. They brought food ideas and mechanical innovations and contributed many words to their adopted language. Eventually, America absorbed more than eight million German speakers; today, about fifty million U.S. citizens claim to have some German heritage. Some of the earliest Germans to arrive were from the Palatine region of Germany; 2,100 of them arrived in a single convoy in 1709 and settled along the Hudson River. Country music singer Tim McGraw is descended from one of these "Palatines"; he found out this interesting fact by participating in the popular television series *Who Do You Think You Are?* The Palatines were followed by many waves of German settlers, and just about every major U.S. city has a substantial population of their descendants.

Before 1871, Germany was not a unified nation, and even in the 20th century, parts of Germany were sectioned off and absorbed by its neighbors. So finding your German ancestors will depend on knowing the specific place they called home until they relocated, whether it is in today's Germany or not. German geography and history are complicated, but taking time to review the history of German-speaking peoples in Europe will help you when you are searching for records.

First, as always, you must begin with a thoroughly researched family history back to the immigrant generation. That task may prove difficult if you are descended from some of the earliest German settlers. But if you can nail down a specific town or village name, you can take the next step. Unlike some other countries, Germany does not maintain a centralized records repository, so you'll need to locate the state (there are sixteen) that contains the right town. A historical map side by side with a modern one will help you figure that out. Since 1871, each German state has conducted a regular census, and most of the returns are still available. Civil records of births, marriages, and deaths date back to

1871; for earlier records, you will have to turn to parish registers—church record books for baptisms, marriages, and burials. Many registers have been kept continuously since the 15th century. Be sure to check the Family History Library catalog for these register records before you write to the parish administrators in Germany.

People whose ancestors came from Romania, Serbia, or Hungary might well have some German heritage; each of those nations once had a significant minority population of Germans. They resided in the area of Central Europe once called the Banat region, which was overseen by the Ottoman Turks from 1552 to 1718; then it was subsumed into Habsburg Austria. The new Habsburg rulers recruited colonists from Swabia, Alsace, and Bavaria, encouraging them to settle several hundred miles from home.

These colonists cleared land, built roads and canals, established farms, and worked mines. They came to be called *Danube Swabians*, after the part of southern Germany where most originated. For almost two hundred years, their descendants lived far from Germany but never stopped being German in language, culture, and identity. Only after World War I, when the Austro-Hungarian Empire was disbanded, did the Banat region get divided up: two-thirds became Romanian, just under a third became Serbian, and a tiny piece remained with Hungary. Today, the name *Banat* is retained only informally and does not appear on most maps. In retaliation for having started both World Wars, most of the German residents from the Banat were expelled. Some went "back" to Germany, where their ancestors had come from, but many headed overseas for a fresh start. For a good overview, check out Joe Beine's page "Resources for German Genealogy on the Internet" (www.germanroots.com).

Also check out James M. Beidler's book *The Family Tree German Genealogy Guide* (2014).

France

Like the Dutch, English, and Spanish explorers and settlers during the 17th and 18th centuries, thousands of immigrants from France came to the New World colonies, but many of them pushed on into the interior or settled in eastern Canada. In parts of the United States, especially in Illinois, Indiana, and Louisiana, French immigrants established the first non-native villages and towns. But the greatest number of French arrivals came in the middle of the 18th century, when about a million French Canadians moved south across the border.

If you manage to identify the immigrant generation and are ready to begin researching records in France, Kimberly Powell has a helpful online article called "How to Research Your French Ancestry" (www.thoughtco.com/how-to-research-french-ancestry-1421947). The title is somewhat misleading; it is a beginner's guide to researching your ancestry *in* France but not all that helpful in getting to that point. The American-French Genealogical Society (afgs.org) provides guidance on researching French ancestry in America and Canada; Canadian records, including the census, are available through Ancestry and FamilySearch. Access to Canadian records in Ancestry requires the pricier international plan, so check the Family History Library's extensive microfilm and online records from Canada before you commit.

The Netherlands

The first Dutch people in what became the United States were colonizers of, rather than immigrants to, a land newly claimed by several European powers. Pushing aside the natives, in the early 17th century the Dutch settled on Manhattan and began to build up the area that became the New York City megalopolis. By the time their New Amsterdam colony was taken from them by the English in the 1660s, the Dutch settlers numbered close to ten thousand. The English takeover of Manhattan and the surrounding areas effectively stopped Dutch immigration until the early 19th century, when it resumed and continued into the 20th. Tracing Dutch ancestry is easier if you are descended from those later arrivals, as the records are more complete and better preserved, but if you descend from the original settlers, you have more American ancestry to track than most people do.

After you have established a documented family history back as far as you can using the usual methods, zero in on the Dutch aspects with Trace Your Dutch Roots: Your Dutch Genealogy Guide (traceyour dutchroots.com/roots), a free site packed with research leads and explanations. It is a tiny place on the world scene, but the country called, with good reason, the Netherlands has had a major impact on American culture and language (e.g., *boom, booze, cookie, waffle,* and *walrus*).

China, Japan, and Korea

The United States and Canada have absorbed millions of people from Southeast Asia, but each group came at a different time and has a different history. The information given here covers three of those groups; information on researching other groups from Southeast Asia can be found at the FamilySearch wiki.

China

During the 19th century, as the dominant European powers established colonies all over the globe, Chinese people left their home country and headed outward, many of them to work in new colonies. A growing shortage of manpower the world over resulting from restrictive laws regarding African slaves left many natural resource exploiters with a problem, and they solved it by hiring Chinese laborers (sometimes called *coolies*, which derives from a Hindi word). The first of three major waves of Chinese immigrants to the United States began occurring in the early 19th century; many were employed on the transcontinental railroad construction project and in the mining industry.

Historians have worked hard to document the racial discrimination suffered by these workers who helped build the infrastructure of a rapidly growing country. They were paid a fraction of what Caucasian workers could get and were regularly dismissed in the media with the phrase "Yellow Peril." Congress passed a law in 1882 specifically forbidding the immigration of Chinese nationals for the next ten years; the ban was eventually extended until 1943. Known as the Chinese Exclusion Act, this law was the first one ever passed that blocked immigration solely based on race. Chinese workers could still land on the shores of America, but they were guest workers on temporary visas, not permanent residents who could become citizens.

Even before the 1882 law, Chinese people were excluded from naturalization, as were all nonwhite people. Under the Naturalization Act of 1790—one of the first pieces of legislation passed to define the parameters for granting American citizenship—Congress limited naturalization to immigrants who were "free white persons." Native Americans and those of African or Asian origin were not invited to apply. Not until 1898, with a Supreme Court decision known as *United States v. Wong Kim Ark*, were Chinese immigrants and their offspring permitted to seek U.S. citizenship. These stark historical facts contribute to the research parameters for documenting the history of Chinese families.

A Chinese person today could have ancestors who lived in the United States for many decades, but their presence, in many cases, will not be as well documented as that of European immigrants. The census counted Chinese individuals, and the vitally significant events of their lives (births, marriages, deaths) created paper records, but because of the 1790 Naturalization Act, they left no declaration of intent or other naturalization documents. Without those documents, the name of the birthplace in China for the immigrant generation must be obtained from other sources, if possible.

A good place to start understanding what those early Chinese immigrants experienced is the National Archives guide called "Chinese Immigration and the Chinese in the United States" (www.archives.gov/research/chinese-americans/guide). It has links to several helpful resources, including a surnames database. FamilySearch offers a record set called China, Collection of Genealogies (1239–2011), which contains digital images of Chinese genealogies from public and private collections. The collection has more than eleven million images and is subdivided by family name and place.

Japan

Before the late 19th century, relatively few people had left Japan and become permanent residents of other countries. After 1868, when imperial rule was restored in Japan (the Meiji Restoration), people began heading for the United States in great numbers. Most of them settled in Hawaii or the North American west coast. A 1907 agreement between Japan and the United States restricted Japanese immigrants to skilled workers, businessmen, and students, along with their families; unskilled laborers were not welcomed. The Immigration Act of 1924 put a stop to almost all Japanese people coming in. By that time, about 275,000 Japanese citizens had made a new home in America.

Many of those Japanese nationals were subjected to internment by the U.S. government following the Japanese attack on Pearl Harbor in 1941. Thousands of Japanese Americans were forced to live in specially built camps and were detained indefinitely while the country pursued war against Japan. The detained lost their property and their freedom, but almost none was ever charged with any crime. This sequence of events generated much misery for the 120,000 people relocated and detained but also created a paper trail for genealogists. The Internment Case Files are held at the National Archives and can be requested. An index called the Japanese-American Internet Data File, 1942–1946 is available in the Access to Archives Database (aad.archives.gov/aad). Search the National Archives' holdings for other record sets relating to "enemy aliens" and persons considered a threat during wartime.

Searching for ancestors in Japanese records is difficult, because Japan has strict privacy laws and does not generally allow public access to vital records; although the records are exceptionally thorough. But if you can establish a family line back to the ones who left, you might be able to establish the *koseki*, or official registration and information record, for your family. If your ancestor is listed in a *koseki*, you are entitled to a copy of the record, which often contains information on multiple generations. Start your online research with Japan GenWeb (sites.rootsweb.com/~jpnwgw) and check out the National Archives of Japan (www.digital.archives.go.jp/index_e.html).

You will not find many records online, but you can research Japanese records practices and the laws that govern access to them. Also worth checking out is a free database called Japanese Immigrants to the United States, 1887–1924, offered by Brigham Young University's Idaho branch (abish.byui.edu/specialCollections/fhc/Japan/index.asp). Immigrants from Japan and their descendants are known historically as *Nikkei*. The Japanese American National Museum in Los Angeles (www.janm.org) is a great place to investigate the cultural history and experiences of this group. You will find described there the International Nikkei Research Project, a three-year collaborative research project on the evolution of Nikkei cultures and societies.

Korea

Immigrants from South Korea came later than those from China and Japan, starting in about 1903. Thousands of Korean orphans were adopted by American families in the years following the Korean conflict in the 1950s, but the number of Koreans in America remained small until after 1965, with the Immigration Reform Act; today about two million people of Korean descent live in the United States. A good place to start researching those immigrants is the SouthKoreaGenWeb (sites.rootsweb.com/~korwgw-s), followed by an exploration of a database recently made available by the Paik Inje Memorial Library of Inje University in South Korea (genealogy.inje.ac.kr/eng/main.htm). Note: the latter site operates only with Windows Explorer.

Native American Ancestry

Professional genealogist Kimberley Powell has put together an excellent, regularly updated research guide called "How to Trace American Indian Ancestry" (www.thoughtco.com/tracing-american-indian-ances try-1420669). She advises the researcher to follow a series of steps, which are not the same one would follow for other ethnic lines. The following is a paraphrase of Powell's advice.

Step 1. Establish Your Family Tree. Interview family members and collect documentation; pay special attention to the places where births, deaths, and marriages occurred. Learn as many variations on given names as you can.

Step 2. Establish and Document Tribal Affiliations. If you cannot identify the tribes that your Native American ancestors were part of, map out the locations where they lived and compare that to historical tribal location maps. The American Indian Heritage Foundation maintains online tribal directories (indians.org/tribal-directory.html).

Step 3. Research the Tribal Background. If you were able to establish tribal connections for your ancestors, your next step is to learn as much as you can about the tribes. Fortunately, a great deal of information that was once difficult to pull together or simply unavailable is now easy to find online and in print. Reliable data on tribal customs can help you weigh family stories against historical facts.

Step 4. Use the National Archives. The federal government managed the affairs of Native American tribes during the years of European settlement and expansion; that management resulted in myriad paper records, most created by the Bureau of Indian Affairs. They include tribal census rolls, records of schooling, records relating to removal of Native Americans from property claimed by the federal government, and the establishment of reservations. The National Archives site (www.archives.gov/research/native-americans) is the best place to review what records and resources are available there. One of the more important record sets at the National Archives is the Dawes Commission Enrollment Records for Five U.S. Indian Tribes. The Dawes Commission, established in 1893, oversaw the exchange of Cherokee, Creek, Choctaw, Chickasaw, and Seminole tribal lands in the southeastern United States for new land in Oklahoma. Administrators of those five tribes still use the Dawes Rolls to determine eligibility for tribal membership.

A thorough description of all the records created by the Dawes Commission is available at the FamilySearch wiki. Also available through the National Archives are the federal census Indian schedules, which are different from the tribal census rolls established through the Bureau of Indian Affairs. The Dawes Commission records and the Indian schedules, like many other National Archives documents, are available through Fold3.

Resources for Native American research have been put together online by Joe Beine (www.genealogybranches.com/nativeameri cans.html). Also, there are excellent wiki entries on this topic at Family-Search ("American Indian Genealogy") and Ancestry ("Overview of Native American Research").

Canada

The resources available for Canadian genealogy are used not just to track immigrants from Canada but also to Canada from Europe and through Canada to the United States. Many Europeans took that indirect route to America. If your family story includes a Canadian connection, you can research Canadian records via Ancestry (you'll need the international subscription) and FamilySearch. On Ancestry, you will find voter lists, phone and address directories, church records, the country's decennial census from the mid-19th century through 1921, passenger lists of people landing at Canadian ports, border-crossing records, an obituary index, and vital records indexes for most of the provinces. FamilySearch has a long list of available indexes as well, most with original record images provided. Then check out Library and Archives Canada

(www.bac-lac.gc.ca/eng/discover/genealogy/Pages/introduction.aspx) and Canada GenWeb (sites.rootsweb.com/~canwgw).

CULTURAL HERITAGE RESEARCH

In addition to your ethnic heritage, you have connections to cultural heritage as well. More than likely an interest group for that heritage is out there waiting to be found. For example, if your family tradition says that you are descended from a *Mayflower* passenger, you can contact the Mayflower Society (www.themayflowersociety.org) and submit a request for an inquiry (there is a modest fee). If your connection is proved, you can join the group more formally known as the General Society of Mayflower Descendants. Likewise, if you have a documented lineage from someone who fought on the colonists' side in the Revolutionary War, you can join the Sons or Daughters of the American Revolution (www.sar.org and www.dar.org). These groups and others like them offer much to members, including assistance and advice about pursuing genealogy interests.

Fraternal unions and clubs were vital to the European immigrants who arrived in the 19th and 20th centuries. Many depended on the literacy assistance and savings plans these unions offered, and new immigrants found a friendly space with people who spoke their language. These organizations also helped those left behind by assisting immigrants with the tricky business of sending money overseas. Not all these groups were focused on such serious things; many were formed for entertainment, such as the dozens of German *Gesangvereine* (singing societies) that sprang up in American cities. If you can identify the club or organization your ancestor belonged to, you might find an online presence, which potentially could lead to an indexed archive of their membership papers. It's a long shot but always worth checking. The city history museums of many large cities such as New York, Buffalo, Chicago, and Philadelphia usually hold items relating to these organizations as well.

Many cultural heritage groups are local rather than national entities, so check your local public and academic libraries as well as local archives to see if they have what you need.

One final bit of advice: if you find that someone has written a book about an ethnic or cultural heritage that interests you, try to get it through interlibrary loan before you spend money for your own copy. Your local public or academic library can process interlibrary loan requests.

DNA TESTING

Nothing changes faster in the genealogy world than DNA science, testing, access, and laws relating to all three. Any print publication that covers the subject in detail will inevitably become outdated, so the best way to keep up with genealogy DNA options and issues is to follow developments in blogs. The best ones are written by people who understand both the science and the laws relating to genetic genealogy. Start with these two: The Legal Genealogist (www.legalgenealogist.com/blog) and The Genetic Genealogist (thegeneticgenealogist.com).

How It All Began

Once upon a time, nobody knew about DNA, but genealogy was already a popular pursuit. Family history researchers knew about proving who was connected to whom, but they worked mainly with documents. Even after the DNA double helix was described by Watson and Crick in 1953, no one guessed what the future would bring.

Fast-forward to the 1980s. Blood type testing had long been available to law enforcement investigators, but this decade brought a new option for tracking down offenders: an analytical tool called Restriction Fragment Length Polymorphism (RFLP). The RFLP test, which required that blood be drawn, became the first to make use of DNA markers—and thus was born the modern paternity test. The new, sophisticated test was also used to track and convict (or eliminate) suspects in any crime where DNA evidence was collected at a crime scene.

Science kept galloping along as it always does, and in the 1990s RFLP analysis was replaced with PCR testing (polymerase chain reaction). This was the test that freed genetic testing from bloodletting—a simple cheek swab sufficed. More baby daddies were identified, and more criminals were linked to their crimes with genetic evidence. But the genealogy world was unaffected until new developments in genetic science during the following decade led to identification of markers that could be used to pinpoint ancestry and ethnic heritage. The practice of genealogy has never been the same.

In short, as a result of the ever-increasing sophistication of molecular biology research in combination with the seemingly infinite resources of the Internet, DNA testing has moved on from helping tie fathers to offspring and criminals to crime scenes to helping family historians find relatives and identify heritage groups. You still need to create a documented, detailed family history with traditional sources, of course; the DNA results are merely supplementary. But for some researchers, the results open up avenues of exploration that were previously unknown. A DNA test will not do the work of creating the family history or tell you the names of your ancestors, but it can prove whether you are related to another person—that is, whether you have a common ancestor. It can also give you a broad picture of your ethnic origins.

What Does a Test Involve?

A DNA test for genealogy results is simple to execute: you order a kit and follow the instructions. Kits are available from a variety of companies, but the biggest three and most reliable bets are Ancestry, 23andMe, and Family Tree DNA. Costs vary, but all three companies regularly offer discounted kits tied to holidays.

First you register your kit; then you spit into a tube up to a marked line, seal the tube, and mail it back to the company. Then you wait for several weeks until you get an e-mail saying your results are available. At the testing company's site, you see not the raw data results but an interpretation of those results in colorful graphic form.

Scientifically speaking, there are three tests that can be done on a single spit sample:

Test 1: Mitochondrial DNA

Mitochondrial DNA (mtDNA) is passed by a mother to all her offspring, so this test can determine direct maternal ancestors. A male's mtDNA is not passed on to his offspring; his children inherit mtDNA only from their mother. In September 2012, skeletal remains were found under a parking lot in England; historians immediately suspected that they had found England's famous hunchback king, Richard III, who died in 1485. When the mtDNA of the remains was compared with that of two living descendants of Richard's sister Anne, this theory was verified; they all had inherited that particular mtDNA stamp from Anne and Richard's mother. An even older specimen, a nine-thousand-year-old preserved corpse from a bog near Cheddar, England, yielded viable

DNA that, upon mtDNA testing, was found to link "Cheddar Man" to living descendants.

Test 2: Y Chromosome

Male-line ancestry is traced through the Y chromosome, which passes down almost unchanged from male parent to male offspring. Shared Y chromosome markers can indicate that two males are related; because last names are usually passed down from the paternal line, many people use this test (Y-DNA) to determine if individuals who share a surname have a common ancestor. A woman who wants to determine paternal DNA history must ask a male related to her father to do the test on her behalf. In 1998, a Y-DNA test indicated that Thomas Jefferson or one of his close male relatives was the father of children by his slave Sally Hemings; because he had no direct surviving male descendants, samples came from male descendants of Jefferson's paternal uncle. It should be noted that DNA science cannot establish genetic relationships with 100 percent certainty.

Both the mtDNA and the Y-DNA tests can determine any individual's *haplogroups*, a general group of people who share genetic characteristics. While not useful to determine relation to another individual, haplogroup data can indicate the geographic region of lineage for both your paternal and maternal lines. The DNA code revealed by both these tests is not useful all by itself; the results must be compared with the results of others before they begin to yield valuable information.

Test 3: Autosomal DNA

The autosomal DNA test (also auDNA or atDNA) can be applied to everyone. It tests more than seven hundred thousand markers on the twenty-two autosomal chromosomes, which differ from the sex chromosomes known as X and Y, to determine connections both maternal and paternal.

Using these test results in combination with documentary research, genealogists can map specific segments of a chromosome to specific family lines and thus help resolve identity and kinship problems. Results suggest a person's ethnic mix—what percentage of his or her ancestry comes from what region of the world. To determine which testing company is best for you, check out Kimberly Powell's article "DNA Tests Available for Genealogy" (www.thoughtco.com/dna-tests-avail

able-for-genealogy-1421838); it outlines the factors to consider.

If you are interested in establishing your genetic connections to other people, remember that results are useful only when compared with other results. Each testing company will compare your results only to others within their database; so unless you go outside that closed system and upload your results into another, third-party database, your results will be limited to a specific pool. In general, if you're exploring genetic connections for whatever reason, it's best to get your results compared with as many test takers as possible. That means, if you've already done the Ancestry or the 23andMe test, you should consider doing the other one as well to increase your comparison pool.

Downloading the raw results from your DNA test is an option at all three of the biggest companies named above, and there are multiple options for you to upload those results outside of the closed databases of the testing companies. Years ago there were multiple open databases; however, in the past year a few popular open-sharing sites (Ysearch, Mitosearch, and World Families Network are three) have shut down in response to a European Union law called the General Data Protection Regulation (GDPR), which took effect in May 2018. This tough new law is intended to protect the privacy of data, including genetic data. Because it is so new, its parameters haven't yet been tested in court— and nobody wants to find out just how expensive it would be to come out on the losing side of a case involving genetic data.

Two third-party sharing companies are still in business as of this writing: GedMatch (www.gedmatch.com) and OpenSNP (opensnp .org). The former was instrumental in helping law enforcement, in partnership with a genetic genealogy specialist, to determine familial matches for Joseph James DeAngelo, the man suspected of being the infamous Golden State Killer. Someone closely related to DeAngelo chose to upload DNA results at GedMatch, which, unlike Ancestry and 23andMe, is open and available to be searched by law enforcement.

Closed databases like Ancestry and 23andMe are not the target of GDPR; those results are not shared with anyone other than the registered test taker. But if someone uploads results to a third-party site such as GedMatch or OpenSNP, and their software allows that data to be shared, those companies are in potential violation of the GDPR law. The law has, at bottom, a positive intent: to protect consumers from a business entity acquiring and selling any person's DNA results without that person's consent, even if the results are not tied to a name. Of course, you might be giving consent without realizing when you click "I agree" without bothering to read the terms and conditions you're agreeing to. Caveat emptor is the rule with genetic genealogy.

If you have questions about the potential legal and privacy ramifications from uploading your DNA results at an open-sharing site, check the two blogs mentioned above for the latest news and info. An excellent book-length resource on this subject is Blaine Bettinger's *The Family Tree Guide to DNA Testing and Genetic Genealogy* (2nd edition, 2019).

Unexpected Revelations

Many people who have excitedly viewed genetic genealogy results have felt smacked in the face by unexpected results. For example, if all the siblings in a family do the same test, they should be shown in the list of genetic relatives to share 50 percent (not 100 percent) of their DNA with each other. DNA distribution has a random factor; the distribution is not going to be identical for all the siblings. In other words, one will get slightly more from one parent than the others. However, if one of those siblings shows only a 25 percent match with the others, that means (pending confirming tests) they are only *half*-siblings (share only one parent). Seeing those numbers can come as a complete shock. In fact, a whole side business in genealogy research has sprung up around this very issue—specialists who analyze genetic results to help people identify their actual heritage when results show something different from the established family story. Genetic genealogy has shown that quite a few family trees have cases of what professional genealogists call *misattributed paternity*.

Health Results

One of the biggest reasons many people want a genealogy DNA test is to obtain health data. What do my genes say about the likelihood I will develop cancer or Alzheimer's disease? One of the three testing companies named above, 23andMe, does offer health-related data, but caveat emptor once again; the data obtained is not as useful as most people hope for. Instead, people who choose to pay extra to get 23andMe's health results will be told whether they are carriers of genetic variants that can lead to certain diseases (mostly rare ones). In other words, you do not get information about whether you yourself will go on to develop a certain disease but rather whether you will pass it on. The health results also tell you the likelihood of certain physical traits, as in whether you have light or dark eyes, straight or wavy hair. You might want to think twice about paying extra to learn something you already know.

If you have health concerns, your best bet is to request tests through your regular physician rather than relying on a genealogy company's summary. The International Society of Genetic Genealogy (isogg.org) offers unbiased (i.e., noncommercial) information and can help you explore the pros and cons of various tests and with interpreting results.

SUMMING IT UP

Not every family history researcher will get to the point of researching specialized subjects or submitting a DNA sample for genealogy results. For others, however, the ethnic and culture research as well as the DNA tests sometimes are the starting point and inspire someone to back up and start a more traditional, document-based research project. The ethnic research can be complicated by language and cultural differences, but you will likely find a community online of people looking for the same thing. Remember:

- Doing cultural heritage and ethnic group research often requires specialized resources; seek out online communities and advice targeting your interest groups.
- Genealogy DNA results can be unsettling. Be ready for potential surprises.

Next: keeping up and sharing your work.

8

KEEPING UP AND SHARING RESULTS

This chapter addresses:

- Blogs, podcasts, and forums
- Conferences, seminars, webinars, and online courses
- Ideas for sharing

Genealogists tend to be helpful people, eager to share what they have found and lend newbies a hand with the task of searching, documenting, and compiling a family history. Many have taken their helpful impulses public with podcasts, blogs, forums, and dedicated sites. Advice and inspiration spill out at no cost; they offer their experience and expertise, pull resources together into helpful guides, and answer questions. In fact, some of the more useful specialized sites, such as Find A Grave, began as one person's desire to share his or her knowledge. Does any other research community have such a profile?

The world of genealogy research changes every day: new databases are added, record access laws are redefined, and subscription sites alter their parameters, including costs. Use the sites and sources listed in this chapter to track changes in genealogical research, to seek help when you hit the inevitable brick wall, and to continue educating yourself in the evolving world of family history research.

BLOGS

The rapid growth of the Internet during the 1990s brought a new kind of publishing. Suddenly, it seemed, anybody who had anything to say could address an international audience and do so without pesky editors and fact-checkers. Web publishing tools developed quickly to accommodate the millions who longed to be heard; in the beginning, these tools were primarily "web logs," a term that lasted about three minutes before it morphed into the familiar *blog*. Initially, users posted their comments into an ongoing "log"; readers scrolled through them. Blog creation took off and has never slowed down; unfortunately, the clumsy scrolling feature remains in most of them. Today, genealogy blogs cover myriad topics, from the general to the micro-focused.

Some people read a few blogs regularly; others sample in and out or use them only when retrieved in a Google search. Some blogs are earnestly informative, while others aim at the funny bone. There are dozens of worthwhile genealogy-related blogs out there. Ancestry and FamilySearch each have an excellent one; use them to keep up with record set availability at these powerhouse sites and other vital news (blogs.ancestry.com/ancestry and www.familysearch.org/blog/en). Britain's counterpart to Ancestry, FindMyPast, has a good blog as well (blog.findmypast.com). Following are a few more worth checking out (given in alphabetical order).

DNAeXplained—Genetic Genealogy

dna-explained.com. Roberta Estes, a scientist and owner of a company providing analysis of DNA results and genealogy help, shares stories and answers questions about genealogy through the lens of DNA testing.

Eastman's Online Genealogy Newsletter

blog.eogn.com. Despite the title, this is a blog more than a traditional newsletter—and a good one. Dick Eastman's eclectic mix of news, updates, and items to ponder is always well written and leans toward the technological aspects of genealogy, such as choosing a family history program or storing your data in the cloud. The blog is sponsored by MyHeritage.

GenealogyBlog

www.genealogyblog.com. This prosaically named but informative blog by Leland and Patty Meitzler will keep you up to date on database additions and changes, genealogy conference news, and genealogically relevant news items, such as advances in DNA technology.

Genea-Musings

www.geneamusings.com. Southern California resident Randy Seaver has maintained this entertaining blog since 2006; it covers a range of topics, from his own family research to discussions of genealogy-related conferences and products. If you like your genealogy news laced with humor, give Randy a look; also check out Chris Dunham's news-oriented blog called *The Genealogue* (www.genealogue.com).

The Legal Genealogist

www.legalgenealogist.com/blog. Maintained by Judy G. Russell, who bills herself as "a genealogist with a law degree," this one delves into the complicated but interesting laws behind genealogy records such as land and property ownership, among many others.

The Practical Archivist

practicalarchivist.blogspot.com. This focused offering from archivist Sally Jacobs states on its About page, "If you need help organizing, preserving, or sharing your family archives, you've come to the right place." Trust Sally J. for the best advice on storing, preserving, scanning, and displaying your family documents, photographs, and other items.

You can find blogs devoted to DNA research, tombstone transcriptions, particular ancestry lines, genealogy software, and assessments of subscription sites. The downside: blogs are usually studded with ads from this company or that, and some of those ads blink. Most blog page interfaces are too "busy"; the scrolling feature, part of blogging since the early days, contributes to the difficulty of navigation. But blogs hold the genealogy knowledge network together, and you'll find something useful in many of them.

PODCASTS

Think of genealogy podcasts as blogs on the air; you get a similar mix of news, research hints, and updates, often in an entertaining manner. There aren't many really good ones, given that creating a quality podcast is more time- and effort-consuming than updating a blog, but a few people have done it. Check out these podcasters if you prefer to get your genealogy discussions through the ear. If the episodes are not available at the dedicated site, search for them in iTunes, Stitcher, or PodBean.

Lisa Louise Cooke

lisalouisecooke.com/podcasts. Lisa loves everything about genealogy, and her enthusiasm has carried her through three podcasts and a blog, four book publications, a video series, and speaking engagements all over the world. Her podcast, *Genealogy Gems*, has been rolling out research tips and sharing techniques, plus interviews with genealogy experts, since 2006. Lisa has also put together a thirty-one-episode podcast for beginners called *Family History: Genealogy Made Easy*, hosts the *Family Tree Magazine* podcast, and teaches courses for Family Tree University. Tap into Lisa's energy when your own starts to dim.

George G. Morgan and Drew Smith

genealogyguys.com. Known as the Genealogy Guys, these two affable experts produce the world's longest-running, regularly produced genealogy podcast. Since September 2005, *The Genealogy Guys* show has offered listeners a mix of news, discussion, and guest interviews in roughly thirty-minute segments. Their voices are reassuring, and their knowledge is seemingly endless.

Scott Fisher

extremegenes.com. The Extreme Genes podcast alternates between lengthy segments and short tip-focused episodes. Fisher has a perfect voice for radio and is an entertaining, energetic, and knowledgeable presenter. You're sure to learn something here.

FORUMS

Have a question about some piece of genealogical information or wondering if anyone else is researching the same family you are? Genealogy-oriented forums reward exploration because discussions are lively and free help is on tap. Experts in tiny pieces of the genealogy puzzle abound. For example, one forum is dedicated to discussing research in German records; another will walk you through the steps to research your Revolutionary War ancestors.

Participants can post images and queries about particular records, and others will respond with translations, explanations, or interesting details about places and records. Usually you do not have to register or join to read forum discussions—only to post. Following are some forums worth browsing or searching.

Ancestry Message Boards

www.ancestry.com/boards. A tightly organized space where you can search by name or browse the messages relating to a particular place. Ancestry attracts a lot of beginners, who often ask forum users questions that could be researched using that very site, but the forum crew usually answers anyway. Do not limit your forum search to surnames; try searching street and locality names as well, such as *Fly Street, Buffalo NY*. That particular set of keywords will take you to an informative discussion of the remodeled Erie Canal docks area once populated by newly arrived immigrant families. Forum users in this instance have posted links to maps and pictures that you would most likely not find right away working on your own. Ancestry users who browse and post to the forum constitute a major knowledge network with potential value for all family historians.

GenForum

www.genealogy.com/forum. Powered by the pay site Genealogy.com, this forum contains more than a decade of archived postings that span a range of topics. You can search by location or surname. Registration is required to post, but browsing is free.

RootsChat

www.rootschat.com. The United Kingdom's largest free family history forum. Some of the discussions are fascinating and not restricted to U.K. interests. One recent back-and-forth involved debunking the persistent myth that the pejorative term *wop* for Italians was originally an acronym standing for "without passport" (it actually derives from the Italian word *guappo*). You never know what you'll find here.

MAGAZINES

For the most part, printed genealogy magazines are a thing of the past. Online publications and knowledge-sharing sites have taken their place. Despite the change in format, genealogy magazines still provide a useful service if you seek to expand your education and research options.

One of the biggest publications for decades, *Ancestry Magazine*, ceased production in early 2010—for the previous twenty-five years, it had provided an excellent and valuable resource (back issues are available through Ancestry and Google Books). Still available online is *Family Tree Magazine* (www.familytreemagazine.com), published since 1999 and with more than seventy thousand subscribers. You can also find articles and news in magazine format at www.genealogymagazine.com, from 1987 to 1999 available in print and now published online at a dedicated site. There are many more publications out there that you can retrieve by Googling *genealogy magazine*; many articles can be read for free.

CONFERENCES

When genealogy in the United States was in its early days, it was practiced primarily by people who were researchers by nature rather than by training. For the most part, these people were self-taught, and they learned through trial and error the best ways to compile and document a family history. Unlike traditional academics, they had few opportunities to meet with like-minded others and even fewer to get access to formal presentations about research strategies, evidence analysis, and document preservation.

Fortunately, the passing of time has brought a new paradigm. Although the genealogy world was somewhat slow to adopt the principles and practices of university-led academic research, it now has dozens of conferences each year featuring powerhouse speakers who inspire their own rock-star following (evidence guru Elizabeth Shown Mills, discussed in chapter 1, tends to attract that kind of attention).

Genealogy's academic conferences and institutes, in general, take place outside the perception of most people, but information on upcoming events and proceedings from past gatherings can be found easily enough. Most blogs described in this chapter contain announcements of upcoming conferences, along with news and reviews of those that have occurred recently. The major genealogical societies sponsor an annual conference—most notably, the National Genealogical Society, since 1979 (www.ngsgenealogy.org), and the Federation of Genealogical Societies, since 1978 (fgs.org). In August 2019, these two organizations announced their intention to merge by October 2020.

There's also the Samford Institute of Genealogy and Historical Research, which has existed since 1964; the National Institute for Genealogical Research, which has been based at the National Archives since the 1950s; Boston University's various programs under the auspices of its Professional Learning Center; and Canada's National Institute for Genealogical Studies, formerly based at the University of Toronto, whose online offerings have attracted thousands of U.S. students. The most recent offerings include forensic and genetic institutes and are grounded in academic principles and practices.

Genealogy conferences are busy events with many opportunities for you to learn, share, and connect. A family historian does not need these gatherings to complete a project, of course, but attending does have advantages, including hands-on demonstrations of software, presentations that can inspire and help you to rethink your strategies, experts in subject areas who provide suggestions for tough research challenges, and a crowd of people who all care passionately about family history. You have hundreds of conferences and workshops all over the globe to choose from—some of them highly specialized. As with almost all academic conferences, you'll pay a registration fee.

ONLINE COURSES AND SEMINARS

If you want to continue learning and interacting with the national and international genealogical community but do not like leaving home, you have many options for online courses, webinars (originally *web seminars*), and training videos to help you take your research a few steps further. Somewhere out there is the perfect course, presentation, or video tutorial for you.

FamilySearch's Learning Center classes are a great place to start exploring self-education on genealogy topics (www.familysearch.org/wiki/en/Classes_in_the_Learning_Center). You can find topics both basic and advanced, usually well presented and produced by America's genealogy experts at the Family History Library. They offer around six hundred free courses in multiple languages, some of which can be downloaded. If you need to work with non-English records, the series of tutorials on handwriting and scripts from country to country is quite useful.

For more formal online instruction, try the following: the National Genealogical Society, taught since 1980 (www.ngsgenealogy.org/learning-center); the Canada-based National Institute for Genealogical Studies, taught since the mid-1990s (www.genealogicalstudies.com); and Boston University, taught since 2007 (professional.bu.edu/programs/genealogy). Brigham Young University, the educational institution most closely connected to the Family History Library, offers free online classes at is.byu.edu/catalog/free-courses. Caution: the BYU offerings are narrower and somewhat less rigorous in their application of current genealogical standards.

Another source of training is the Legacy Family Tree Webinars site (familytreewebinars.com), which pulls together offerings from a variety of organizations, most of which are free to view live and for a short time thereafter and then are archived and available for a modest fee. Watching one of these webinars is like sitting in a conference meeting room listening to an expert presenter but without the traveling. Coursera (www.coursera.org)—one of the bigger companies offering free massive online open courses (MOOCs)—has several genealogy-related offerings that can be sampled from the comfort of home.

While usually not free, some of the courses available through Family Tree University (www.familytreemagazine.com/store/university) are worth checking out. Family Tree University is the online education program created by the publishers of *Family Tree Magazine*. You'll find a variety of formats: online courses that "meet" online, independent study courses that you complete on your own schedule, and webinars, live and recorded, by genealogy experts.

Finally, large genealogy societies, state libraries, and library organizations regularly offer webinars; if you belong to one of those hosting societies, you can usually get access anytime at the group's site. Even if you do not formally belong, these educational offerings are usually available for free for a short time. It pays to join or at least stay aware of a society near where you live.

TELEVISION AND WEB SHOWS

Genealogy has attracted the interest of growing numbers of people in the past few decades; television producers have capitalized on that interest with shows such as *Who Do You Think You Are? Finding Your Roots*, and *Genealogy Roadshow*.

Who Do You Think You Are? began, like some other acclaimed American television offerings, with a British original that appeared in 2004. Adaptations of this series have appeared in the United States, Canada, Australia, Ireland, Sweden, Denmark, and the Czech Republic, each providing that country's viewers with a rapidly unfolding family history for some well-known person. The American version premiered in 2010 and has been a popular hit. *Finding Your Roots*, a series produced by PBS, began airing in 2012 and is hosted by Harvard professor Henry Louis Gates Jr. In addition to traditional genealogical research, these shows highlight the use of DNA testing to trace distant and recent connections.

Genealogy Roadshow, an idea borrowed from an Irish original that began airing in 2011, is the latest to arrive, and it's got a twist—instead of tracing the history of famous people, it features ordinary people who think that they have a famous connection. For example, someone's family lore has it that Abraham Lincoln was an ancestor, or someone possesses an object that might have belonged to Martha Washington. Using the popular *Antiques Roadshow* as their model, a handful of genealogy experts travel to selected cities and meet with people who bring their potential treasure/family story for assessment. Local historians join in the hunt for verification.

All three of these shows are slickly produced, informative, and entertaining. But genealogy-related airings are not restricted to the television screen. If you enter *genealogy* into a YouTube search box, you will retrieve a variety of videos, many of them posted by Ancestry and other subscription sites or by bloggers and podcasters.

SHARING

Sometimes family history research can feel like a lonely pursuit, but that feeling disappears when, after posting what you have discovered, someone contacts you to say, "Our trees connect!" Sharing is vital to all areas of research. Without publication of results, scientific research has no validity; genealogy research is no different. The sharing paradigm allows us to learn what others are doing and to stay plugged into the knowledge network.

You can share your family research results in many venues. The biggest subscription site, Ancestry, makes it easy to create and post data files on-site; other users can be invited to view (if set to *private*) or retrieve in a search (if set to *public*). You can also create a shareable tree with other software programs: MyHeritage and RootsMagic are two of the more popular ones, but dozens of others are out there.

Family history data is stored in a format known as GEDCOM (stands for *genealogical data communications*), with the extension *.ged*. The data is saved in ASCII text format (the equivalent of a *.txt* file), which can be opened by other programs. This software was developed by the LDS church in 1984 to facilitate the sharing of genealogical data for church purposes, and it has become a widely used standard in the years since. Some software programs use their own data-formatting extensions but usually allow you the option to "save as GEDCOM." Do not even consider purchasing family history software without this option.

You can share documents and pictures by using a service such as Dropbox (www.dropbox.com), the basic form of which gives you two gigabytes for free. If you have lots of documents and pictures to store and share, Google Drive offers fifteen gigabytes of free storage with options to upgrade to more. There are other file-sharing services out there as well, all of which are useful if you wish to share your entire document file for a particular line of a family tree with another research-minded family member. You could always put the documents on a flash drive or CD and mail it, of course, but cloud storage makes that process seem old-fashioned.

Genealogists have come up with many clever ideas for sharing their research results and getting family members interested; the blogs, podcasts, magazines, and forums discussed here frequently deal with this subject. Here are a few:

- Share family photos on Facebook or Instagram by posting pictures connected with birthdays and anniversaries. First, find a downloadable Excel file called a "birthday calendar" by Googling *birthday calendar download*. Pick the design you like, and then start filling it in with the dates you have collected and input into your tree. Then, check the calendar each day—is it someone's birthday or anniversary? Post a quick note with some photos! Other family members will appreciate the sharing and might return the favor by offering more pictures and info.
- Make a narrated video showing a slideshow of family photos and post it on YouTube—then use social media to share the link.
- Once they are digitized, print out new copies of the best family photos to distribute and frame (use premium-quality photo paper).

For more sharing ideas, check out the ever-reliable Kimberly Powell's article "5 Great Ways to Share Your Family History" (www.thoughtco

.com/great-ways-to-share-family-history-1421879).

SUMMING IT UP

Opportunities for expanding your genealogy knowledge have never been easier to find. Doing family history research in the 21st century means spending a great deal of time online, and that is primarily where continuing education takes place. Remember:

- Genealogy blogs are ubiquitous; you can easily spend hours wandering through them, or you can hit the best ones for updates on the ever-changing world of online resources.
- Some bloggers and podcasters maintain a tight subject focus, while others take on the whole science. Find the one that's right for you, wherever you are in the process.
- Online forums are full of freely shared advice. Check them to see if others have already solved your problem or answered your questions.
- Genealogy conferences are great places to get inspiration and guidance and to meet the rock stars of family history research.

9

FINAL THOUGHTS

The key to success with a genealogy project is to embrace its complexity: let the process absorb hours and even days. Search for records, of course, but don't just download, label, and store them. Study each one carefully, gleaning every bit of data you can and noticing what those records imply. The people whose living presence inspired their creation once breathed, cried, and hoped. Their realities will come into sharp focus when you take time to study the records. Sometimes a single line, number, or date can stop your breath as understanding dawns. The records are literally just pieces of paper with writing on them, but figuratively they are your window into the past. They can help you understand those people from long ago and learn to differentiate what was unique and what was common between their experiences and yours.

The past, even the distant past, is far more than a collection of data points. It was and always has been about *stories*. For humans, narrative has always been essential to their development as a species. It is one thing among many that sets us apart from animals—not just the habit of telling stories, but the drive to do so, the almost primal need to re-create experiences for others. Whatever facts you discover are useful only when they connect with the narrative of someone's life. Use the information in the records to piece together the stories and do your best to tell them. Family history research is about connecting the land of the living with the land of the dead, making sure that the people behind those names and dates don't get lost. Each family-connected record you fish out of the ocean of paperwork pins a once-living person to a time and place and connects that person to the still-living world. All those people long ago could not imagine you, of course, but you can imagine them. Do the research for them, for yourself, and for the generations to come.

Of course, you'll have questions no old records can answer; the answers were inside the minds and hearts of people who did not record the facts about their lives for their descendants. Most of us go along, as no doubt they did, thinking that nothing special can be said of us. But those who came before did something extraordinary—they lived in the past, a world we cannot visit or even really know. Many of them showed tremendous strength of body, mind, and heart as they went about their ordinary lives. Wouldn't it be wonderful if we had their own words to tell us what those experiences meant to them?

Someday *you* will be the one long gone, so in addition to researching the past, do something now to tell the story of your own life so that people you cannot even imagine will feel connected to you. Get the facts down, but also talk about the *how* and *why* of things. Record the story of your life so someday the people who come after will know, in your own words, what it was like to be you. However ordinary your experiences seem, they will be exotic to someone a hundred years from now. Do this soon and without worrying what will become of your information, who will hear it or read it. Someone will, and that someone will be very glad to know you.

APPENDIX

Suggested Questionnaire for Genealogy Interview Subjects

These questions can be modified, and follow-up questions can be asked at any point. As a supplement to the information gained during a semiformal interview, you might also want to record the comments of your subject as he or she looks through old family pictures, which always prompt memories and stories.

Personal

1. What is your full name?
2. Why did your parents select this name for you?
3. Have you ever used any other names or had a nickname that appeared in records?
4. When and where were you born?
5. Who were your godparents/birth sponsors, and why were they selected?
6. Do you remember any stories that your parents shared with you about your birth?
7. Where were your parents living when you were born?
8. Where did your parents live before that?
9. What other family members lived nearby?

Household

1. How big was the earliest childhood home you remember?
2. Were there any special items in the house that you remember?
3. Give the addresses of any home you lived in as a child.
4. What books were in the house?
5. What kind of car did the family have?
6. What were some of the rules in your family/house?
7. Is there anything else you'd like to say about your household(s)?

Parents

1. What are/were the full names of your parents?
2. When and where were your parents born?
3. When and where were your parents married?
4. How did your parents meet?
5. What were your parents' occupations?
6. What is something each of your parents often say/used to say?
7. For each of your parents, give a few words that describe that person's personality.
8. How did your parents enforce discipline?
9. What songs do you remember your parents singing?
10. Did either of your parents play a musical instrument? If so, what training did they have?
11. What books do you remember them reading aloud to you?
12. What were their favorite foods or special things they would cook?
13. Where did your parents attend school? What degrees did they earn?
14. Is there anything else you'd like to say about your parents?

Grandparents

1. What were the full names of your grandparents?
2. When and where were each of them born?
3. What were the names and birth dates of your grandparents' siblings?

4. What were their homes like?

5. What were the names and dates of birth for their children other than your parents (i.e., your aunts and uncles)?

6. What did your grandparents tell you about their lives when they were young?

7. What do you know about where your grandparents came from or where they lived when they were young?

8. For each of your grandparents, give a few words that describe that person's personality.

9. Is there anything else you'd like to say about your grandparents?

Other Family

1. What are the full names of your siblings?

2. When and where were your siblings born?

3. What nicknames did your siblings have as children?

4. For each of your siblings, give a few words that describe that person's personality.

5. What were your favorite foods?

6. How were holidays (birthdays, Christmas, etc.) celebrated in your family? Did your family have special traditions?

7. What were/are the names and ages of all your first cousins?

8. Who was the oldest relative you remember as a child?

9. What relatives or family friends do you remember going to visit or remember visiting your home?

10. What do you know about your family surname?

11. Have any recipes been passed down to you from family members?

12. Are there any physical characteristics that run in your family?

13. Are there any special heirlooms, photos, Bibles, or other memorabilia that have been passed down in your family?

14. Which family members served in the military?

Childhood

1. What is your earliest childhood memory?

2. What illnesses or health problems did you have as a child?

3. What chores did you have?
4. Do you remember any fads from your youth? Popular hairstyles? Clothes?
5. Who were your childhood heroes?
6. What were your favorite songs and music?
7. What kind of pets did you have, and what were their names?
8. What was your religion growing up? What church did you attend?
9. What did you do on summer vacations from school?
10. Who were your friends when you were growing up?
11. What world events do you remember?
12. Where did you go on dates?

School

1. Where did you go to grade school, and what years?
2. Where did you go to high school, and what years?
3. How did you get to school?
4. Have you kept in touch with classmates from grade school or high school?
5. What were your best and worst subjects?
6. Who were your favorite and least favorite teachers?
7. What school activities and sports did you participate in?
8. Have you attended any of your high school reunions?
9. Give the college(s) you attended, with years, major(s), and degrees earned.

Hobbies and Recreation

1. What kind of games did you play growing up?
2. What were your favorite toys and why?
3. What are some of your most memorable family vacations?
4. What did your family do together for fun?

Work and Career

1. As a child, what did you want to be when you grew up?
2. What was the first job you ever had?

3. What was your profession, and how did you choose it?
4. What other jobs besides those in your chosen profession have you had, and when did you have them?
5. If you could have had any other profession, what would it have been?
6. Where were you when you heard John F. Kennedy had been assassinated?
7. Where were you when you heard about the planes hitting the Word Trade Center on September 11, 2001?

Military Service

1. What branch of service were you in?
2. On what dates did you enter and leave the military?
3. What places did you live during your military service?
4. What were your duties?
5. Were you ever injured in the line of duty? If so, what were the circumstances and what were your injuries?

Spouse

1. When and how did you meet your spouse?
2. Where did you go on your first date?
3. Where and when did you get married?
4. What memory stands out the most from your wedding day?
5. Where did you go on your honeymoon? How was this place chosen?
6. Where was your first home after marriage?
7. What do/did you admire most about your spouse?

Parenthood

1. What are the full names of your children?
2. Why did you choose your children's names?
3. Where and when were each of your children born?
4. Where were you when each of your children was born?

5. Do you remember anything that your children did when they were small that really amazed you?
6. What is the funniest thing that you can remember that each of your children said or did?
7. What was your proudest moment as a parent?
8. What lessons would you like to pass on to your children?

Lifetime Changes

1. Where have you lived as an adult? List the places and years that you lived there.
2. What days do you consider turning points in your life?
3. What accomplishments are you most proud of?
4. What nicknames have you been given as an adult?
5. What is the one thing you most want people to remember about you?
6. What was the most memorable gift you ever received?
7. What is something that you wish was the same now as when you were growing up?
8. Who had the most positive influence on your life? What did he or she do to influence you?
9. Do you have any hereditary health problems?
10. Have you ever won any honorary degrees, awards, prizes?
11. Have you ever met any famous people?
12. What organizations and groups have you belonged to?

Travel

1. Where have you traveled to?
2. What was your favorite place?
3. What is the longest trip you have ever gone on? Where did you go?

NOTES

I. GENEALOGY—AN OVERVIEW

1. An earlier version of this section appeared in the author's column in *Kentucky Libraries* 76, no. 1 (2012): 22–23.

2. *About Family Search*. www.familysearch.org/en/about.

3. *Archives*. www.familysearch.org/records/archives/web/services.

4. An earlier version of this section appeared in the author's column in *Kentucky Libraries* 75, no. 3 (2011): 12–13.

5. An earlier version of this section appeared in the author's cowritten article with Rosemary Meszaros in *DttP: Documents to the People* (Spring 2018): 7–12.

6. boards.straightdope.com/sdmb/archive/index.php/t-493641.html.

7. Gladwell, M. (2000). *The Tipping Point: How Little Things Can Make a Big Difference*. New York: Little, Brown.

8. Kiviat, B. (2006, October). "Change Agents: Are You Sticky?" Time.com. content.time.com/time/subscriber/article/ 0,33009,1552029,00.html.

9. See "What's in a Name? A Closer Look at Family Surnames" (www.genealogy.com/articles/research/88_donna.html) and "Ancestors in the Records: Naming Patterns" (www.understandingyourancestors.com/ar/na mingPatterns.aspx).

10. Watch the whole scene at www.youtube.com/watch?v=_3nxoMci3HI.

11. Steerage Act of 1819, 3 Stat. 488 (1819).

12. Act of March 3, 1893, 27 Stat. 570 (1893).

13. Steerage Act of 1819, 3 Stat. 488 (1819), Section 4.

14. See, for example, the public-domain documentary *Island of Hope, Island of Tears* (archive.org/details/gov.ntis.ava15996vnb1).

15. Naturalization Act of 1906, 34 Stat. 596 (1906).

16. Safford, V. (1925). *Immigration Problems: Personal Experiences of an Official*. New York: Dodd, Mead & Co. (full text at the Hathi Trust Digital Library, www.hathitrust.org).

2. THE BEST FIRST STEPS FOR A RESEARCHER

1. An earlier version of this section appeared in the author's column in *Kentucky Libraries* 75, no. 1 (2011): 4–5.

2. www.evidenceexplained.com/index.php/content/quicklesson-2-sources-vs-information-vs-evidence-vs-proof.

4. GENEALOGY RECORD TYPES

1. Cuno, K. M., and Reimer, M. J. (1997). "The Census Rregisters of Nineteenth-Century Egypt: A New Source for Social Historians." *British Journal of Middle Eastern Studies, 24*(2), 193–216.

2. Scheidel, W. (2009). *Rome and China: Comparative Perspectives on Ancient World Empires*. New York: Oxford University Press, p. 28.

3. Wiseman, T. P. (1969). "The Census in the First Century B.C." *Journal of Roman Studies, 59*(1–2), 59–75.

4. Blake, K. (1996). "First in the Path of the Firemen: The Fate of the 1890 Population Census." *Prologue: Quarterly of the National Archives and Records Administration, 28*(1). www.archives.gov/publications/prologue/1996/spring/1890-census-1.html.

5. Act Regulating Passenger Ships and Vessels. 1819. Ch. 46, sess. II, 3 Stat. 488.

6. Immigration Act of 1891. Ch. 551, sess. II, 26 Stat. 1084.

7. www.libertyellisfoundation.org/genealogy/ellis_island_history.asp.

8. en.wikipedia.org/wiki/List_of_Ellis_Island_immigrants.

9. Svejda, G. J. (1968). *Castle Garden as an Immigrant Depot, 1855–1890*. www.npshistory.com/publications/cacl/castle_garden.pdf.

10. Naturalization Act of 1906. Ch. 3592, sess. I, 34 Stat. 596.

11. Married Women's Citizenship Act. 1922. Ch. 44 1, sess. II, 42 Stat. 1021.

12. Robertson, C. (2010). *The Passport in America: The History of a Document*. New York: Oxford University Press.

13. An earlier version of this section appeared in the author's column in *Kentucky Libraries* 77, no. 4 (November 1, 2013): 22–23.

5. ONLINE RESEARCH—THE BASICS

1. Hafner, K. (2007, March 11). History, digitized (and abridged). *New York Times*, p. B1.

6. ADVANCED RESEARCH TECHNIQUES AND SPECIALIZED RESOURCES

1. www.thelongridersguild.com/hopkins2014.htm.

2. Smolenyak, M. (2004, April–June). Steve Morse: A genealogical mensch. *Genealogical Computing*, pp. 27–29.

3. Morse, S. P. (2008). A one step portal for on-line genealogy. *Federation of East European Family History Societies Journal*, *16*, 117–133. net.lib.byu .edu/~tke8/Hist 354/Readings/vol_16.pdf.

7. SPECIALIZED SUBJECTS, INCLUDING DNA FOR GENEALOGY

1. www.census.gov/programs-surveys/acs.

2. Washington, R. (1999). "The Southern Claims Commission: A Source for African American Roots." *Ancestry*, *17*(4), 30–36.

3. Gambino, R. (1977). *Vendetta: The True Story of the Largest Lynching in U.S. History*. Garden City, NY: Doubleday.

4. Borsella, C. (2005). *On Persecution, Identity, and Activism: Aspects of the Italian-American Experience from the Late 19th Century to Today*. Boston: Dante University Press, p. 239.

RECOMMENDED READING

Adams, S. R. (2008). *Finding Your Italian Ancestors: A Beginner's Guide.* Provo, UT: Ancestry.

Alzo, L. (2016). *The Family Tree: Polish, Czech, and Slovak Genealogy Guide.* Cincinnati: Family Tree Books.

Beidler, J. M. (2014). *The Family Tree: German Genealogy Guide—How to Trace your Germanic Ancestry in Europe.* Cincinnati: Family Tree Books.

Bettinger, B. (2019). *The Family Tree: Guide to DNA Testing and Genetic Genealogy* (2nd ed.). Cincinnati: Family Tree Books.

Board for Certification of Genealogists (2019). *Genealogy Standards* (2nd ed.). New York: Ancestry Publications.

Burroughs, T. (2001). *Black Roots: A Beginner's Guide to Tracing the African American Family Tree.* New York: Fireside Books.

Chater, K. (2017). *How to Trace Your Family Tree in England, Ireland, Scotland, and Wales: The Complete Practical Handbook for All Detectives of Family History, Heritage, and Genealogy.* Leicestershire: Hermes House.

Colletta, J. P. (2002). *They Came in Ships: A Guide to Finding Your Immigrant Ancestor's Arrival Record* (3rd ed.). Orem, UT: Ancestry.

Haley, A. (1976). *Roots: The Saga of an American Family.* Garden City, NY: Doubleday.

Holtz, M. D. (2017). *The Family Tree: Italian Genealogy Guide—How to Trace Your Family Tree in Italy.* Cincinnati: Family Tree Books.

Jones, T. W. (2013). *Mastering Genealogical Proof.* Arlington, VA: National Genealogical Society.

Luxenberg, S. (2009). *Annie's Ghosts: A Journey into a Family Secret.* New York: Hyperion.

Maxwell, I. (2019). *How to Trace Your Irish Ancestors: An Essential Guide to Researching and Documenting the Family Histories of Ireland's People* (3rd ed.). London: Robinson.

May-Levenick, D. (2015). *How to Archive Family Photos: A Step-by-Step Guide to Organize and Share Your Photos Digitally.* Cincinnati: Family Tree Books.

Mills, E. S. (2017). *Evidence Explained: Citing History Sources from Artifacts to Cyberspace* (3rd ed.). Baltimore: Genealogical Publishing.

Robertson, C. (2010). *The Passport in America: The History of a Document.* New York: Oxford University Press.

Roulston, W. (2018). *Researching Scots-Irish Ancestors: The Essential Genealogical Guide to Early Modern Ulster, 1600–1800* (2nd ed.). Belfast: Ulster Historical Foundation.

Ryskamp, G. R. (2009). *Finding Your Hispanic Roots.* Baltimore: Genealogical Publishing.

Smolenyak, M. (2010). *Who Do You Think You Are? The Essential Guide to Tracing Your Family History.* New York: Viking.

Szucs, L. D. (1998). *They Became Americans: Finding Naturalization Records and Ethnic Origins*. Salt Lake City, UT: Ancestry.

Szucs, L. D., & Luebking, S. B. (2006). *The Source: A Guidebook of American Genealogy* (3rd ed.). Provo, UT: Ancestry. Full text available for free at wiki.rootsweb.com/wiki/index.php/The_Source:_A_Guidebook_to_American_Genealogy.

Tepper, M. (1999). *American Passenger Arrival Records: A Guide to the Records of Immigrants Arriving at American Ports by Sail and Steam* (revised and enlarged ed.). Baltimore: Genealogical Publishing.

Wyman, M. (1996). *Round-Trip to America: The Immigrants Return to Europe, 1880–1930*. Ithaca, NY: Cornell University Press.

INDEX

ABOUT THE AUTHOR

Katherine Pennavaria is a professor at Western Kentucky University and coordinator of the Visual and Performing Arts Library at WKU. She is the author of *Genealogy: A Practical Guide for Librarians* (R&L, 2015) and *Providing Reference Services: A Practical Guide for Librarians* (R&L, 2017) and writes a regular column on genealogy for *Kentucky Libraries*. Katherine has presented at numerous national and state conferences and participated in webinars; topics include genealogy record types, search strategies, and resources beginning researchers need to know about. She has published articles in *Libraries and Culture*, *College & Research Library News*, *Library Journal*, and the *Word-River Literary Review*.